Ramblings

An Insight into Human Demeanor

Dr. Munir Cheema

Printed in the United States of America
Library of Congress Control Number: 2023922786
ISBN: Softcover 979-8-89174-192-8
e-Book 979-8-89174-193-5
Republished by: PageTurner Press and Media LLC
Publication Date: 12/14/2023

To order copies of this book, contact:
PageTurner Press and Media
Phone: 1-888-447-9651
info@pageturner.us
www.pageturner.us

Contents

"Read, in the name of your Lord Who
created all that exist
He created man out of a germ cell
Read, Your Lord is the most benevolent
He has taught man with the pen
The things that he knew not."

Al-Qu'ran

Introduction

How did this book come to see the light of the day?

It was my good fortune to be in Boston Massachusetts when I listened to an inspiring lecture by President Clinton. Amongst myriad of subjects on world affairs he exhorted the audience to write their life stories. He had written his and his wife was writing her's. I was no writer, but the idea kept buzzing in my head, and hence the 'Ramblings.' After its publication, was it gratitude or goad, I do not know why I sent him a copy with the note, 'you pushed me into writing this book, now you will have to read it!' And I forgot all about it. I was humbled at the courtesy and civility of the man when he actually acknowledged the book. While typing these lines I am watching on the tele with admiration the unending applause, the standing ovation at Wimbledon as Roger Federer enters the central court as a spectator. Reminds me the dialogue Satan had with God at the inception of this world, "why create a man that would turn into a monster." God's answer, "I know what you know not."

God must have such men in His mind, who are utilizing their position and wealth for the good of mankind.

WILLIAM JEFFERSON CLINTON

December 1, 2009

Dr. Munir Cheema
6408 Tone Drive
Bethesda, Maryland 20817

Dear Munir:

Thank you for sending a copy of your autobiography. I believe it's good for people to write about their lives, and I appreciate your thoughtfulness in sending me a copy.

All the best to you.

Sincerely,

Bill Clinton

Now I know what makes men great.
It is the humility and service to humanity.

The title of the book has now become an emotional odyssey.

Chesapeake is a picture postcard archipelago of small, beautiful islands in the greatest estuary in America. It is so peaceful and so close to the Capital that during the weekend it is a trendy holiday resort for the Washingtonians, while people have the leisure to read books.

Dick Wilson, Editor of a newspaper wrote a review for "Ramblings." I had never known or had the honor to meet the gentleman but always wanted to thank him in person for his kindness. After over a decade, this time when I was finally all set for the pilgrimage, his secretary pulled the rug from under my feet with a shocking news, 'Mr. Wilson has died!'

How deeply this neglect pains me? A famous poet has abridged my feelings and lament:

'Hamaisha dair kar dehta hunh main'
Alas, I am always late.

Munir Niazi

We keep on waiting for the right moment to express our yearnings. There is no right or wrong moment. It is here right now. Reach out and touch someone's heart.

As a mark of reverence to the dear departed soul, I am complying with his bidding.

"Dr. Cheema Ramble on."

He probably is the only reviewer who has read the book page to page!

Read:

"Dr. Cheema is Pakistani by birth, which gives him valuable insight into the workings of that part of the globe. In Ramblings he shares his travels, ranging far and wide, observing as he goes and holding forth on many subjects.

He is a keen watcher of the passing parade; he reaches out, wherever he happens to be, gathers in, and organizes whatever anecdotal or observational nuggets are laying around and puts them on the page for us to read. One thing leads to another, and we're off on a series of observations, experiences (other people's as much as his own) and essays. Which is to say, Dr. Cheema tells a story with panache.

Ramblings starts off with his appointment as physician to the president of Pakistan, and that leads to an aside about the Hippocratic oath which, in turn, leads to a story about Lord Moran, who was the personal physician to Winston Churchill. From there we venture into a discourse on recent history of the Indian subcontinent. And that takes us all the way up to page 3.

As the stories ramble on, you are caught up in the moment. Dr. Cheema keeps himself at a distance, not allowing his ego to come into play. Ramblings is not a celebration of the good doctor. When he is in the scenario, Dr. Cheema comes across as a reliable, interested, objective observer who's trying to give an honest account of what he sees and feels.

Ramblings holds its reader's interest no matter how far afield the subject wanders. Perhaps it's because of the easy, coherent writing style; or maybe it's because that's the nature of the universe: everything is connected to everything else. On his first experience with the Western world, Dr. Cheema recalls with delight his first encounter with electronic doors at London's Heathrow Airport.

On a deeper level he recognizes the vast chasm between his early life in Pakistan and his new life in the U.K. as he gives us the details of his emotional and intellectual journey.

Much of the book is taken up with Dr. Cheema's experiences as a practicing physician, in and out of the military, dealing with other people's tragedies. It's here where he reveals himself as an individual with a large heart that sometimes seems on the verge of breaking.

One of my favorite threads in the book is Dr. Cheema's deep analysis of Pakistani life and history. He describes in very readable style the processes now at work in that country as well as the momentous and complex effects of the British colonial legacy.

I started reading this book expecting to promptly put it down. Instead, I've read it through with pleasure. There is much of practical value here for Americans — especially considering our current involvement in a far-off war. I, for one, have obtained more fascinating and real information about the politics, geography and people of Afghanistan and Pakistan from Dr. Cheema's ramblings than I ever learned from the news media.

I've been surprised by the strength of my positive reaction to Ramblings (Rosedog Books). It's been a good read and a good ride; you've probably noticed that I enjoyed it."

Ramble on, Dr. Cheema.

Dick Wilson

Foreword

I have been lucky enough to meet Dr. Munir Cheema personally, during an unforgettable luncheon at the Harvard Faculty Club attended by him, his wife, and daughter Farah. As I have also met Dr. Cheema's son Omar, I can proudly boast acquaintance with the major cast of Ramblings. A fine family they are, successful by any measure – and a credit sufficient even to rival the considerable professional achievements of Dr. Munir Cheema. That he understands the importance of family, friends, and relationships, is one of the prime transformers of Ramblings from another set of memories into an educational and entertaining book about life.

For those with prime interest in medical anecdotes Ramblings does not disappoint. As is evidenced by the popularity of U.S. television shows such as E.R. (which, I must confess, I have never had the pleasure of viewing), the raw material of human suffering and its relief – or helpless observation – provides compelling reading. Dr. Cheema's stories of healing, like Ramblings as a whole, are candid in their content and conversational in their tone. And, thankfully for most readers, Dr. Cheema is not writing a surgical textbook: there is sufficient factual medical content and explanations to inform readers without burying them in Latin phraseology and medical esoterica. Given the broad – literally, multi-continental – scope of Dr. Cheema's experiences, any reader interested in geographical disparities in approaching medical care will find Ramblings fascinating and enlightening. One knows instinctively that it is easier to get an MRI at the Massachusetts General

Hospital than it would be in some of the locales described in Ramblings but reading Dr. Cheema's reminisces offers the reader a true insight into the challenges and rewards of caring for patients in the nether regions where he has practiced.

Beyond materia medica, however, lie what are arguably the true gems of Ramblings. Dr. Cheema surely has written a book about what it was like to be a surgeon, but he has also written about what it was like to be human. Ramblings encompass such a wide range of human experiences that an overview would be impossible to realize in any Preface. Let the reader be assured, however, that within the following pages lies a narrative which evokes myriad sensations of fascination, joy, melancholia, mirth, and, above all, unceasing interest. Yes, readers of the chronicle of Dr. Cheema's experiences will be entertained, but I offer the humble opinion that if enough of them adopt even a facet of his Weltanshauung, the world may become a better place.

Stephen H. Thomas.

MD. MPH. FACEP.
Director of undergraduate Education in Emergency Medicine,
Massachusetts General Hospital.
Harvard Medical School.
Boston. Massachusetts.

Professor and Chair, HMC (Government of Qatar) Dept. of Emergency Medicine. Chief of Service, Hamad General Hospital Emergency Department.

Weill Cornell Medical College in Qatar. Barts and the London School of Medicine, Queen Mary University of London.

Preface

A Chinese saying: "The palest ink is better than the sharpest memory," stimulated me to collect my thoughts and reduce to writing the events of my life because memories mellow with March of time and the fervor to sit down and write fades away. I do not know for sure why I am writing this book and I will not put forward any excuses for doing so. I thought I had something to say, may be not very wise, important, or instructive, and to preserve what I have seen, felt, and learned during my career as a surgeon, which took me to a number of countries in Asia, Europe, America and Africa. Every fisherman loves to boast of the fishes, both real and imaginary, that he had caught in the good old days; and every traveler likes to spin a yarn. I am a surgeon and I fear, I have a rather prosaic imagination; and so I will rely on my memory, not imagination and say in plain words what I have experienced and felt as a person and as a surgeon in the last half a century.

Most airline pilots have logged more mileage and a lot of other people certainly have traveled farther, visited more countries and seen more than I have. But a doctor, I think, has more opportunities to see the pleasant and the unpleasant sides of life, observe the exhilarating and saddening aspects of human nature and experience the joys and sorrows of human condition. The medical man has the unique opportunity of becoming a part of every social group if he is genuinely interested in men and their affairs. He can experience their ethos and passions, their hopes and sorrows and their miseries in disease and ecstasies in health, almost like a member of their family. I do not think any other person can get so close to people. Medicine is one place where all the show is stripped off human drama. Doctors are in a position to see the human race in its natural naked state, physical, mental and moral.

The life has been full of toil, travel, and adventure. The memories of my travels, all of which are not pleasant, are still fresh in my mind and I cherish them as the most valuable and unforgettable experience of my life. My going around the world a couple of times in eighty days may not be as full of suspense and excitement as that of Jules Verne's extravagant romance 'Around the World in Eighty Days' but for me they were wonderful and memorable journeys. Traveling by road through Europe and Middle East is another adventure that I will always remember. My sojourn in black Africa was also a pleasant and valuable experience that gave me an opportunity to meet a lot of wonderful people.

My stay in South Korea, Japan, Iran, and many other exotic lands will always be a part of my memory that I treasure most. I stayed in Britain for six years and traveled across that beautiful land and visited many remote, out-of-the-way places not explored even by very many natives. In all parts of the world where I worked, I had the opportunity to see and—-study lot of human beings; Common ordinary folks who looked different from the people among whom I had lived the first quarter century of my life. Yes—-they looked different, but they were not different. Like us they toiled; enjoyed the pleasure and braved the suffering and the ills and disappointments of human existence as we did: day in and day out, to earn enough for their families; and, like us, enjoyed what little joys life brought them. They looked different since they carried the burden of different cultural fabric of life. The journey has not only been a geographical exercise, but it also explored the key dynamics of hearts and minds of different people and is indeed an intellectual and an emotional odyssey. This strengthened my belief that all people are alike, despite the conditions and climates in which they live; that the divide of color, creed and race is only skin deep, and that, "All people," as a famous maxim says, "are children of God."

An astronaut put it even better. After finishing their space mission, he radioed NASA at Cape Canaveral, "we are coming home!'

Wherever I could, I took my family along. They shared all the inconveniences and tribulations of traveling, settling in new places and then packing up again for new destinations like gypsies and soldiers. My family and I shared every adventure and misadventure that came our way. This experience strengthened the ties that bound us together. I can, based on my experience, tell with confidence to every family, particularly the families of young people: Travel together, if you want to discover one another and become a real family.

Munir Cheema

Washington. DC
4th July 2023

1

Surgeon To The President

Once, a senior English surgeon and distinguished Professor of surgery with a silvery head was bestowed upon a singular honor, more coveted than knighthood: He was appointed the surgeon to the Queen. The news arrived on the day he was to deliver a lecture to his class in the medical school. Happy and excited, he wished to share his joy with his pupils. Keeping a composed exterior on his English poker face, he broke the news to his students in a straight, unemotional manner, "Boys and girls," he said, "I have been appointed surgeon to the Queen." The announcement was received in so complete a silence that one could hear a pin drop. Perhaps the students were digesting the significance of the honor conferred on their teacher. Then suddenly the whole class stood up and loudly started chanting in unison their national anthem as is the custom on such occasions:

"God save the queen!"

Perhaps they were only celebrating the news in the traditional British way and not referring to the surgical skill of the professor, but the professor felt a little embarrassed. My friends made similar comments when in 1988 they heard the news of my appointment as Surgeon to the President and the Prime Minister of Pakistan. I presume it was all in a light vein, but traumatic deaths of a couple of heads of state lead somber thoughts to the theme of the British national anthem. I did feel a little embarrassed. I also knew that even if a head of the state or the government, or some other important person for that matter, dies a perfectly natural death, someone who loves to imagine wolves lurking behind every bush would ascribe it to some sort of conspiracy, pointing directly or indirectly an accusing finger in some direction.

The appointment of military physicians and surgeons to look after the President and Prime minister's health in Pakistan is perhaps, the legacy of long military rules or continuation of tradition of British viceroys. The rulers from the military naturally felt that they were more comfortable in the hands of a military physician or surgeon, who, despite not being a member of the fighting force, was one of them and had undergone all security checks like them. Military doctors may not be professionally more competent than their civilian brothers, but they usually have no political ambitions and affiliations. Their professional ethics and military discipline ensure that they would pose no problems or embarrassments for those in power. Of course, all medical men take the Hippocratic Oath before beginning medical practice and I know that they, excepting certain unscrupulous individuals, do abide by it but the military discipline makes the military doctors secure more conscious of their obligations. This scrupulous adherence to professional ethics and discipline has during the last fifty years enabled the military doctors to keep their jobs despite the changes in the fortunes of the persons in power.

The Hippocratic Oath requires the doctor not to divulge to anyone whatever he sees or hears in connection with his professional practice, or not in connection with it, in the lives of men that ought not to be spoken abroad. This reminds me of Lord Moran's memoirs. He was the personal physician of Sir Winston Churchill, and he published his book long after the death of that great Englishman. The book makes engaging reading, but it attracted a lot of controversy. The book was severely criticized on ethical grounds. I do not know whether he should have made public the personal and professional information about his illustrious patient even when he was dead and buried. It goes to his credit however that he never betrayed any secret about his patient's state of health or his ailments when doing so could have caused him political damage or weakened his position as the leader of the British nation in the critical years of the Second World War. It can be said in Lord Moran's defense that all great men become a part of history after their death, and that the truth about them must be recorded.

The course of events in the Indian subcontinent in the fourth decade of last century would perhaps have taken a different turn if a Parsi physician of Bombay had not strictly followed the Hippocratic Oath. He kept the very serious ailments of Quaid-e-Azam, (great leader) the founder of Pakistan a closely guarded secret locked in a heavy chest in his office. Dr. JAL Patel's professional ethics has earned him a place, an honorable place in the annals of medicine and because of his moral code he helped change the course of history in the subcontinent. The incident is also a testimony to the Quaid's astuteness: his evaluation of people was perfect.

Closer at home in our country, President Ayub Khan's tight grip on the reins of power loosened when he suffered a heart attack. He survived but was never his former confident, decisive self again and had to resign his office. If poor health had not impaired his will power, the tragic and climactic events that followed his eviction from the President's house might not have taken place. One may differ with some of his politics and criticize certain flaws in his character, but none can doubt his patriotism and take away the credit he deserves for the economic development of Pakistan. Had the good work that had been done in this field during his tenure of the office of president continued after him, this country would have built a strong economy.

Perhaps one of the most interesting aspects of working close to the corridors of power is the opportunity it gives of observing certain traits of human psychology. One soon finds out that, those who look like gods from a distance and behave like gods in their well-appointed, posh offices are no stronger and no better than ordinary human beings. Not only the feet, but their entire body is also made of clay. These little Caesars have many facies, or perhaps they have no face at all but only masks for various occasions and eventualities, and they put them on and peel them off according to the demands of circumstances. They treat their subordinates and the common people with characteristic bureaucratic arrogance but stoop to any level to earn the pleasure of big Caesars. Of course, the most effective way of doing so is sycophancy, the art of praising, flattering people in power and always agreeing with what they say. The sycophant has no principles, no loyalties, and no self-respect. He is the worshipper of the rising star. When one-star falls, he turns his face towards the new star that rises on the horizon without any guilt, without any qualms, without any remorse. Such people throng the corridors of powers and unfortunately, they do thrive. The art of sycophancy is a subtle art, and it deceives and disarms even the most discerning and self-effacing person. There is no effective armor against flattery. Only a few noble souls who are deeply conscious of their 'humanness' escape the snare of the flatterer: those too full of truth to deceive and too full of wisdom to be self-deceived.

I was called to the Presidency to attend President Zia only a couple of times, but I remember him vividly. Once he had problem with his gall bladder and needed surgery for its removal. Those were the days when anyone who mattered would go abroad, even for petty procedures. In fact, a senior officer's wife was flown abroad for Burns at a stage when all she required was intravenous fluids. The poor lady wasted millions in foreign exchange on chartering planes for herself and her entourage and paying the fat fees of private hospitals in UK and USA, but she died of a condition that could have been easily and perhaps more effectively treated at home. Everyone in those hospitals where she was unceremoniously dragged must have been laughing in his sleeves at the medical judgment of those who had advised her to go abroad.

For General Zia-ul-Haq, the President and supreme military commander of the country therefore, going abroad for treatment was no problem but he seemed to have faith in Pakistani doctors and insisted that he would undergo the necessary operation in the country, which he did. In fact, he had a few surgical procedures done, all in the country. I think the General was a very shrewd man, not as naïve as his exterior, like pomaded hair lacquered to his head and sad sunken eyes had us believe. In fact, it was this docile deceptive demeanor that foxed many, especially those at the helm of affairs that brought him to the top, and how they regretted their judgment for a very long time.

He knew that the top Pakistani surgeons were inferior to none in the world and that he would not find better treatment in any hospital abroad. He had complete confidence in the professional competence and moral integrity of Pakistani physicians and surgeons and never entertained the idea of going abroad for treatment. When someone suggested it to him, he would laugh it off. He was not afraid of death and believed that when the appointed hour arrived, none could postpone it; not even the best physicians and surgeons of the world.

One may question his many decisions and a lot many people, particularly politicians hated his guts, because he was wily enough to see through their hypocrisy. He was a God-fearing man and would not miss any opportunity to help the needy. The General had nerves of steel: once he had made up his mind, he had no misgivings about it. After making momentous decisions that shook the world and chilled the spines of the bravest of men, he could fall into deep, peaceful sleep without any pills; such strong were his convictions.

His historic decision to challenge the Russians and give all-out support to the Afghan *Mujahideen* was taken at a time when the whole world including America was convinced that it would be impossible to check the Russian march from Afghanistan towards warm waters. General Zia had even the audacity to call President Jimmy Carter's offer of help in the Afghanistan war a 'peanut' and refused to accept it. Still smarting from the humiliating experience in Vietnam, in Afghanistan Americans saw a God sent opportunity to avenge the defeat without shedding a drop of their blood and they persevered with General Zia who finally relented, and they provided Afghanistan material support. The protracted war finally ended and Russian bear retreated with a bloody nose and its tail between the legs, leaving behind a war-ravaged country and millions maimed, dead and displaced.

It is height of callousness that after the Afghans drove out the Russians, their American benefactors instead of helping build the devastated country, chose to apply sanctions on same Afghans. The paradox of American politics is that they are welcomed into a country as friends and then must leave it as 'Ugly Americans.' Some think-tank in America need to research to find out how they manage to do that! Scores of countries in the Middle and Far East are glaring examples of this strange phenomenon. If one visits a small town in the middle of that vast continent, it will become obvious to anyone that an average American is an honest, decent, God-fearing man who happily goes about his daily life, enjoying watching his favorite teams, Baseball, Basketball and Football; without worrying too much about the problems that beset the globe. Here dollar is the king, life is sheltered and the media reigns supreme. Whatever the TV screen feeds Americans, they believe it verbatim, without ever making any attempt to read between the lines. For an ordinary American his state is his country, and the world ends at the shores of Atlantic and Pacific: beyond that there is a void, a dark space with which he or she has nothing to do.

Once the dust settles down and the historian can see and evaluate the events of the eighth decade of the nineteenth century in its true perspective; it will become clear that the Russian bear's defeat in Afghanistan was what exploded the myth of its invulnerability, reversed its expansionist designs, and led to Soviet Russia's disintegration. It is a pity that the Afghans who challenged one of the superpowers of the world and forced it to its knees were not able to settle their internal differences and bring peace to their war-torn country. The obvious thing that did happen was the vacuum left after the exit of Russians. To avoid this vacuum, poor General cried hoarse that the Russians are not let go scot-free, till Afghans evolve a system for transition; form a government of some sort to run the country. But his hand-picked prime minister was hell bent to sign Geneva Accord that guaranteed nothing. Russians did not leave Afghanistan because of any accord; they were leaving anyway, as they had been bled white. Their exit resulted in a bigger vacuum: because as soon as the soviets left, so did the Americans; they had managed a veneer of respectability after Vietnam. While the battle to win the war in Afghanistan had been won, the war to win the hearts and minds of Afghans was lost and for long shall the Americans regret and pay dearly for this betrayal.

General Zia's dealings with his staff, particularly the doctors who attended him, were so friendly that it was a pleasure to meet him. While there would be a grand reception in the President house on any state occasion, he ensured that all the lesser mortals like drivers and other staff of the luminaries and government functionaries were served with refreshments at another floor of the President house.

General Zia was perhaps the only military chief and the president who appreciated scholarship. Not only he esteemed the Engineers and the Educationists but also, he seemed to have a special soft corner for the doctors. Whereas most military generals seemed to have inherent complexes against the specialists, General Zia to their chagrin, promoted physicians to the highest ranks. At one time there were four Lieutenant Generals in the Medical corps. This has never happened before and never again will. The number of institutions that were raised during his tenure thus improving the lot of the patients by improving the standard of treatment proves the point. His dealings with other arms also were simple, recognition of merit. To command will always remain the innate right of the military commanders.

Another commander who showed some deference to academics was the Air Chief, Air Marshal Asghar Khan. After a passing out parade for the pilots whereas the chief guest he pinned flying badges on the chests of the pilots, the underlings, and the hangers on and the sycophants pumped him to preside over the convocation also and confer degrees to the graduates. He declined the offer on the plea that wearing academic regalia, the ceremonial gowns were the privilege of the learned and the scholars, not the soldiers; pen and sword are way apart.

After having met him for the first time, I awaited a call from the Presidency, which soon arrived when he stumbled and fell while strolling in his lawn and sustained an injury. I went to see him at his residence that to my surprise did not look much different from any other senior army officer's. His room was as plainly and sparsely furnished as I found mine. After I had attended to his injury, he said, "While you are here, why don't you have a look at my toes. They have been bothering me for years. The skin specialist keeps giving me one ointment after another, but we are getting nowhere." I looked around for a small table or a seat of some kind so that I could bring it close to the sofa he was sitting on and examine his toes. I noticed a small settee in one corner of the room and went for it. While I was picking it up, the President also raced for it and said, "Please doctor sahib, let me pick it up; it is not your job." Saying this he gripped one side of the table while I held onto the other. We both hung on to the seat each hoping that the other would let go. Fortunately, an attendant arrived in the room and unlocked us, settling the matter by taking the small table from both of us. I examined his toes. I had been suffering from the same condition myself and after experimenting with various medicines I had found one that proved to be effective. By chance I had a couple of samples of that medicine on me and I gave them to him. He returned one saying that it might be of use to some other patient.

Whenever General Zia used to suffer any muscular aches and pains, and which was quite often, he would send for his doctor who would examine him and having not been able to find any definite cause except rheumatism would advise physiotherapy. Initially he would go to physiotherapy department in the hospital for the treatment but then he noticed it wasted lot of his time and the movements of the president in town caused lot of inconvenience to people on the roads and patients in the hospital. So, one day he asked me to send a physiotherapist to his residence. The senior most JCO who retired as a Captain was selected, who would come to President House in style to treat him. The president found this treatment very beneficial. For a good physiotherapist, it is not only his professional skills that are important but also his personal conduct, bedside manners, and his public relations. He or she must be likeable and an interesting person. While working in England I noted that most of the physiotherapists were comely young girls and since they knew the importance of exercise were well groomed. Dedicated, pleasant charismatic young ladies who would charm or may be shame their patients into extensive physical exercises, who would happily cooperate. I noticed that several consultants were married to physiotherapists. In the primordial days of cardiac surgery in Pakistan, a couple of teams from London assisted our surgeons in establishing proper surgical units. What went on inside the operation theatre not many know but after the surgery, I am sure a number of patients, particularly the elderly owe their health, in fact life to a physiotherapist we well remember, Nicky. It is because of her that the morbidly and certainly the postoperative mortality decreased. The high-profile cardiac surgeons owe their glamour to her; the postoperative mortality before her arrival used to be appalling.

Captain Sadiq had a warm personality, would immediately develop a rapport, get involved and win over his patients even before starting his treatment. This is extremely important as moving a painful part of the body, following an injury or an operation, most patients are reluctant to cooperate unless they are convinced and have full confidence that this treatment despite some pain is beneficial to them and will do them good. I have high regard for the physiotherapists. While in England I rated them above the rest as they made the post operative period of patients smooth, decreased greatly the morbidity, may be also mortality, particularly after hip and chest surgery in old folks who because of dementia and senility were uncooperative.

As an orthopedic surgeon I consider a physiotherapist as one of the most important members of our surgical team.

So, whenever the president needed any treatment, he would send for me and I in turn would ask for the physiotherapist who would do the needful. Soon the president found out that the doctor was quite redundant, if not useless and started bypassing me and would send for Captain Sadiq on his own. The physiotherapist developed so much rapport with the president that he would recommend him to his relatives and friends for the treatment of all aches and sprains on his own even without my knowledge.

During Afghan war against the Russians when Afghans were called Mujahdin (holy warriors) and not Taleban (Terrorists) and things were hot, the head of CIA along with his wife visited Islamabad for first-hand knowledge of the situation on the ground. Mr. Bush, later President Bush suffered from some Arthritic problem that would bother him episodically and he would need urgent medical attention. Being an American and with fingers on purse strings, he was accorded a red-carpet welcome. In the evening he was due to meet all the Afghan leaders. Just before this meeting Mr. Bush suddenly had one of his joints locked and was in excruciating pain that pinned him down. President Zia, his host got worried and thought of sending for the doctor. But then he remembered the old routine; send for the doctor, who would send for the physiotherapist. Writhing in pain Mr. Bush with his very worried, silver haired graceful wife dotting on him, could not have been able to see, in that state the Afghan leaders who had traveled far from their war fronts for this meeting. Captain Sadiq arrived in a flash. Expert as he was in his field, he gently manipulated Mr. Bush's joint and with a clonk it unlocked, and the pain suddenly disappeared. The Bushes were impressed with the efficient treatment. They both were delighted and thanked the physiotherapist profusely. Giving him his visiting card, Mr. Bush invited him to visit them in America whenever he happened to be in USA. Captain Sadiq very respectfully acknowledged the invitation but soon forgot all about it, as it was very unlikely that he would be visiting America.

Captain Sadiq had two daughters and it so happened that they both got married to two young men who immigrated to America. His only son, a Captain in Pakistan army unfortunately died in an air crash. Many years later feeling lonely after his retirement, he and his wife decided to visit their daughters in America. While in US, Captain Sadiq one-day fell ill; He had urinary infection, rigors, and high fever. So high that he had to be taken to a hospital, where he was promptly admitted despite his protests. He had gone there under the impression that the doctors would give him some medicine and he would return home. Being a visitor and guest of his daughter, he did not want any financial burden on her. Man of average means he feared he could ill afford hospitalization in America, where he would have to pay in dollars. Not covered by health insurance, he knew too well how expensive American hospitals could be.

After a few days in hospital his fever settled down and he felt well enough to plead to his doctors to discharge him. Fat hospital bill being on his mind all the time. Instead, doctors put him through the mill and with a battery of sophisticated tests had all his systems thoroughly checked, while Captain Sadiq remained a very worried man. One day while rummaging through his scant belongings he happened to come across the card Mr. Bush had given him many years ago. Mr. Bush had been president of the country and had since retired and was leading a quiet life. The events of that day when Bushes visited Pakistan came to his mind and he thought of getting in touch with them. He wrote to the ex-President how he had come to America on a short visit and that he had been taken ill and how sorry he was that he would not be able to have the pleasure of seeing them this time. He wondered if such an important person like President Bush would even remember him or acknowledge his letter.

Next day there was flurry of movements in the hospital, with lot of pinstriped suited gentlemen coming and going. The hospital administrator and several other people whom Captain Sadiq never knew or had even heard of came to show courtesy and enquire about his health and his room got filled with bouquets. He was suddenly whisked to a VIP suite. Captain Sadiq was worried sick; he could ill afford hospital stay what to say of a penthouse. He saw several motorcades coming and leaving hospital and what seemed very important people visited him enquiring about his welfare and respectfully asked if they could do anything to help. Then arrived a bouquet, biggest of all from the governor of the state with a note from President Bush saying how pleased he was to have Captain Sadiq in US and apologized for not being able to come personally to see him.

Captain Sadiq felt very embarrassed and was regretting why ever he had written the letter that caused so much commotion. After ten days he was discharged from the hospital; and with lot of apprehensions, he asked for the hospital bill. No one would talk about it. When he insisted, the bill was presented; just over a hundred dollars that Captain Sadiq if he so desired could pay in installments!

General Zia would always try to see off his visitors at the door, however busy he might be. Some people said that he put on these affable, courteous manners to impress and deceive people. I do not know whether his good manners were the expression of the nobility of his soul or a mere mask to deceive others, but I wish more of us would put on such manners.

One of his old colleagues a retired Major, who must have served with him sometimes during his early military career, was granted an appointment by the president for some personal problem. He arrived late one evening in his old rickety car. The battery of the car had worn out and at times would not start ignition. The Major therefore parked the vehicle away from gaze outside the Presidency on a slope to facilitate push starting the vehicle on his return. After the visit, despite his protests the president insisted to see him off and continued walking out to the car beyond the gates of the president house. Once inside the car the Major could not start his car as the battery was low. The president called a soldier standing guard outside the gate and they together gave a push and ran after the car to push start the vehicle. To the embarrassment of the Major the car would not start. The president pushed harder and on third attempt the engine of the car came alive. Waving good night to discomfit Major the president came back in the house.

Before going to bed the president rang him up to ensure that the Major had reached home safely without any further trouble enroute.

I visited the President House several times after General Zia-ul-Haq's death before my retirement from the Army and gave medical advice to some of his successors, but I never met a more considerate and courteous person. It is not the ailments of the occupants of the President and The Prime Minister's houses that linger in my memory but their manners and etiquette, or lack of it.

I had seen President Zia only a couple of times and I never deluded myself with the thought that he would remember my face or name for long, but he did. On the morning of the 14th of August 1988, the 40th anniversary of the independence of Pakistan, the ringing of my telephone woke me up. It was my father-in-law at the other end of the line. He wanted to know if I had seen the list of Independence Day's honors list in that morning's newspapers. He told me that the list included a Col. M. A. Cheema who had been awarded Sitarai-Basalat. Shaking up languor of sleep I was in that fugue state between dreaming, waking, and sleeping when one is far from one's best, I told him that there were lots of Col. Cheema in our army and it was difficult to tell which one of them was awarded the medal and fell asleep again. Several telephone calls followed, and I repeated the same answer. I could not convince myself that it was I on whom Sitara-i-Basalt had been conferred. Why on earth I thought, should I be awarded a medal? I had done nothing extraordinary. The military medals are gallantry awards generally given to the members of the fighting forces for some extraordinary act of valor. A few more telephone calls finally confirmed that it was my name. I felt rather embarrassed and thought of the things that my friends would say about this honor. I was afraid that they would think that the medal was a reward for sycophancy or a result of someone's ability to pull a few strings. I wondered how I would be able to look them in the eye and explain why this medal was awarded to me.

I found out later the pains the President had taken to ensure that this honor came to me as a complete surprise. He did not know me well enough, but I guess he remembered my name and whatever little service I had rendered to him. I believe he must have gone through my credentials and gathered some information about me in a very discrete manner, without letting anyone suspect the purpose of seeking that information. The result was that those who write citations which are read out at the time of presentation before the chief rightly did not have any basis for a proper reference or was it their subtle sense of humor! All the citation could say was that I was a colonel in the army and a surgeon and then added a comment or two about my physique to give some sort of substance to an otherwise an anodyne description. After exhausting the scintillating revelation, I was presented the medal.

A man who is not grateful to his benefactors is seldom grateful to God, his creator. I therefore decided to thank the President in person for this favor and find out the reason for his act of benevolence. Alas, the occasion never arrived.

The C-130 aircraft he was traveling in, mysteriously crashed on the day I was to see him. I carry this sense of gratitude with me to this day and will feel relieved only when I have thanked him in the Hereafter. With this medal, there were some monetary awards as well. I decided to write this honor after my name but forego the material benefits.

But old, experienced hands took wind out of my bloated sails with the statement, "In military the difference between a medal and a court martial is razor thin," and narrated this story.

There were two small third world countries who had a long-running dispute over their border which was like a line on the sand and small skirmishes kept on erupting between the two armies over the border. Once a young energetic commanding officer was posted on one side of the banana republic who thought of resolving the problem once for all. After careful planning he amassed his troops and invaded the other country bringing the border line across a rivulet, thinking the physical topography would become a peaceful border. The heroic effort was applauded across his country. There was lot of fanfare and patriotic fervor. Once the army unit returned triumphally there were rows of cheering crowds welcoming the soldiers. Graffiti and rose petals were showered in the streets from both sides of roof tops. The officer was mentioned in dispatches as the only casualty was a dead horse. His name was recommended for a gallantry award to the ministry.

Because of battle the relations between the two countries soured, and the matter was taken up in the United Nations for arbitration. The name of the officer kept climbing in the ministry red tape despite objection from the ministry bureaucrats for loss to exchequer of a dead horse. The officer was finally approved by the ministry for the gallantry award. In the meantime, diplomatic efforts brought peace between the warring nations and things cooled down at the border. The old border was restored, and the officer was now incremented for an unnecessary battle and a warmonger. It was recommended he be court martialed!

2

Life In A White Coat

I still remember vividly my first flight to London, where I went for FRCS in early sixties. The only route to travel to England those days was to catch a flight from Karachi, which was previously the capital of the country. It was an Air France flight via Athens to Paris, where I was to board another plane for London. To reach Karachi, I took a plane from Lahore. There used to be only a few flights daily. Although I took one of the late flights, when I reached Karachi there still were a few hours before my flight to London. My brother in-law, a senior officer, a Captain in the Navy, had come to receive me. Since there was plenty of time, he took me home to his island residence. There we had dinner and what turned out to be a memorable talk, the depth of which I did not, in fact could not register fully then, but his words haunt me to this day, even years after his death. His comments seem to be permanently etched in my mind. Especially when things do not move the way I would like them to. He was a seasoned sailor who had sailed over seven seas and had seen the world.

He said, "I am pleased you are going abroad to improve your qualifications but mark my word, your life is going to change forever after this. From now on your peace of mind will leave you for good. You will never be the same man again." His advice fell on deaf ears, but he carried on, "When you will come back, that is if you decide to, you will always keep comparing working conditions in England with your chaotic local conditions. You will wish to change things but will not be able to. You will find stone walls built around you. Therefore, you will wring your hands and sulk and suffer; hit your head against the walls and will undergo mental anguish and frustration for rest of your life. Ignorance indeed would seem to be a bliss. On the other hand, if you decide to stay behind and join the rat race, you will always keep on yearning to come back to where you belong; fish out of water, like a salmon swimming back to where it came from. Although the professional world would be excellent, you will always feel and look like a second-rate citizen in a first-class world. If you decide to cut off your roots and try to behave like the Brits: by uncomfortably following their customs of pubs, drinks, and promiscuous living even then you will neither be accepted nor would be at ease with yourself and would indeed suffer from all sorts of complexes. So do whatever you might, from now on peace of mind will always elude you."

I did not quite fathom the depth of his sermon then, as my mind was set anxiously for takeoff time. Being not fully aware of the facts that he knew, what I did not know at the time and in euphoria of exploring a new world I did not register a lot of things he said, but now looking in hindsight he was absolutely right. My friends who have stayed behind are as unhappy as I sometimes become when things do not move my way. Thoroughly confused I took off from Karachi in the dead of the night.

My naïveté though amusing to remember today is difficult to comprehend. Howsoever we may crib about the chaos our country is in, because of inept political leadership; we have come a long way from those days. The world today has shrunk to a global village, what with invasion of cyber space with satellites, cellular phones, and the lot; today's communications are indeed astounding. We in our country today enjoy nearly the same comforts and facilities as anywhere else in the

West. Imagine life in early sixties, when there was no television, and the telephones were a rarity. Means of communications were rudimentary. Going to the West was like going to a fairyland, or to the other side of the moon. Overnight I had crossed the chasm from my medieval youth to the modern world.

I landed at Heathrow airport in March '64. I had written earlier on, to a friend to receive me at the airport. He was nowhere to be found. The airport seemed to me like a fantasyland, even though Heathrow now is many times bigger and more complex than in those days. I carried my baggage and walked towards the 'Exit' sign. In front there was a closed passage at the end of which was a big glass. I came close to it and was looking for the way out, when suddenly to my great surprise the big glass without even my touching it slid open. I was taken aback, bewildered, and astonished. I had read 'open sesame' only in Ali Baba stories. But here it was for real. It was my first experience of the modern world of sensor doors.

After having gone out of the door in the waiting lounge I looked everywhere for my friend but could not find him. I saw a telephone booth but had no idea how it functioned with coins. I was standing next to the booth, trying to figure out how this contraption worked, lost in wonderland, when a kind looking gentleman read my blank foreign face. He asked me, "Do you want to ring some place?" Of course, I wanted to. I did not have any coins and took out the only ten-pound note I was carrying. That used to be the total foreign exchange we were entitled to according to regulations. Without asking he took some coins from his pocket and connected me to my friend. My friend who had been held up due to some emergency told me to get on an airport bus and then take a taxi to a certain student's hostel, where he had booked a room for me. This hostel was close to the Pakistan Embassy in the poshest area of London, where a mortal like me could never afford or imagine living. I still remember the address 15 Chesham Place, Lowndes Square. The chimney of the hostel kitchen would spew the tart curry smell, to the chagrin of the high society of London in the neighborhood!

My friend came to see me in the evening. He brought some medical magazines with him and asked me to start applying for the jobs in my specialty, starting from the lowly residents. I took his advice and wasting no time spent the night writing applications, The response was electrifying. In the next couple of days there were three calls, including one telegram. Since I needed a job quickly to settle down, I thought a hospital that sent a telegram seemed more desperate to hire me. I informed them that I would be attending the interview. I was under the impression that this hospital was in London, as the night before I had spotted a Crewe Road in the London A to Z directory. So, the hospital should be on this road. Next morning, I came out of the hostel and asked a taxi driver to take me to the address of the hospital. The driver looked at the letter, smiled at my youthful bewildered foreign face and said, "This place Crewe is over a hundred miles away. You will have to take a train to get there." Since I had no idea of the geography, I took his advice. He dropped me at Euston railway station, a grim cast iron and brick Victorian legacy, where I caught a train to Crewe.

While it was freezing cold outside, the train was well heated and very comfortable, and I enjoyed my first ride on British rail. When I got out of the railway station at Crewe, I had no clue about the whereabouts of the hospital. I was wondering what to do when a kind looking man stopped his car and seeing my blank face asked me where I was heading. I showed him the telegram from the hospital. He asked me to hop in the front seat and said, "I will take you there." I had difficulty understanding why everyone was so helpful. I was not used to it in my country. What sort of people are they? I wondered. They were not even Muslims!

The hospital was way out of town, and I felt very embarrassed that this Samaritan had driven so much out of his way to drop me. I thanked him most profusely. He advised me, "If they give you this job, take it." The interview seemed only a formality. The consultant was very nice and took me around the hospital. My predecessor, whose stay in that hospital had been cut short, was also a Pakistani, with whom they seemed thoroughly, disgusted. This character apparently was of such fair complexion, almost an albino that everyone took him to be an Armenian. He had unfortunately not left a good impression. I was amazed, that having been bitten once, why they were taking a risk again. They must be desperate, I thought. I immediately accepted the job. The consultant took me for lunch in the cafeteria. He introduced me to every one present. I found out later that this consultant was a very famous surgeon. I had already started liking the place. The atmosphere was very friendly. I left for London in the afternoon where I found several letters waiting from other hospitals for further interviews. I settled for the bird in hand and decided to forego other offers although my friend advised me that I should look for a job in London. He himself seemed confident about getting a job in a teaching hospital.

He was the son of a senior federal minister back home. He had arrived in London with high hopes, that a friend of his father in the Embassy, a medical advisor, and a retired British high ranking official in the British medical hierarchy would find him a job before his arrival. He seemed annoyed that this had not happened so far. The British Medical Advisor, a much-respected elderly Englishman, took this class fellow of mine to a famous teaching hospital in his Rolls Royce to see the administrator of the hospital, with whom they had an appointment. The Advisor introduced my friend to the administrator and asked him to fix up this young doctor in his hospital, as he was the son of a very important person and a bright young lad aspiring to rise in the profession. The administrator was polite and courteous. He quietly opened a drawer and pulled out a copy of the British Medical Journal, the famous BMJ that my friend had given me the very first day. At the end of the journal were displayed all the advertisements for the vacant posts in the National Health Service. He asked my friend to apply for the jobs. My friend was taken aback. He had pinned such high hopes on this interview on account of the accompanying Lordship, who protested that no heed had been paid to his presence. The administrator was unmoved.

In disgust they left his office and came out in his secretary's office, a slip of a girl who was busy typing some letter. The fuming Lord said that he wanted to ring up someone. The girl, who knew the Lordship continued typing, momentarily looked at the nobleman and quietly said, "Sir, the public telephones are out in the hall!" I thanked God I had taken the right course of applying for the jobs, in a country where, unlike in Pakistan, institutions stood taller than men.

I joined the post of Resident the very next day. Since I knew the geography of Crewe now, I had no difficulty finding my way. I reached the hospital this time in a taxi. The porter outside the hospital, whom I had never seen before greeted me warmly. He took my suitcase, my total belongings, and said, "Your room is ready sir, I will take you there." We climbed upstairs to the doctor's residences. The room was well lit, warm, and tastefully furnished. I marveled at the hospitality. A note on the table said, my Muslim dinner was lying in the oven. I thoroughly enjoyed well-cooked sumptuous English food. Things had gone so well that I did not realize I was in a foreign land. Next morning, I started seeing patients. I worked very enthusiastically to impress my consultant. Everything was new but everyone was most helpful.

When I returned to my room, it was nicely cleaned, and everything was spick and span as happens in good hotels, but my nightclothes were missing. Had these been stolen? I thought it would be in bad taste to start complaining right away and took another pair out for the night. Early the next morning, the nightclothes washed and pressed were lying outside my door. This became the routine. I did not have to do a thing. The food was served in time, everything moved like clockwork. Since all my mundane chores were taken care of and I had nothing else to do, I worked day in and day out, quite often through the night untiringly. This certainly impressed everyone, thanks to my predecessor, who had lowered their expectations.

My consultant, a father figure, and a kind man wanted to ensure that I spent my time for the purpose I was in England for, FRCS. While I was assisting him in an operation one day he commented, "It rains almost every day in England. You must ensure you remain dry. There are two ways, either you buy an umbrella or buy a car. If you want to pass your examinations, I recommend that you buy an umbrella." I figured out the wisdom of his advice later, when I saw my other friends who had bought cars soon after their arrival, going astray. They either returned without qualifying, or with company. Some never came back home.

A very important basic fact of life that I learnt very early was that one should not feel shy of learning from any quarters. The ward sisters were very experienced and there was so much that I learnt from them. The theater sister used to be a terror, who would scare even the consultants. The result, the theaters were pristine clean. There was hardly any infection; unlike the place I worked last at home, where almost every case got septic. I soon discovered that the doctor was not necessarily the most important person in the hospital. There was dignity of labor. Everyone took pride in his or her job. The ward sister would not let the consultant do a ward round at lunchtime. She would say proudly, "My patients are having food." The consultant too would retreat meekly. I had not seen anything like that at home. Even the porter, was a well-respected man. He would do his errands with a style. One thing was obvious; everyone did his or her job most efficiently, without a care in the world for the superiors. So unlike what transpires in our country where the only reason for working is to win the favors of the superiors and where not hard work but sycophancy is rewarded. Here there seemed a self-imposed military discipline. For every one work and punctuality had become second nature. Everything else was secondary.

Coming as I did; from a disorganized and disorderly world I found the system odd but very efficient and tidy. But I could not help wondering that everyone here was a slave of habit. That time here was a tormenter, a ruthless tyrant that controlled them absolutely. Everyone was terribly afraid of and to it everyone was utterly subservient. Perhaps for the fear of retribution or flogging, not physical but mental; no one dared defy the clock; so, everyone did work according to clock; and unlike us they only lived to work. Deep in my mind however I thought that perhaps to let go, at least at times, get off the whirling globe and step out of stream of life and leisurely stretch out for a while was good to unwind; as we did at home, most of the time! The only place they would let themselves loose was when they were not quite themselves, in the pub. Then I realized I was in a country, where people had been free for generations and their thinking was different from mine. In my land we had been subjected to invasion after invasion since times immemorial; ruled till the 20th century by the British and now in 21st by the Americans. In our subjugated world it never paid to stand up or tell the truth. Centuries of invasions had changed our psyche. To survive before an army of invaders one had to lie low, hide the assets, tell half-truths and be a sycophant. It never paid to stand up and be counted; whosoever tried, broke, vanished and was never heard of again. However enlightened one may have felt when British ruled my land, the fact remained that our mind set and thinking habits due to carrying heavy burden of cultural luggage for centuries had been enslaved. Whereas these people were free for generations and had no hesitance to speak the truth, act right, and do what they willed. Britain was not only free; it was bastion of the free world, where all the free thinkers, even heretics from all over the world who were persecuted and hounded in their native lands, found refuge.

When I compared myself to these people, I realized that there were not only differences in geography of thinking, but there were also differences in our very mindsets. Over the years the very alchemy, may be even our genes had changed due to generations of subjugation and that now we were dealing with not physiology but pathology of thinking. Insecurity was the reason for our morbid behavior. After being physically free it takes at least three generations to feel free. Then spinning webs of rationalization and perhaps self-deception I consoled myself that, like me they were also slaves though of a different master.

I also found out that personal relations with other people would last as long as one did one's duty. If one did not do his or her job, one could not last long. And certainly, would be excommunicated, politely but subtly ostracized. In contrast to my country, where everyone knows who indulges in bribes, is corrupt, insolent, and instead of helping causes obstruction in work for graft, yet not many have the moral courage to show their indignation. There is no social pressure. In fact, because of their ill-gotten wealth they are considered respectable individuals. Corruption therefore is bound to thrive. The difference in the two cultures was stark.

Here, even the porter of the hospital commanded great admiration. He was omnipresent. In his spare time, he was a handy man and in emergencies he would stand in for the telephone operator, transport patients and prepare death and cremation forms; he did all sorts of odd jobs. He was the most informed person who knew about all the scandals and the inside stories of the hospital. He seemed to be the head of hospital grapevine. It was important to be on his right side. So I soon found out.

An Indian doctor was working in the emergency department. All sorts of patients thronged the place. It was difficult for the casualty medical officer to admit a patient in hospital unless it was a real emergency, otherwise the medical and surgical registrars, who regarded hospital beds as their personal property would lynch him. There was no way one could admit a patient with a common cold or a sprained ankle and get away with it. There was always dearth of beds in the hospital.

It was quite usual to have scores of drunks brought to the hospital every Friday night. Some time it was difficult to tell who was suffering from a real medical problem when the patient was not sober. The casualty officer had to be very careful that he did not send away a seriously ill patient home, to die. It would be scandalous, in fact lethal, particularly for a foreign doctor.

An elderly patient arrived in the hospital in the dead of night with a cough and chest pain. The casualty medical officer was in two minds, about admitting the patient. If he were not a cardiac patient, the medical officer would have to face the wrath of an irate registrar. On the other hand, if he sent the patient home and something happened, it would be disastrous. The casualty medical officer remembering previous unpleasant encounters with the registrars chickened out. He reluctantly sent the patient home. The ill at ease casualty medical officer then went to his room to snatch some sleep.

Next morning the porter met this doctor in the corridor and informed him, "Doctor, that patient you sent home last night died of a heart attack, soon after he left hospital." The casualty medical officer was stunned. He immediately thought of losing his job and maybe his license to practice in England, as the General Medical Council applied the rules very strictly; unlike in our country, where its presence is hardly felt.

The poor doctor was still in a trance, thinking about his Medical Defense union and imagining local newspapers flashing headlines on the front page, "The Asian doctor turns away a dying patient from hospital!" The porter must have had a soft corner for the Indian doctor. He spoke again, "But don't worry doctor, I saw to it that all went well." The doctor could not believe his ears, but hesitantly asked, "What did you do?" The porter explained, "The patient had walked out of hospital with your prescription and the medicine in hand. He collapsed in front of the hospital and died. When I saw him, he was stone dead. I took away the medicine and prescription from him and turned him, so that it looked as if he was coming to hospital, instead of leaving it. That is how the police found him lying in the street, clutching his chest and brought him to our mortuary for disposal!"

How important the nursing sisters were in a hospital was evident when a new sister arrived in a teaching hospital. She was preparing the ward for the round of the Professor whom she had not yet met. She had the ward spick and span, but a clogged sluice worried her. She had sent for a plumber to open the drain a couple of times, but he had not arrived yet. She was waiting for him impatiently, when suddenly a man with a long white coat arrived. She was so charged that before he could open his mouth, the sister gave him a piece of her mind for being late and ordered him to open the drain immediately before the round started. The man quietly went and worked on the blocked drain and with some effort managed to open it. He then washed his hands and with some muck still sticking on his face and his coat, he reported to the sister saying, "Sister I have opened the drain. Can we now go round the wards and see the patients, I am Professor Smith!"

The dignity of labor was clearly reflected, when a sister was looking for a porter and could not find one, she mumbled to herself, that it was much easier to get a consultant in the middle of the night, than find a cleaner in the middle of the day!

I was working very obediently and efficiently under my consultant. One day for some reason he asked me to admit a patient out of turn in the ward urgently, for an operation the same day. Knowing the set up well, I politely suggested that it would not be possible to operate on him the same day. The operation list had already been submitted to the theater sister, who did not take any change in the routine kindly. The consultant insisted, so I did as I was told. When the patient was being operated upon while I assisted the consultant, the theater sister charged in. She let hell loose on me. Since I had done it at the behest of the consultant, I was hoping he would come to my rescue, but he was hushed as a mouse, pretending that he did not know what the fuss was all about. I had to brave her wrath. After having spent her fury, she marched off. Signs of animation started appearing on the consultant's face, once she had left and he quietly whispered in my ear, "Thank you Mr. Cheema for bearing the brunt!"

A new registrar was posted in the unit where I was working as a resident for the last six months. I was familiar with the routine and understood the sensitivities of the staff better due to my longer stay than this new arrival. The registrar in his thirties, a thoroughbred British gentleman, was a peaceful, happily married man. He was a content family man, raising his numerous offspring in utter bliss, so much so that he had not achieved much academically yet. I, on the other hand having cleared my Primary of FRCS, was studying for my finals. Being new to the hospital he was also not clear about his jurisdiction.

Every time an emergency arrived after working hours and he wanted to operate, the sister in charge of the theater, a middle-aged spinster, known for her temper, would block his way. She used one pretext or another, like theaters were being cleaned or theater staff was busy doing this or that, whereas I, a foreigner a lot junior would have no trouble booking the theater. The Registrar after the refusal of the sister would ring up his consultant and complain about the uncooperative sister. The consultant, in turn, would telephone her and after some pampering would request the sister to let the registrar operate. The operation would then be carried out but with a lot of bad taste in a charged atmosphere.

This was becoming a routine. The emergency would arrive. The Registrar would ask the sister for the theater. She would refuse. The Registrar would ring the consultant, who in turn would intervene and the operation would be performed. The consultant was getting a bit fed up with these frequent calls, sometimes at odd hours. Once the Registrar had to ring him up in the middle of the night as a serious emergency had arrived, asking for the consultant's recommendation to the theater sister. The consultant who was probably sound asleep exploded on the telephone. So loud that even I, sitting next to the Registrar could clearly listen to his outburst. "Look here Peter," he blew up, "You will have to sort out these matters yourself. My House officer has no problem." Then he thought aloud, "Next time I appoint a Registrar I will make sure he is unmarried!"

During weekdays I was so absorbed in my work that the time flew. It was the weekends when I felt lonely. The local boys on the other hand used to look forward to weekends. During Christmas holidays the English doctors would do everything in their power to get away from the hospital whereas I would volunteer to work during Christmas, since there was so much fanfare in the wards and theatre. Later I found another healthy pastime to kill time during weekends. I would travel by bus or train on Friday evening to Lake District and trek for miles together during the next two days. Due to long weekends, I managed also to explore Yorkshire dales and Scottish Highlands and the beautiful lochs. On one occasion I trekked the entire length of that beautiful scenery that spans between the two ends of Loch Ness.

For a new arrival in a foreign land, it was understandable to feel lonely at times, particularly during the long weekends. But it was interesting to note that even a mature Registrar had similar sentiments. A senior surgeon, who was our surgical registrar back home, had also decided to come to England at this late stage for a fellowship in surgery. He was staying in the doctors' quarters. Along with him was another of his colleague, now a famous surgeon, whom the army along with his wife and children had sent for FRCS all expenses paid. We used to notice this senior surgeon unusually depressed. One morning the army surgeon and I were trying to cheer him up. He said, "I have come here leaving my family behind and feel very lonely. I wish my family was here." Thereupon the army surgeon, a colorful character who would not miss a pretty face when he saw one said, "I wish my family was not here with me!"

The army used to send these upcoming officers, some even with their families to London for postgraduate qualifications and on job training. Some seized this opportunity to study and learnt, while others just whiled away this precious occasion. There was a special cell in GHQ that dealt with these arrangements.

Miss Penelope Pope was the secretary of the Royal College in London who was in charge in arranging placements of military doctors from Pakistan in various specialties in the college. Col Mohsin Paul (later Major General, a very handsome and highly intelligent officer) was the man in GHQ dealing with the careers of officers in the medical corps and coordinated with Miss Pope for sending Pakistani doctors to England for higher education. The two would liaise well in time to fill the various slots in the college. Whereas Miss Pope was efficient and ran a very smooth arrangement, Col. Paul due to various agencies involved would be bogged down with security clearance, foreign exchange etc. of the army red tape and at times would find very difficult to send doctors in time for the courses. On one such occasion one officer was delayed for over a month and Miss Pope refused to accept him as the course was well in progress. Col. Paul tried his best to have the officer adjusted, but to no avail: Miss Pope would have none of that. Telephone connections were difficult those days but somehow Col. Paul managed to get through to Miss Pope who was infuriated at the request. Even after discordant argument Miss Pope would not budge from her stand and refused to accommodate the officer. Frustrated, Col. Paul gave up but could not help sniping at her, "All right Miss Pope," he said, "If you would not listen to me, so be it, but remember this will be the first occasion when Pope denies Paul!" The officer was promptly adjusted.

If one looks at the world map it becomes difficult to locate a small country like Pakistan, but in the world of sport, it is interesting to note that this tiny country has been world champion in hockey, cricket, and squash. Pakistan in the field of hockey even then was a household name. Unlike in Pakistan, in England hockey was more popular amongst women. Doctors preferred more rugged sports like Rugby and surprisingly not cricket as I had assumed. Our hospital had a very strong nurse's hockey team that had won many trophies. For their practice matches when they ran short of female players, they used to hunt for any available person who could hold a stick and fill the empty slot. On one of such dire occasion, they trapped me. I tried to excuse myself by saying that I cannot play hockey. "A Pakistani and cannot play hockey. That is impossible." They did not believe me and dragged me in the hockey field. Sheepishly curbing my male chauvinistic ego, I joined them at the expense of being labeled a sissy. The standard of their game was amazing. They were not hard hitters of the ball but their stick work was mesmerizing. They sailed the field as if in a dream and netted the goals superbly. I would feel very uncomfortable since I had difficulty even stopping a shot.

I also vividly remember a sweet old lady of around seventy who had come to see me in the orthopedic outpatient clinic of an English hospital for some problem in her knee joint. Walking with a stick and wearing a dandy hat she looked cute. She slowly limped into my clinic. To examine her thoroughly, I asked her to slip into the adjacent examination room, undress and show me the offending part. While I was examining her notes and X Rays, she opened the door ajar and standing there stark naked asked me sweetly, "Dr. Should I take my hat off as well?"

I also cannot forget the face of an elderly lady of over sixty who had brought her even older gasping husband to the emergency department. The old man had a heart attack at home and was rushed to hospital in a precarious state. The poor lady in tears sat outside the emergency Operation Theater of an old county hospital in the midlands. She was broken down and was very frightened of what was coming next, while we struggled inside to save his life by artificial breathing and pouring all the drugs we knew of in his veins. It looked a lost battle when even the defibrillator could not jolt his failed heart into action. Exhausted and drained after hours of struggle we then went through motions to complete the formalities of disposing off the dead body while his poor wife sat out frozen in fear of the inevitable, still hoping against hope.

It is a strange fact that if the patient survives every member of the team of nurses and doctors even after working whole night, would still feel fresh despite being physically tired and sleepless. But if the patient died after all your efforts, everyone felt a personal loss, in fact a feeling of guilt or failure. The tired body would make you feel as if your whole blood had been drained.

After the death, awaited the most painful event; the duty for the team of exhausted team of doctors and nurses who had treated the patient. A role that everyone hated. Facing the next of kin; the ordeal of informing the family that their loved one has died. I thought the senior sisters were the right people for this painful job, as they knew the local culture much better than I did; being a foreigner and a young raw resident. But they insisted that it was a doctor's duty to break the news, which of course I never believed for a moment. I am sure the thought uppermost in their minds must be that the gravity of the loss would perhaps be diluted and diffused through the filter of a foreigner's tongue. It went to their credit though that they stood by me during this painful hour.

Away from the busy emergency department, in the quiet warmth of a secluded place and with a cup of tea, the poor old woman sat in a chair surrounded by a couple of sympathetic senior sisters when I was invited. They would then stare hard at me to quickly announce the sad news and get it done with. I would run short of words, dry mouthed, with a lump in my throat and would mumble and believe myself close to a break down before breaking the terrible news. Mercifully then the sisters would take over. May God bless them. But I always wished they would spare me this agony, as they amongst themselves were more than competent, being very experienced to handle such matters involving human interaction and emotional matters.

I understand they now have chaplain to perform this obligation.

The vast experience gathered over the years has not done much to cure this aphasia, consoling someone in grief. Nothing can shield you from compelling and distressing emotions. You feel tongue tied and just do not know what to say to the dying patient who is terminally ill. What hope can you infuse in a person who has just lost a dear one? Death seems to invalidate our active, heroic posture and optimistic attitude. One runs short of all the pearls of wisdom. Not even the masks we wear for sterilization can mask our expressions. Only consolation for a person in grief is your presence, just be there. No oratory skills are necessary.

A well-respected clerk lost his only son, a young dashing pilot in an air crash. Suddenness and sadness of the tragedy attracted crowds of people at his residence soon after hearing the terrible news. The grief was so intense that everyone sitting around the clerk was stunned as if thunderstruck and there was pin drop silence. Finally, the clerk himself broke the ice. He said, "I think I will say something. What has happened is indeed heart rending and we are all stricken with grief, but I have no doubt at all in the wisdom of Lord and His scheme of things. Whatever has happened had to happen the way it has happened. There are no two ways about that. What I request you all is to pray for the deceased and for me that God give me strength at this old age to bear the terrible loss."

I would take pride in our Eastern family values and how we stuck together, in contrast to Europeans where I was told that people changed spouses like coats and marriage was only a seasonal sport. The next day, the bereaved old lady we were consoling the night before was rushed to our hospital in a state of shock.

Defying energetic resuscitation, she promptly died. The nurses filled in the details of the Performa—-Death Certificate of the old lady and asked me to write down the cause of death. Confidently I wrote down, "Bereavement." Sisters objected that there was no such cause of death in the official list and wanted me to incriminate a human organ. Reluctantly I changed it into "Broken heart," which they later conveniently translated in the medical jargon as "Heart Failure." Such sudden emotional deaths, after hearing a shocking news like bereavement now have a medical name, Takotsubo syndrome. (Stress cardiomyopathy)

During my stay as a resident in a surgical firm in the East End of London, an urgent call came from children ward of the hospital to see a young infant who had been persistently vomiting. I went to see the child. He was a few months beautiful old baby with blue eyes who could not hold anything down. I examined the infant and while I was there the baby vomited. I clerked the patient and presented him to my elderly consultant; grizzled and neat as a squirrel he was very keen to teach anyone who came his way but despite his best could not get into a teaching program. Listening to the history he was very excited, and we went to see the child. The consultant was a very methodical man and always went step by step and would rap me on the knuckles and would be quite annoyed when I tried to cut corners. He asked the mother to feed the baby and then hold him in her lap with his belly bare for his inspection.

We the residents in a state of high anticipation and full of excitement peered closely at his abdomen, some standing, and some crouching craned to get a good look at the tiny infant. The consultant said, "Soon you will see peristalsis in this abdomen and then this child will vomit." I was at a distance and could not see any peristalsis, but the child promptly vomited. The consultant said, "This is what is known as a 'projectile' vomiting and is typical of the condition child was suffering from." He then had the baby laid flat on an examination table and said, "Now we all will feel his belly and I will demonstrate a tumor in the abdomen." All the residents one by one palpated the abdomen. Some were convinced they could feel the lump, others were not so sure. With the baby bawling his head off I could not feel anything in his tense abdomen, but I attributed my inability to feel the tumor to my inexperience and my thick fingers. The consultant said, "This is a typical case of Pyloric Stenosis with all the classic signs and since medical treatment has failed, surgery is the only way out."

The baby was operated upon, and I assisted the consultant. I could not feel the kick one usually gets while confirming the pre-operative diagnosis at operation. It was disappointing to find that on opening the abdomen there was no tumor and everything seemed normal. The consultant nevertheless performed a pyloroplasty and closed the abdomen. I was skeptical of the diagnosis. Postoperatively the baby was no better and continued vomiting after every feed.

We were all baffled, but I continued to visit the child every day. One day a student nurse drew my attention to the back of baby's head. There was a small bruise hidden in his flock of thick hair and child resented any touching. I thought there was also some swelling. I ordered an X-ray. This startled everyone. There was a fracture of skull and we all felt very uncomfortable. The neurosurgeon drained a hematoma from the skull and the child got better; the vomiting stopped.

This was my first encounter with a battered baby. In early sixties there was no such term in the surgical books. This now has the dubious dignity of a diagnosis, 'Battered Baby Syndrome.' I can recall that night I could not fall asleep. I kept turning and tossing in bed. The sweet innocent face of the blonde baby with blue eyes kept haunting me. How could a man be so inhuman to man, let alone his own blood and flesh? It was a very traumatic experience. How can one label it a disease, it is a heinous crime. I recalled the translation of a verse in the holy book: The ethereal heights a man can reach and the abysmal depths he can plummet into. Then I remembered about the day God created Adam and Satan pleaded why create a man who would turn into a monster and God admonished him, "I know what you know not."

In those days many foreign doctors were working in National Health Service of Britain. Doctors from India and Pakistan, whether like me, they were product of schools who's medium of instruction was not English, had no problem in communicating with their seniors, the hospital staff, or the patients because they had studied medicine in English. I must however admit that those who had studied in English medium schools had an initial advantage over us. They could speak better English with a correct accent. But we were their match, if not better, in written English, thanks to our teachers in high schools who laid great emphasis on correct grammar and syntax.

I was trained in schools where the medium of instruction was not English, unlike an English medium school, or a convent type monastery. The teachers however laid a lot of stress on correct grammar and our written English was reasonable. However, the students from the English medium posh and expensive schools had an edge over us poor lot as they spoke fluent English in the correct accent. We, the natives, always thought in Punjabi, translated that into Urdu and then having transferred our thoughts in that language finally spoke in English. There was a delay and unnecessary waste of energy in the process because words are a mere lens to focus one's mind. When we translate through different languages how blurred a lens can get and the words bereft of the meanings in the minds.

When I started working in British hospitals, looking around at other doctors gave me a lot of confidence. There were doctors from Europe and from the Middle East who's medium of instruction in the medical schools was not English and when they spoke, it was cold-blooded murder of the English language for which we had so much reverence. The language these Italians, Greek or Arabs spoke was atrocious. Even I would find it difficult to control my mirth and sometimes it led to hilarious situations.

A Greek house officer was recently appointed in our hospital. His English was hopeless. Though very handsome and quite overconfident, he did not know much medicine either. I had a head start on him being better in grammatical English due to our hard task teachers. In the outpatient department there was often a lot of rush. The SHO had to see close to fifty patients in one afternoon. The registrar also had a similar number of patients. The consultant would see complicated patients, the new arrivals, operated cases, and the one's he fancied. There would be no time to waste, in fact no time even to think, as we had to clear all the patients in that session. The sisters running those clinics saw to that. It was like a conveyor belt system. The sisters would not let you rest for a moment. This Greek doctor was taking his time to settle down to the great annoyance of the sisters who wanted him to dispose of patients quickly, there being a long list for one afternoon. The sisters usually were part timers, married, with children to look after and were in a rush to get back home and look after their household chores.

This Greek Casanova was new to the routine of the place and was not yet sure of himself. He would suddenly get up and March off to the consultant's room and would seek instructions for the disposal of patients, even concerning small things. Had he been popular with senior sisters, they would have been more than willing to sort these little problems for him. Instead, he was more popular amongst the younger student nurses to the great annoyance of the senior spinsters! After every few minutes he would walk to the consultant's room next door and take a patient along with him and seek his advice on petty matters, like should he repair a cracked plaster or not.

The consultant a firebrand, short-tempered old man, tolerated these intrusions for a while. He himself was busy in his own hectic schedule. One could see from his bald scalp and face going crimson at the sight of this resident that he was reaching his flash point. He tolerated him a couple of times and was getting quite restless of the frequent peeps in of this Greek doctor. He did not want to be rude to him straightaway and that too in the first week and showed rather unusual patience, which, I am sure; he would not have done with me. When the Greek doctor got up again the fourth or the fifth time and stuck his head between slightly ajar doors into the consultant's room, the consultant detonated even before this doctor could open his mouth. "Look here Dr. Papadopoulos, I am not going to see any more bastards for you." The Greek doctor was stunned but remained unnerved at this outburst. Dr. Papadopoulos, however had a patient in tow, he opened the doors wide and dragging the elderly respectable looking gentleman in the room said, "All right sir, please see this bastard for me and then I promise I won't bring any more bastards to you again!"

During a recent visit to England, it was painful to see the discrimination against the Asian physicians. Any European doctor who's medium of instruction in medical school was not English was free to walk in without any restraints and work in English hospitals; whereas Asian doctors had a lot of custom-made obstructions and hurdles to cross before being admitted. Goal posts were constantly being moved to their disadvantage, sometimes even in the middle of the game. The benevolent fair system I had fond memories of, is now only a dream. Our discrimination against the native English was understandable but discrimination on account of the amount of pigment in the dermis and not the neuron in the brain is not only unjust but also cruel, despite the 'equal opportunity' rhetoric. I think it remains a dream as Martin Luther King saw it when people would be judged by 'the content of their character' and not by color of their skin.

It is sad to see that Britain shrinking to its shores, not only into a small island but working hard to become a mini-European county. Commonwealth, a relic of the past is but a club of poor relations. It is only a question of time before even that will be disowned. The greatness and strength of Britain was in her character, compassion, and fair play and not in her size.

I keep wondering though how I would like to remember Britain. As the country that had the biggest palaces and oldest castles, its rock stars or its beautiful people or a society whose people created great music, art, science, and literature. A society that produced best scientists, teachers and artists and excelled in medicine, literature, and philosophy. Her doctors who through their academic and scientific curiosity changed the shape of medicine by discovering Penicillin, the mother of all antibiotics and by discovering DNA which through its Geno metric theory has unearthed new vistas in the treatment and prevention of diseases hitherto unexplored. British scientists who pioneered such earth-shaking discoveries like Television, Radar, and Jet Engine: though American with their better marketing skills high jacked the commercial benefits.

Yes, I remember Britain for all that but most of all, for the decency of its people who believed in justice and fair play. A country where kings abdicate thrones for love and princesses ditch crowns for the lack of it: or a country that would give asylum to the most wretched, even those who abused her hospitality. People, who felt the pain of fellow human beings, for a famine in Africa, a natural disaster in Asia or any catastrophe anywhere in the world. It is them who used to open their doors and hearts for the oppressed and downtrodden. Yes, despite my latest experience I would like to remember Britain that way.

The people of the Raj still remember Britain fondly.

Is it the stars that decide your fate or is it the other way round, I am not sure. Why I went to Britain and not America for my postgraduate training depended on which flight I got first. Those were the days when few doctors ventured to go to America. The influence on us due to British colonization was intense since all our professors had returned from England after high qualifications and had those coveted alphabets after their names; FRCS and MRCP. We all dreamed of and harbored secret fantasies of specialization in heroic fields and clamored to achieve these well-respected degrees.

Pakistan, like California is a long strip of land stretching from Arabian Sea at one end to the highest mountains of the world on the other. The temperature varies from freezing cold to boiling hot at the two ends. The Himalayans and Kora Karam range of mountains have ice-covered glaciers and world's most challenging peaks, like K-2 and Nanga Parbat, (naked mountain) daring mountaineers from all over the world. Numerous falls and deaths of climbers due to freezing speak of the treacherous mountain cliffs. The country was carved out of colonial India in 1947 after a bloody birth when over a million people were butchered and even more maimed and displaced. Located in the cradle of Indus civilization there is admixture of locals and invaders, Buddhist, Mughals, European and Muslim races. There remains a very strong Hindu influence. The physiognomy of its people varies from Mongoloid albinos, through Caucasians to jet black Negroid. The country is uncomfortably nestled in between India and Afghanistan. Because of fear and insecurity Pakistan is living beyond its means to defend herself. Its history is checkered and has survived onslaught from its neighbors, losing half of the country in 1971. Afghanistan gave the country millions of refugees, Kalashnikov culture and prominence in the world press, when Russians invaded Afghanistan and notoriety when they left her. Whenever in the headlines, it is always for the wrong reasons. It has lived up to a Chinese curse or is it a prayer, "May you live in interesting times." The people of Pakistan have never seen dearth of 'interesting times.' Fighting for its survival it reluctantly had to go nuclear when its big neighbor, India detonated an atomic bomb. The West, USA has courted Pakistan whenever it suited them and jilted her again many a times. Due to their patronage the military dictators have had heydays and the country has seen more dictators than democracy in its turbulent history. Interestingly, there is more democracy in the country when military is in power than an elected government.

The people of Pakistan are highly skilled craftsmen, and all the time are jumping fences, eager to travel abroad. Because of Raj for over a century customarily the people of this land have deep Western influences and the doctors always craved to study in England, I am being one of them.

America those days was a far-off land and only those who could not fit in English system ventured to go there despite the incentives, like arranged passage to America with an assured job before leaving home. Unlike today the demand for Asian doctors those days was extreme. Over the years the trend has changed and now America is the Promised Land for everyone particularly the doctors.

When I went to England, I had no idea how I was going to pass my exams except following the footprints of my senior colleagues who roughed it up. Most took a month off before the examination and sweated hard burning mid night oil. When I started my career, I was thrown at the deep end; swim or sink depended on me. I was just a pair of hands; learning was my problem and I learnt everything the hard way; academics were my responsibility. If I wanted to get a postgraduate degree, I would have to work for it on my own. Although this on job training had its own merits, I was never encouraged nor coached for my degree. In fact, I remember when a fortnight before my finals I went to my consultant expecting he would let me off so that I could sit down and work on the books since in hospital it was difficult to find any spare time, he said, "yes you must travel to London and reach the examination hall well in time. You do not want to be late; make sure you are there at least half an hour before the appointed hour as the traffic in London can be unpredictable!"

On the other hand, now since I know the American system better, I find the teaching program excellent, structured, and integrated; in fact, so well organized that now even the British are copying it. There are daily rounds and conferences where you are grilled and polished. There is a program director that is your mentor, and you get personal attention, and he watches you like a hawk and ensures that you are properly trained. The result is that even a below average medical graduate who went to America did far better than us. The difference between the two systems was obvious. Whereas we with English training were more conservative, may be pragmatic, those with American training were overconfident, outspoken, and aggressive. An average medical graduate excelled exponentially and as someone remarked that the American system could groom even half-wits into professors, while it was the other way round in Britain. Also, the lavish praise the Americans can shower on their protégée is in sharp contrast to the constipated British testimonials.

As is the custom, a European resident after completion of his tenure as a houseman went to his English consultant for a Reference and got just one liner, "During his stay of six months here Dr. Papdouplas worked entirely to his own satisfaction."

3

Life In Uniform

Coming from the genial academic atmosphere of a great teaching hospital in London as I did to the strictly controlled life of army barracks was like entering a totally different world. For first few months I was a 'recruit' rather than a doctor, not a very comfortable position for a doctor.

The first day a batch of recruits joins the army, and the instructor, usually a *havaldar* (sergeant), orders them to line up and march in step, they have stepped into a new life in which breaking step is considered an unpardonable error. The sergeant orders, 'Left, and the recruits bring their left feet forward. 'Right', he yells, and the recruits place their right feet forward. The commands continue in loud, monotonous pitch 'Left, right, left, right, left... left... left..., about turn, left, right, left... left... left, halt. In the first few days the recruit finds it difficult to keep in step, but same daily routine has its effect and by the time the training ends his responses are so completely conditioned that he finds it difficult to fall out of step. There is nothing the soldier will do, for the rest of his life in uniform, without being ordered: nothing more and if possible, nothing less.

When I joined the army there was a story going round the barracks and the wards: A nursing orderly in a neuro-surgical ward was given clear orders to 'record pulse and blood pressure of a certain patient every half-an-hour.' The patient had suffered a head injury. The soldier dutifully kept on jotting down the steadily dropping figures on the record sheet. When the surgeon came to see the patient, he found him nearly dead as his blood pressure had dropped to a nearly fatal level and his pulse had become imperceptible. When asked why he did not inform his superiors about the deterioration in the patient's condition, the orderly answered that he was told only to record the findings and there was no mention of informing anyone.

On joining army, I was provided with an orderly (Batman) to look after the stiffness and the razor-sharp crease of my uniform. He was a middle-aged soldier who apart from half a dozen children had not contributed much to life. He still wore the lowest rank and was not a very willing worker. I would have been better off without him but an officer worth the name was not supposed to do any chores with his hands. On arrival in the officer's mess, I drove my car in front of my room and asked the Batman to bring in the entire luggage from the car. He brought in everything, all the luggage from the boot of the car, including the toolbox and the spare wheel.

It is grilled in the mind of a soldier day in and day out that he is to do only what he is told. To think too much is not a martial trait. The soldier's job is to obey and not to reason why. Army needs soldiers not thinkers. This kind of attitude may be a virtue in the fighting man, but not in a doctor who must think and reason all through the process of diagnosis and treatment. When I was working in London, a couple of army doctors were attached with our hospital for training in surgery. They were Majors in rank and senior to all of us, the junior registrars. Soon they became the laughingstock of the entire hospital staff. The consultant did not rate them very high and would not trust them independently even with a simple procedure. He used to ask them; "Don't you fellows know anything else except, Yes Sir?" Those days the military doctors did not enjoy much of a reputation in the medical circles of the United Kingdom. The jewel of the English crown was the National Health Service that maintained very high professional standards. So my adviser, Sir Watson Jones hit the ceiling when I told him that I would be leaving Hammersmith Hospital and going home to join the army. "Join the army!" he exploded, "You cannot be serious!" For the first time in one year, he officially summoned me to his office for a serious discussion. He told me that I did not realize how lucky I had been—working in one teaching hospital after another despite being a foreigner. "You have worked your way up to a position from where you are poised to easily make it to the top. This desperate step is not necessary, as I believe you have sufficient ability to make a career in other walks of life."

When he realized that his persuasion was falling on deaf ears and that I was stupid enough to throw away what I had earned so painstakingly, he almost lost his cool, "Are you out of your mind?" His logic was no doubt correct; but then man does not live by logic alone. In the duel between head and heart, the heart always wins. Also, life is shaped by not only from the opportunities seized but also from the ones passed over. I kept on wondering though what if this mistake; a wrong decision cost me my career. Then I consoled myself by philosophizing, taking a crutch of our faith; that had Adam not made a mistake by touching the forbidden fruit while enjoying the luxuries in heaven, this beautiful world would not have come into being. I realized that God wanted us to make bold decisions even if these at times turn out to be wrong. By making decisions we exercise the autonomy conferred on us. Then I remembered the famous saying of Ali (peace be upon him.) "If things go my way, I am happy because that was my decision, but if these do not, I should be even happier because that is God's will." But decisions we must make; luck favors the bold. The important thing is to reconcile with the verdict even if it is against your liking as quickly as possible and not keep on sulking—what if? No one knows what is in store for him and what may happen next moment.

My father, to whom I was very deeply attached, had died while I was in England. I could not even see him being buried and felt extremely guilty. My elder brother had recently visited London and left me a one-way ticket to Pakistan as an emotional feeler. I had appeared for an interview with the then Surgeon General of Pakistan Army, Gen. S.A. Mian, who was visiting London in 1966. He was a surgeon himself and naturally painted a very rosy picture about life in the army. He was extremely annoyed when I told him my consultant's views about army doctors.

It seemed the way events had come together; the course of my fate was set. With mixed feelings and a heavy heart, I resigned from Hammersmith and cancelled my contracts with other hospitals where I was earmarked for the next couple of years and returned home.

I had been once before selected in the army. This was soon after my going to college after matriculation. One day while loitering in the corridors I noticed some boys including a couple of my buddies filling out some forms in the presence of an army officer and his staff who were visiting our college.

I asked my friends what it was about. They told me that they were applying for a commission. "Commission; what is a commission?" I asked. The only 'commission' I had heard of was a commission agent's fee that he received from illiterate peasants for selling their produce. Some agents were unscrupulous, and they never let go an opportunity to fleece the poor rustic farmers. The other 'commission' did not exit those days when the bureaucrats, politicians and even the heads of the government would ask for cuts from the foreign investors even from the agencies which gave loan to the country!

One of my friends handed me a form. Since everybody was filling in the forms, I too filled one without knowing anything about this commission. Then one day when I had all but forgotten about the incident, I received a letter asking me to report to Inter Services Selection

Board (ISSB), Kohat for tests and interview. I was confused but now knew what this commission was all about. I was not sure whether I wanted to go in the army, but I decided to go as the army was to pay all expenses and a friend of mine was traveling to Kohat. I accompanied him, telling my parents that I was going on a college trip. At the ISSB, jumping walls, clearing obstacles, climbing ropes was an interesting experience. We had also to fill numerous forms and take written tests. One test required writing names of the objects shown. This was very simple, though I could not surmise the purpose of such trivial exercises. Someone told us that we were being psychoanalyzed.

I was young and athletic and cleared every physical test easily with time to spare. We stayed at Kohat for three days and really enjoyed ourselves. On the third day, a very noble looking graceful Colonel, the Commandant, had us gathered in the hall, and addressed us. I remember his speech vividly. He said, "During the last three days we have tested you chaps thoroughly, and now we know more about you than you know about yourselves." I was amused. How could he know more about us than we ourselves did? "Some of you", he continued, "are excellent, some good, some average, some below average and some rotten to the core. The army does not want any one from the two extremes. We want just the right sort of people in the army, those who are neither excellent, nor rotten to the core. We just want the middle sort of stuff. So those of you who have not been selected take heart, you were too good for the army." He was a decent man and did not mention the other extreme. He then read out the serial numbers of successful candidates. I was one of them. It was satisfying to know that I was slightly above 'the rotten to the core' class. I was rather pleased with myself, but my selection did not give me much euphoria. The other boys who passed the test were ecstatic. Those who failed were crestfallen, but the address of the Commandant, I guess, did console them that all was not lost. We pocketed our result sheets and left for our homes.

Back home I did not breathe a word of what I had done to anyone. In fact, I forgot all about it. Sometime later when my elder brother, an Air Force officer, happened to be home on a short visit, a registered letter in an official envelope addressed to me arrived. My brother opened it. It was a call to report to the Pakistan Military Academy, Kakul. My brother was furious: "How dare you? We want you to be a doctor and not a soldier." Looked like he knew the difference. He was so authoritative that I dared not open my mouth to tell him that I had no intention of enlisting in the army and that I had gone to Kohat just to have some fun at state expense. He was not only behaving like a big brother, but he was also the big brother. In disgust he tore the letter into pieces. That was the end of my 'commission'! I keep wondering though what course my life would have taken if I had joined the Pakistan Military Academy (PMA) in early fifties.

I know the course the life took for a friend who joined PMA as I was about to do once. He did very well for over one year, but then had a problem with his superiors. He was thrown out of PMA only a few months before graduation. This was a very traumatic experience that left him devastated. But he is a strong character. He picked up the pieces and started all over again. He went to college again, and with hard work and perseverance, passed his pre-medical, got admission in a medical college, became a doctor, and then joined the army once again. He excelled in his specialty, and after a distinguished career as a surgeon, he retired as a Brigadier.

The officer who threw him out of PMA was once brought to him in agony due to retention of urine. My friend now a renowned urologist operated on him and relieved his pain. At the time of discharging his grateful patient from the hospital, Brig. Iftikhar who had shown him extra-ordinary respect and given full protocol due to past connections said to him. "Sir, you must have done some good things in your life but the best thing that you did, I guess, was to throw me out of PMA. I would not have been what I am today but for what you did to me. May God bless you."

How small events decide our fate is indeed amazing. One of my colleagues, now a famous surgeon, hails from a village. After passing Secondary school examination, he applied for admission to King Edward Medical College Lahore. He was confident of getting admission as he had secured good marks. However, he got a bit worried as days passed and no call for an interview arrived. Perhaps he was not short-listed, he feared. The communications in mid-fifties were rather slow and uncertain. Post used to be the only way of reaching people. The telegraph was, of course there, but it was used only in great emergency; the arrival of a telegram was associated with the news of death, accident or some other terrible happening. He was thinking of traveling to Lahore to find about the fate of his application when one afternoon, while he was coming back from his farm, he saw a couple of urchins trying to fly a kite. The kite would not take off because it was made from ordinary office paper, and there was no breeze either.

One of the boys requested him to help fly the kite. My friend obliged the little boy by holding the kite with his both hands spread above his head. As he was going to throw it in the air, he noticed the writing on the kite. It was a familiar name his eye had caught, his own name in fact. Instead of releasing the kite, he gave it a closer look. The kite was the call-up notice from King Edward Medical College! He was to appear for interview next morning. The postman must have thrown the letter somewhere or given it to someone to deliver it to the addressee, but instead of reaching my friend it fell into the hands of those little boys; his fate literally hung by a thread, and fortunately, both for him and his many grateful patients; the thread held. Somehow, he managed to travel for the interview despite the dirt roads made almost impassable by floods. Major General Rafi rose to be a Professor of Surgery and is now a leading surgeon of the country. This tenacious surgeon might have missed the interview had he refused to oblige the kite-flying boy.

In the sixties it was an ordeal for a doctor to find employment after graduation. There were more candidates than the jobs available, and it was impossible to get one without recommendations or links with higher ups. One of my friends who had neither, made frantic efforts to find a job and tried every avenue; from Secretariat to Health Directorate and Mayo Hospital; but without luck. One day somehow, he got wind of some vacancies in Mayo Hospital Lahore. The only man he could approach was a lowly clerk in the hospital. My friend sought his help. The clerk told him bluntly that there was no question of finding a job without some influential person's recommendation. Then seeing the rustic looks of my friend he relented and said, "I am only a small fry and cannot help you, but I will share a small secret with you. There will be a very stiff competition for all these posts except one where you may have semblance of a chance. We have a professor here who deals with urinary problems; he is as foul mouthed as the stuff he deals in. He is so ill tempered that no one likes to work with him; it is likely that there would not be many applicants for the vacancy in his department. So, try your luck in Urology." My friend was not sure what Urology was and whether it fell under the domain of medicine or surgery. Since he was desperate for a job, he picked up the courage to see this professor. As luck would have it, he got the job. What fate had in store for him he never knew? Urology was then a new specialty, and my friend did not know the ABC of it. He was a hardworking man; he also learned to live the notorious bark of his superior. Soon the professor began depending on my friend and encouraged him to write a thesis on the "Treatment of Renal failure with peritoneal dialysis." That was as far the kidney diseases could be treated those days. Transplant then was only a dream.

After the completion of the paper the professor asked my friend to add a line in his 800-page thesis, "May be ours will be the department where first kidney transplant will be performed in the country." It was my friend, when he had joined Army as a lateral entrant like me, who organized the first successful kidney transplant in the country under the tutelage of his chief. Since then, transplants have come a long way, ethics of the donor sale not withstanding and are routinely performed up and down the country. In Rawalpindi alone there are more than half a dozen centers. Luckily for my friend, army retired him when he was at his peak. Col. Shah now heads an excellent hospital dealing with kidney diseases and has performed thousands of transplants assisted essentially by a couple of efficient technicians. After pioneering renal transplant, he is now planning other transplants like Bone marrow and Liver. He is thankful to the professor whose reputation frightened young doctors, to let him work under him. May God bless the soul of the professor whose bite was not as bad as his bark!

Working in an army hospital was a new, rather trying experience for me. Here army protocol was considered more important than the professional competence. Everyone working in the hospital, from an orderly to the Commanding officer, it seemed, had only one aim in life: to hold on to his job and strive for the next rank by pleasing his superiors, whatever it took. I wondered why these fellows said 'yes sir' to their superiors when they knew the answer should be in the negative. I soon found out that it paid to trek on the beaten tracks. It was prudent to follow the practice prevailing in the army, "whosoever made a decision made a mistake." On donning the uniform and wearing the lowest rank of a Lieut. I was interviewed by the commanding officer and spent some time in his office while he was trying to indoctrinate me. He unnecessarily barked at his staff trying to impress me. When a senior officer would ring him up he would reflexly stand up to Attention shun in his chair and nervously punctuate every sentence with 'yes sir' at least a couple of times. He would seek the advice of his seniors even for petty matters. Looked like he had spent his entire life stepping around the necessity of ever making decisions or taking a stand. I was amazed to see the stark difference of his attitude in dealing with his subordinates and seniors. What sort of a leader this officer will make, I tried to visualize. From his self-interest, lack of loyalty to his subordinates, a picture emerged of a personality deficient in something other than intellectual acumen. Later I found out there was no dearth of such characters.

Wearing uniform made one obligatory to certain protocols, like you must salute your seniors and reply to the salutes of the juniors whosoever they might be, quite unlike the British custom where one never spoke to strangers and would not talk to anyone unless formally introduced. I was advised that till such time I recognize the ranks on the shoulders it was best that I salute anyone wearing red. By volunteering crisp salutes, I surprised quite a few bewildered sepoys (foot soldiers) wearing red berets of the Army Medical Corps. A young sublet fresh from PMA was seriously offended when the senior JCO did not salute him and complained to his commanding office. Both were marched before the commanding officer who as a punishment ordered the JCO to salute the officer one hundred times and asked the officer to reply to his salute every time. By the time their arms were exhausted no one could tell who was saluting whom.

Everything was a parade and done strictly in accordance with instructions; whatever the senior said was right. I realized that the centuries-old traditions of army discipline had made incursions in the army medical corps as well; that needed to be motivated more by professional integrity and compassion than by feudal spirit or any other consideration. A doctor should feel free to discuss and differ in diagnosis, differential diagnosis, and treatment without any worry about the ranks and uniform. For a doctor there must be no curb on flight of his thoughts and—to wonder why, whereas the policy for the rest of combatants in the army is, 'theirs is not to reason why;' shoot first anything else later.

Doctors in the army were divided into generalists—the administrators and the specialists. If the two worked like a team and complimented each other the working would be smooth, but unfortunately there was a big divide between the two and most of the time they were at loggerheads. The specialists were further divided into graded, custom made locally trained and classified; properly trained. The graded ones after some time would return to administrative cadre if they did not achieve a post graduate qualification. But quite a number of older lots were calcified if not fossilized. Then there was a bigger picture, relationship of doctors with the rest of the army.

A senior officer, the Surgeon General once, delivered a lecture to a batch of new lateral entrants in the medical corps. He jotted down on the blackboard: "Who are you?" This abrupt beginning baffled everyone, but he then set out to answer that question himself. "First of all, you are an officer, then you are a doctor and last of all a specialist." Then he said, "If you do not get these priorities right, you will always be a misfit." This dilemma lasts the whole life of a military doctor. Who is he? The army hierarchy will like him to be an officer, stiff and proud in his well starched, immaculately pressed uniform. The doctor would like to excel in his profession even with scrubs and concentrate on patientcare rather than worry about the way he marches, turns about or salutes. In this confusion, doctors in uniform often behave like an officer with his patients and a doctor where he should be an officer.

A class fellow of mine from same medical school also joined army about the same time as a lateral entrant. He decided to clear this ambiguity as to who he was once and for all albeit at a great cost. My friend, a buoyant personality was posted as an independent surgeon to a military hospital in the Northwest, close to where I was working. Being very dynamic and ebullient he worked very hard and soon made his mark as a competent surgeon, to the annoyance of his commanding officer, who had not been able to practice as a specialist as he could not attain any post graduate qualification. He had been therefore reduced to or elevated as a general duty medical officer (GDMO) and appointed as commanding officer (CO). He was always on the lookout to tame Major Asif and thought he should realize the import of CO.

My friend had put on the list an emergency, acute appendicitis to be operated on a morning when there was also a visit of the hospital of a senior officer. He was not a doctor but a combatant and was the recommending officer for promotion of the CO. Naturally the CO wanted my friend to be present in the receiving line, not only as a duty but also to help augment the prestige of the CO. The surgeon, who had already had a few unpleasant encounters with the CO, was getting fed up with these fencing matches. He would be given unsolicited and unwarranted advice about the patient care and would be summoned to CO's office at odd hours; sometimes from his operation theatre when he would have to change into uniform and come for the interview which could have been easily postponed. Outside the CO's office he would be asked to wait till the CO was less busy. My friend was getting bit fed up with these pinpricks and there was little love lost between the two. So, when this senior officer visited the hospital, the surgeon was operating in the operation theatre and was not present at the parade to receive the visitor.

Somehow the absence of the surgeon was brought to the notice of the visiting dignitary in a way that it sounded a big deal; espionage or may be a mutiny! Instead of sorting out the incident gracefully the CO thought of settling old scores. An issue was made of an event that a prudent person at best would have ignored.

The surgeon was charge-sheeted and ultimately court-martialed. It was very inconvenient for me, as I was the surgeon who had to give emergency cover to his surgical patients, the surgeon being under arrest. Once in the middle of a night I was asked to see a patient in his hospital and being an old friend, I thought I should go and see the prisoner. The intentions of visit were not all that noble; there was a vested interest involved. I wanted to suggest it to him that instead of languishing in a room alone why does he not see some of the acute surgical emergencies. To sort them out I had to travel from Peshawar putting my life at stake on those notoriously dangerous roads, where two surgeons had died already. Instead, he got agitated, became furious and started hitting the ceiling with mouthful vocabulary; the Kashmiris living in Punjab are famous for. Outside the officer's mess guards were posted to ensure he did not run away.

It was a ludicrous sight and we both laughed our heads off at the absurdity of it all. Surgeon under arrest; Charge, he was doing the job he was employed for! The whole situation was ridiculous, and I hated his arrest since I had to travel for hours to deal with emergencies of his hospital in his absence, sometimes twice a day. The journey in the hot summer was unpleasant and dangerous on the winding dirt roads. The military juggernaut took its time to come to a conclusion, guilty or innocent and it was an ugly sight to see a FRCS surgeon being marched back and forth to the court escorted by the soldiers totting guns as per army rules; only the handcuffs were missing. The slow iron wheel of legal proceedings dragged on and on. Finally, the court declared him guilty. He was not put before a firing squad but the whole saga was sickening, and it took a heavy toll.

One must find some sort of middle ground between what a specialist wants and what the establishment wants. If one hung on for a while, the army traditions would find inroads to tame him and then would break him down into safety of compromise. I was terribly confused and unhappy for quite some time: Would I follow the court-martialed surgeon or the two Scottish Majors at Hammersmith Hospital who did not know anything except 'yes sir'?

There was a wide divide between general duty medical officers who had the authority and the specialists who wanted to achieve professional excellence and loathed the way they were hounded. The eccentricities and sensitivities of a good specialist if tolerated and pragmatically tamed can be head strength for those who command. Administration is the job of GDMOs; specialist skills are far too precious to be wasted in paperwork, indents, and desk jobs. At least that was how I was trained in England. But it was not so in Pakistan. Looking back what I find is the doctors who used their profession as a launching pad and got more involved in planning and other organizational matters contributed much more than I with my tube vision approach did, and they built such prestigious institutions like that of pathology and cardiology.

I later found out though the hard way, that establishing institutions of excellence did not have much to do with the professional priorities but how well were you connected with those wielding power and the power laid with the combatants and not with the doctors. The heads of medical corps were never groomed for their new assignment and therefore only marked time of their short-term last posting. Only plans they had in mind were personal as to where they could be rehabilitated after retirement. There was little they could contribute in a year or two; most never even tried and just petered out. A man who all his life has looked through the iris of the eye with an ophthalmoscope or concentrated on inside of a cell seeing through the turret of a microscope, when suddenly exposed to bright full picture usually gets so dazzled that he cuts a very sorry figure amongst the well-entrenched career combatants and never could become a member of the club, let alone the kitchen cabinet. How could an outsider who felt so bereft possibly stress his point of view? So, they usually ended up in appeasing the combatants and becoming yes men.

I knew that the only way to make your mark was through rubbing shoulders with the army top brass. My English training however forbade me to do that; it seemed so unethical—like jilting; like having an affair with your neighbor's attractive wife.

I had chosen to be an orthopedic surgeon. When I started working in military hospitals, my superiors laughed at the notion of my practice of being only an orthopedic surgeon. I was told I would have to do everything. This caused me a lot of frustration. The medical hierarchy in the army wanted jacks-of-all trades, whereas my natural ambition was to excel in my chosen specialty. I wish I had been allowed to start orthopedics as a separate specialty then, rather than decades later when I was at the fag end of my career in army. Perhaps this department of surgery in the army would have attained high standards by now. One result of not allowing the organization of orthopedics as a separate department was that when men who mattered whenever they needed specialized orthopedic treatment; they either went to civilian institutions or abroad, raising serious aspersions about the quality of treatment in military hospitals.

The first few months in the army, as I have already said were very discomforting for me and, as I soon learnt, for other lateral entrants. Some of them soon quitted the army; those who stayed were never happy. I do not know why I did not leave when I felt so unhappy, but I guess it was because soon after my training I was posted out as an independent surgeon to a very busy hospital in another cantonment where I did not have time for myself and got engrossed in the professional problems of sick patients.

9

Independent Surgeon

In my new assignment as the only surgeon for a very busy hospital I had to do all kinds of operations. In the beginning, I rather conceitedly felt that I had been converted from a sports car into a good's train. But soon I got so busy and involved in my work that I had little time for nostalgia or self-pity, though sometimes I would give myself airs like a martyr who had sacrificed his career for his family and the country!

The first posting that saved me from a break down was a remarkable event for several other reasons. The surgeon I relieved was an old friend, Major Siraj-ul-Jannat, now a General in Bangladesh army. He lived in a comfortable stone house on a hill. He was very pleased to see me, and we talked for hours remembering all the old days spent together. When he found out that I was still unmarried, he was quite dismayed.

He was the surgeon who conducted all the protocol duties in Pakistan Embassy when the Surgeon General had interviewed me in London. We had been together in Hammersmith Hospital. I was employed as a Registrar, and he was doing a course in Urology at the Royal Postgraduate Medical School. Earlier on we were also together in a FRCS course conducted by the British professors at the Royal College of Surgeons in Pakistan. To ensure neutrality and fair play in the examinations they brought along all the equipment from London, like x-ray films, histology slides and other materials.

I still remember his hilarious reply to a famous anatomy teacher during the examination. He was sent to recognize a histology slide under a microscope while the examiner waited. Once he had seen the slide he was required to return to the examiner and tell him his diagnosis of the tissue he had just seen. He looked at the slide, raked his brain but could not make head or tail of it. To him it looked a section of either the thyroid or the lung or perhaps the breast. Since the examiner could not wait forever, he settled for thyroid. So, when the examiner asked him what the tissue was, he answered it to be a thyroid. The examiner, a very famous surgeon almost a legend who rose to become the President of the Royal College of Surgeons, hummed pensively. He asked him to go back and examine the slide again. The young candidate once again peered down the microscope, but still he could not make much of the jumbled mass; so, he came back and repeated his diagnosis of thyroid.

The examiner looked at him from head to toe and blew his cheeks as in a whistle but kept his temper and sent him for the third time to look at the tissue very carefully. Even a most naive student would have understood that there was a problem with his diagnosis otherwise why on earth the examiner would send him back and forth to the microscope. My friend now could see the writing on the wall that he was going to fail this time. This made him desperate to read the specimen correctly, but the more intently he looked at, the more confused he became. Like us, he had worked very hard for the last six months, day in and day out knowing fully well, that even in London the pass percentage was extremely low. Even on the third attempt he could not make out what the tissue was. The colors of the slide like that of a kaleidoscope added to his confusion.

By now he knew that it was not a section of the thyroid gland, but being at a loss as to what it was, he decided that his best chance was to stick to his diagnosis. With all the confidence he could muster, he said, "Sir, this is a section of the thyroid gland." The examiner was really annoyed, and this time the very patient senior teacher lost his temper. He said, "Look here, young man, I have sent you once, twice and then for the third time to see the same damned slide and you come back each time repeating it is the thyroid. It is not Thyroid. This slide is a section of a breast." The young man stayed calm and collected and, with an innocent expression on his face said, "Sir I knew why you were sending me back and forth, again and again to the same slide, but I can swear that this slide is not that of a breast. However, since you insist, it must be a breast. But it must be an English breast. I can assure you that Pakistani breasts do not look like this." The examiner stared at him in total bewilderment for a full minute, and then exploded into a hearty laughter. He called the other examiners to his table and told them what this candidate had just said. It goes to his credit though that he passed my friend. How could I have not remembered this character?

So, as I have already said we had a lot of things to discuss when I went to take charge of that cantonment hospital. He said, "When I came from England and was posted here, I did not have a decent house and we lived in a small barrack. Using all my influence and connections as a surgeon, I have only recently managed to acquire this house. It is a pity I am posted out so soon. I want to ensure that this house goes to a surgeon, but the only way you can get this house is by acquiring a wife." I told him I had no plans to get married soon. He was a sincere friend and obviously wished me well, or so I thought. He said, "I don't care about your program. For the sake of this house, get married quickly before we lose it."

Reluctantly, I took his advice and got married. That eventful day fell on 1st of May, the Labor Day. Since then, every day has been a Labor Day; at times May Day, May Day. I am not so sure now if Siraj was my friend!

This reminds me of a friend in Foreign Service. He, after his graduation from the Civil Services Academy, was sent for training to USA. While driving there he met with a serious road accident in which both the cars involved were totally smashed. The occupants of the other car were some East Asian girls from a Himalayan protectorate. After the problems of the accident got sorted out, my friend a lonely soul started dating one of those girls and eventually got married to her. One may call it marriage by accident. Unfortunately, it did not turn out to be the best of marriages. Many years later in a party his wife was bragging about this accident. "Had I followed the legal path," She said, "This man would have gotten years in jail." Someone who knew the family well commented that now the poor fellow was in for life!

After my interview with the General in the Pakistan embassy he asked me to report to a military hospital in London for a medical examination to ensure that I was fit for the army. I found this Milbank Military Hospital a rather weird place. Most of the people I came across were elderly and had gray hair. Two elderly British Lieut. Colonels carried out my medical examination. They seemed on the last leg of their service and one of them had snow-white hair and a long flowing beard. He looked like Father Christmas. They were talking about the policy of recruitment in the army. With my clothes stripped, one of them oldies said to the other colonel, while he measured my height and girth of my chest, "After decades of research the European armies have formed a policy for recruitment of officers. PULHEEM comes first of course. But we have come to conclusion that there are four categories of people who present themselves for induction. First category is of people who are intelligent and hard working. We accept them straight away. They make excellent staff officers, but they must not be made commanders, as they will ruin the army. The second category is of people who are intelligent but lazy, would not do much with their own hands. This is the category that makes good commanders. In that position laziness is an asset." The Colonel with the beard seemed a loyal type and resented the remarks about the commanders of the army. I am sure he thought that before a recruit the picture of army should be painted rosier.

The Colonel who was very fond of talking would not allow any interruption. He did not let Santa Clause butt in. He waived his hand to silence him and carried on. He said to the bearded Colonel, "I want to tell you a story," He started off, "A customer entered an animal pet shop looking for a pet. He could not make up his mind which animal would suit him. The salesman finally brought him close to a cage in which there were three parrots and started praising the birds. He said this first parrot would be an excellent company and I can recommend him strongly as he speaks three languages, English, French and Spanish and he is a very friendly type. The customer seemed impressed and asked the price, 'Fifty pounds,' said the shopkeeper. The customer wanted to know about the second parrot. The shopkeeper started again and said, 'this parrot, Sir is a genius. He knows everything about calculators, their use and the working and will be an asset. He can solve any complicated problem on calculator in no time and will be a great help at home and in your office.

The man was impressed and asked the price. 'One hundred pounds,' said the shopkeeper. The customer thought he might know something about the third parrot as well before deciding. The shopkeeper warned the customer about the third parrot and said, Sir, this fellow is too costly, and I would not recommend him. I suggest you settle for any of the first two. The customer asked the price, 'Five hundred pounds,' the customer was very astonished about the high price. He could not help asking what was so special about this parrot that he had such a high price tag and what was that this parrot could do. The shopkeeper was perplexed and did not know how to answer this question. He said, "I will be frank with you; quite honestly, I do not know what this fellow can do. He sits quietly in the cage and does nothing, but the other two parrots that are so clever address him as Sir!" The Colonel then continued his classification of men.

"The third category is of people who are stupid and lazy. Army accepts them as a welfare drive because no one else will take them and in the army they do pretty well. The fourth category is of people who are stupid and hard working. Beware of them. This is a dangerous class. They are a menace to humanity and are walking disasters. Shun them at any cost." Although they were talking to each other I sincerely hoped they were not alluding to me as in that room there was no one else present. Both had worked as medical officers in British India and knew Urdu words, which are used in routine conversation and insisted on practicing them with me. They had fond memories of Gymkhana at Lahore. They were rather easy-going old gentlemen and did not take much pain in finding faults in me. I was getting the impression they thought I would fit in very well in the last category despite my knock-knees.

Being young and enthusiastic, in this new hospital of the army I set out to cure the world. Luckily, I got a very cooperative anesthetist who rose to be professor in his specialty (Brigadier Salim). So, I worked day in and day out, performing all sorts of operations. I filled the three surgical wards up to the brim. No patient was ever turned away if he had a faintest connection with the army. What little experience I had of military hospitals had told me that the people who deserved my attention the most were those who had least nuisance value: the poor families of soldiers posted to far flung borders and the retired soldiers who could not make both ends meet. The officers could look after themselves and their families. So, I tried my best to help those who really needed it: old soldiers, their families and even distant relatives were welcome. One ward was reserved for the pensioners with prostates, hernias, and old age fractures. This busy schedule kept me well occupied and I all but forgot my past.

It was my training in civilian institutes that had taught me that for a doctor whatever his attire medicine was a patient-doctor relationship, but I was beginning to realize that in the army there was more to it, and I was still living in the past. Being new, pips and stars were odd and yet did not over-awe me, or the absence of these marks of higher ranks failed to attract my attention whether the man wearing or not wearing them was a genuine patient.

Once while I was examining very intently a patient laid bare on a couch in my office, in walked an officer wearing a red cap to see me. I kept on doing what I was doing. The soldier at his sight sat bolt upright as I tried to lay him down. I think the officer expected me to follow suit and jump to attention. Instead, my face showed some annoyance for the unannounced intrusion. When I ignored him and continued to examine the patient, he had to tell me who he was. I still thought that it was irrelevant but asked him to take a seat while I finish my examination. He was not impressed and further informed me that he was holding such and such position, implying he was a very important person. I did not know what to say but asked him that now he can take two seats.

I quickly learnt to cope with the routine work of a military hospital. Most of the cases required simple, routine operations and I had been dealing with such operations as an SHO in English hospitals.

The Surgeon General, who was also a general surgeon and had interviewed me in London, came on a visit to the hospital. Seeing all the senior citizens, he was furious. "This is a military hospital, not a geriatric home," he exploded. But I did not change my ways. A patient was a patient never mind his exterior. Sicker the patient, more attention he should get. In fact, because of such sermons, I was developing a determination to practice medicine professionally, uncompromisingly, cleanly, honestly—even exactly, as far as exactness was possible in medicine. Surgery however is an exact science.

The kick that I got by doing good to so many, stimulated me to work harder. The army culture did not encourage that. My seniors were not exhilarated, as they had to cope with my demands for additional supplies of surgical equipment and unnecessary work. I knew that all I had to do to be in their good books was to follow the beaten track and to do bare minimal.

I noticed that the culture in the army was not patient orientated, but rank (of the patient) orientated; risks (not to the patient but the military doctor) determined their professional decisions. So, to clear my thoughts I sat down one day and charted out, how a professional surgeon should behave. I visualized, that he should behave with honor, keep his standards high, leave nothing to chance, use his utmost skills and fight savagely to treat his patient; come what may. How far did I succeed, there are no double-blind trials to tell.

To crave for ranks when becomes the only criterion, profession takes a hind seat and the professional growth of military physicians remain stunted, because in their dealings they become compromisers, the politicians, and the sycophants. To survive and succeed in any bureaucratic establishment, the old hands who should know what they are talking about say, one thing is important: pass the buck on, never volunteer. Lie low; do not stick your neck out. The best way not to make mistakes is not to make any decisions. No work, no mistakes guarantee a good ACR; the only criteria to rise in military hierarchy. Mediocrity and anonymity is the safest choice. Docility and humility are the hall mark of a good officer. Most of the outspoken and outstanding officers are weeded out during field service and never attain red tapes.

Surely there are better ways to make your mark. Sycophancy and beating your drum with one, and if possible, with both the hands will surely take you far. Humility seldom attracts attention and keeps you out of trouble. About humble people, Churchill used to say about his successor that he had plenty to feel humble about!

A senior Colonel, trained during the Raj, was visiting our hospital. He went around different wards. A young doctor, who had learnt the tricks of the trade rather early, was recently posted as a Captain. Trying to catch the eye of the superior officer and win some favors he would post himself at all vantage points. Being a typical adulator, he was dancing in attendance. The Colonel was too shrewd not to see through sycophancy. The young Captain seemed to have the knack of giving most stupid answers. The Colonel a thoroughbred swallowed a lot but when he could take it no more had to tell him off on several occasions. He felt rather guilty for scolding the young man so often. After the round while going for tea, he thought of soothing this Captain's ruffled feathers. He wanted to say something friendly to him. The Colonel asked the over enthusiastic Captain. "Are you married young man?" The captain stuck his chest out and said proudly, "Yes sir, I am wedded to the profession." Making an immense effort to keep his cool the Colonel pleaded, "When you do get married young man, please do not molest your wife like you do the profession!"

5

Military Medicine

One day a young recruit came limping to the hospital with pain in one of his legs, which he said, had persisted for the past few weeks. His superiors, I was told, did not pay much attention to his complaint, thinking that the young lad was putting it on or was 'scrounging' as it is called in the army. After examining him I got his leg X-rayed. The radiograph alarmed me. It showed new bone formation in one cortex of his Tibia. In an English hospital such an X-ray would have frightened anyone: the diagnosis—-a bone tumor; the treatment—-an amputation. I admitted him in the hospital and just to be very sure did a bone biopsy. The report, when it arrived after a few days, turned out to be of no help at all. Rather it complicated the matters and confused me further. The pathologist described the lesion as he saw it in the slide and ended up saying, "Malignancy cannot be ruled out. Correlate with clinical findings." In plain English it meant sorry mate I cannot help you, so keep me out of it and make up your own mind whether you want to chop off the leg or not. I was very perturbed. I asked a couple of friends and consulted several surgeons. No one was of any help.

I had sleepless nights thinking of some way to help the young man without amputating his leg. Luckily, another young lad with a similar complaint and a similar X-ray picture arrived the following day. Is this thing contagious? I wondered. I knew malignancy was not. Then a third recruit with an identical problem arrived. Three in a week, surely this could not be malignancy. The feeling of relief that descended on me that night, I can still savor. By the end of my tenure in the hospital I had collected over a dozen such recruits, treated them, and written a paper on Stress Fractures. In those days when we did not know much about the subject, Stress Fractures were seldom diagnosed clinically. I, too, was very ignorant about this malady till those three recruits had limped into the hospital.

Stress Fracture of a bone is like the nervous breakdown of a person. The easy going, particularly urban, young boys not used to tough physical exercise when suddenly exposed to demanding military training, develop this condition, and their bones literally start to crumble, particularly the bones of the lower limbs because of the cumulative effect of repeated stress.

Although I performed every type of operation, I was no virtuoso. I kept on cursing myself for coming back only a year after my fellowship from England. I should have worked a bit longer to gain more practical experience. Each patient was a different problem and a new challenge. I had not performed all the operations in the book. In England I was dependent on my consultants for decision-making. Here I had to make all the decisions myself, without much help from anyone. I felt extremely lonely and vulnerable. Everyone expected me to be an expert in all branches of surgery, after all I had the prestigious abbreviation FRCS after my name; but I knew how ignorant I was. I felt honored with the crown of omniscience but was cursed with the awareness of limitations and fallibility. The faith the patients reposed in me was a humbling experience, and I felt very uncomfortable, but to keep them comfortable and for their benefit I kept a confident façade. I had an intense fear of failing the patients who had placed their health, in fact their lives, in my hands. Far from feeling pleased with each addition of skill and experience that every case brought me; I grew more and more distressed as time went on. Even for simple operations I would read books and journals; to be sure that no mistakes were made, and no old lessons forgotten. Then sick with all kinds of apprehension I would go to the operation theatre in a state of daze and uncertainty; but, fortunately, this sense of inadequacy left me as soon as the operation began as I tried to convince myself that in surgery bold decisions which can be risky have to be taken.

In British system the doctors felt protected and comforted by the fact that they could always yell for help when stuck; and get it. Organizational structure of hospital medicine contributed to distancing doctors from their patients. Care of the patients in hospitals was fragmented for patients and physicians. Here I needed help and advice virtually every day, but there was no one I could turn to. No one could share the responsibility of making difficult decisions. The loneliness was killing. I was my own consultant and my own resident. Only the Lord above could help. Every difficult, complicated case was a challenge, and I realized that to run away from a challenge was not manly. So, I used to think hard and long over unusual cases till I had made one firm satisfactory diagnosis and then memorized and repeated in my head all the steps as how to proceed.

A young soldier had a ruptured appendix and was brought to the Operation Theater for surgery. The diagnosis had been delayed and he had developed peritonitis and was a sick man. With a tube through his nose and drips running I was concerned about his health. Before operating upon him I wanted to be doubly sure about the diagnosis and once again went to the operating table to palpate his abdomen. As I reached him the soldier went into a convulsion; all his four limbs suddenly stiffened. I was horrified as to what new neurological complication had set in now. My mind was put to ease by the attending theatre JCO when he explained that the soldier was being respectful to a superior officer. And in the condition that he was, that was the only way of his expressing 'shun'! Young man was on deathbed, and he still remembered army protocol.

Should one compliment his superiors for the training imparted to him or feel sorry for the poor lad, I was not sure, but his plight brought a silent prayer on my lips.

One day, well past lunchtime at the end of a backbreaking operation day I was looking forward to going home and putting my feet up. I put on my uniform, tied my shoelaces, and wearily walked out of the operation theatre when I saw a JCO with a young boy in tow. The boy's arm was in a sling. The boy, I guessed, must have broken his arm a few days ago, and the JCO must had found it convenient to bring him to the hospital only now when I had packed up to go home after a tiring day. The prospect of going back to the operation theatre made me uneasy. The JCO gave a smart salute and held up the boy's x-ray and his referral paper. The signs of annoyance must have been visible on my face, and I made little effort to conceal my grumpy look as I yelled, "Is this the time to bring this boy to the hospital?" The JCO was cool and polite. He apologized for his untimely intrusion and very respectfully said, "Sir I hate to bother you with this problem at this time of day, but this boy is a nuisance. He makes me mad. So many times, I have told him not to climb up trees at this hour when it is time for the surgeon to go home. But, sir, he is a complete nut. Despite my warnings he did climb up a tree and fell, breaking his arm when it was your packing-up time. Sir, I am extremely sorry. I promise you, sir, to chop off that tree as soon I go back so that you are not disturbed at such odd hours; a thousand apologies, sir." I did not know which way to look, and to conceal my embarrassment immediately took the young boy to the theatre.

All people are not alike; some would put you to shame with their politeness and extreme decency. One of my younger colleagues working in the same hospital in which I did, had a few years-old son he was very fond of. One day the child started having vague lower abdominal pain on the left side that parents did not take much notice of. It was a weekend and on Saturday the pain worsened, and my friend gave him some painkillers. On Sunday, a holiday the child had fever and the father prescribed some antibiotics. In the evening the child vomited, and the mother of the child asked my friend to get in touch with me—-surgeon in the same hospital. The father a very soft-spoken polite man, I have great regard for did not want to 'disturb' me on a holiday. The entire night the child kept fretting and could not sleep and kept his mother awake who now noticed some swelling and bruising of skin over his left scrotum and the child would yell at any handling of it. The distraught mother woke up her husband and pleaded him to consult me. My friend would not think of waking me up, as he thought, I being a very busy surgeon with an operation list next morning, deserved a good night sleep. I am sure due to scolding by his wife early on Monday morning he relented and rang me up. The first question I asked was had the child hurt himself: the parents were not too sure. I asked him to immediately bring the child to the hospital, fearing the worst, torsion of the testicle. I rushed to the hospital and reached Emergency Room before they did. Examining the child, I was horrified and took him straight to Operation Theater. On exploration, unfortunately my fears proved right as the testicle by then had gone gangrenous and only treatment left at that stage was, its removal. It took me couple of days to persuade the distraught mother to let me operate and fix the remaining testis to prevent a similar disaster.

I was posted to a Military hospital in the Northwest of the country where we were allowed to see some private patients. One morning a German lady was brought to our hospital. She had been seized by agonizing abdominal pain during the night. She and her husband had recently arrived in the area to help set up a local paper industry. The investigations revealed a big stone, the shape of a stag horn, in one of her kidneys. It was indeed surprising that, despite harboring such a big stone for a long time, she did not have any symptoms of any kidney problem before.

The lady was huge, to say the least. Her weight was beyond the scales that we used in our hospital to weigh patients. She had to be taken to the storeroom where we had a larger balance. Having diagnosed a kidney stone, I prescribed symptomatic treatment and advised her husband to get the stone removed surgically when they went back to Germany. I was conscious of the disdain of foreigners for facilities available in local hospitals. However, her husband, a middle-aged Engineer, opted to have her operated in Pakistan. I looked at the girth of the German lady and my heart sank. I thought to myself, 'Good grief! How would I find the kidney in this mountain of a lady, what to speak of the stone? It would be like searching for a needle in a haystack.' So, I tried again, "There is no urgency about the operation. The pain will subside with medication, and you can plan the operation according to your convenience when you get back to Germany." After all I thought, this stone had been lying there for years and it could stay there for some more time without giving much trouble to the lady. I also told him that in case they had any problem they were welcome to consult me again. I heaved a sigh of relief seeing the back of that immense lady as the couple left.

I was young and raw and despite my resolve to accept every challenge, I did not like the idea of finding a needle in such a huge haystack. I would be hopelessly lost in that mountain of fat, I thought.

While I was inexperienced, the anesthetist I worked with, a very kind senior specialist was highly experienced. He would not treat me as a surgeon but as his son, and always encouraged and inspired me. He also ensured I did not get into trouble with the establishment. I am indebted to him to this day. May God bless the soul of Col. Minto.

After a few days the German arrived again and informed me that he had made up his mind to have his wife operated upon in Pakistan. I was not thrilled. I wondered why he wanted to have her operated here in Pakistan despite my unenthusiastic attitude. I just did not have the courage to say, 'look here friend your wife is very fat, and I don't feel up to it;' Oh, the agony of saying no, which would have been an admission of defeat that no surgeon worth his salt would like to accept. The only way for a surgeon to excel in surgery is to have confidence in himself and go for the surgical procedures that might at first appear slightly beyond his reach. To accept a new challenge is the only way to improve his skills, otherwise he will shrink and wither away. I knew that a surgeon cannot afford to be timid, but I must admit that this job was too much for me. I tried again in my broken German to make him change his mind, but my repetition of 'akhtung, akhtung' cut no ice with him.

The German's English was better than my German, riddled with 'akhtungs', but we were getting nowhere. The more I tried to change his mind, the more determined he became to have his wife operated upon by me. He was confident that all would be well. I was not so sure. I cursed my German and German's English, which failed to shake him off. All sorts of thoughts crossed my mind. Perhaps this fellow, smart, and handsome, was not very fond of his fat and huge wife; and wanted to get rid of her by having her operated upon in Pakistan. I suspected that he was somehow convinced that she would bleed to death right on the operation table in my theatre. There must be another woman waiting for him somewhere in Bavaria, I told myself, and I was being used to remove the mountain that stood between them. I was afraid that my career as a surgeon might abruptly come to an end if this woman died in my operation theatre. Serious complications were real possibilities. Why can't I be firmer, I cursed myself, and say one firm final 'no', but doing so seemed as difficult as operating on that lady.

The lady was admitted, and the day of operation arrived. It was a humid sultry August morning when we started the operation in our rather inadequately air-conditioned operation theatre. The big lady won't fit on one operation table, so two operation theatre tables were laid side by side for her, still her ample body overflowed the tables. The anesthetist was an expert in his field, and he put her to sleep in no time. Now it was my turn to take over and do my job. A cold shiver ran through my spine.

The anesthetists after putting the patients to sleep usually find the proceedings rather dull, and either settle down with their crosswords or find some other more interesting occupation to kill time. Obviously, my surgical dexterity was not fascinating enough to hold the attention of this very experienced anesthetist who had seen many masters at work.

He, therefore, decided to keep the German sitting in his office next door informed of the proceedings in the theatre by a minute-to-minute running commentary.

My system was overproducing adrenaline. I sweat profusely even on ordinary days, but this was an unusual day with an enormous patient daring me to do what I could. The stuffy theatre and the oppressive humidity of the month of August made things more difficult for me. My heart was pounding furiously, and I could hear the thuds, but I did not know whether my face was flushed or sallow. I thanked my stars that there was a mask on my face, and no one could see it. This must be one of the many reasons why surgeons wear masks in operation theatres. I asked an assistant to wipe the sweat from my brow, rallied my strength and disregarded for the moment all the terrible things that could go wrong. I took the scalpel in my hand, looked at the enormous lady on the table, heaved a deep breath and gave a big whacking incision over her abdomen, right where the kidney was supposed to be in that baby whale.

After that I was in a trance, oblivious of the world around me. I forgot everything—the stifling humidity, the rickety old air-conditioner, my apprehensions, the nationality of the patient, the presence of other people in the room; even myself. My eyes and ears were shuttered from the distant land that I had left behind, my mind unmindful of all the worries of the world. Time seemed to have stopped. My every sense, like touch of fingers had enhanced that only a blind person can experience. Bent over the patient like a stork, my eyesight had changed into a tube vision and all I could make out was the incision and all that mattered at that moment was how to get on with the operation. Then the anxiety that I had experienced before the start of the operation was suddenly lifted and I became my normal self. The pounding in my chest gradually became quieter and gentler till it ceased to bother me. I felt like a person who is afraid of jumping in cold water in the freezing winter but when, after a lot of dithering and dodging, he takes the plunge, he finds that all his apprehensions were ill founded.

It took me quite some time to cut through the fat under her fair skin, and soon both my hands were buried in the big incision. Even at a depth of half a foot or so there was no trace of the muscles of the abdominal wall that I had to traverse before reaching the kidney. At last, I saw pink muscles in a sea of fat, and wondered why nature makes the job of surgeons so difficult by collecting the fat right under the incisions. She had a lot of fat and all of it at wrong places. Being a hard-working German housewife, she also had well-developed muscles. I told myself that once I found my way through the muscles the proceedings would be simpler. But when I had cut through the muscles, I found myself confronted with more fat; there was no trace of the kidney. I prodded everywhere to locate the kidney but could not find the maroon structure till I had cut through that second stack of fat. By then my arms had disappeared into the incision up to the elbows. Mercifully, the size of the stone made it easy to locate it. A sense of relief and utter bliss descended upon me: at long last I was close to the journey's end.

By now my assistants and I knew what we were trying to do; the comforting sense of routine was re-established. Sutures were stitched and cut with almost automatic precision. Mine and my assistant's hands moved together as in a symphony. A case that started as a daunting challenge gradually petered out into a job. What we were doing was nothing new but different and we had to be precise like acrobats on the high trapeze as if there was no net below. But these techniques we had practiced many a times, and this helped us to carry on.

My anesthetist in the meanwhile was constantly on the move, leaving the theatre every few minutes to cheer up the husband sitting next door by describing in detail how I was getting along. The stone was finally removed, and we started the retreat, closing the wound layer by layer. When we had completed the operation, and I was taking off the blood-stained gown, I overheard the anesthetist in his office assuring the husband, "It is all over, the operation is finished, and your wife is fine." "I am sure she must be all right," replied the German. "Tell me how the surgeon is?" He asked.

How is the surgeon? Never in my life have I heard such words from a patient's relative at the end of an operation. They wafted on my ears like rose petals and soft sweet music. Suddenly all my weariness disappeared. The patient and their next of kin seldom appreciate what the poor surgeon, undergoes both physically and mentally, during a long, difficult operation. They are only concerned about the welfare of the patient. But this man was different: he had the decency to feel concern for the plight of the surgeon instead of selfishly worrying only about his wife's condition. Later, when I met him, he apologized most sincerely about the bulk of his wife and then thanked me profusely. I cursed myself for suspecting this noble and considerate man of trying to get rid of his wife through me. Every year a Christmas card arrives from Germany and reminds me of what I went through on that sultry, stifling August forenoon.

The lesson learnt; tension is necessary for any creative work; tension is natural reaction when you face a crisis. Tension is harmful only when you are more concerned about it than the crisis you must deal with. Surely one should take all the safety measures because it will be a stupid man who attempts cartwheels at a precipice.

In the late sixties of the last century, before the Russian invasion of Afghanistan, the road through the historical Khyber Pass used to be a very popular route for European tourists coming to visit Asia. My hospital was located near the Mercedes workshop. Most of the German tourists driving through mountainous terrain of Afghanistan visited this workshop for necessary repairs to their cars. Almost every morning I would find a group of foreign tourists of all sorts camping in my lawns: some were simple, innocent tourists out to see this part of the world, but most of them were junkies, young boys, and girls, visiting Pakistan for fun and drugs. The route was also popular with Pakistanis returning home from Europe. Several of my friends driving back from Europe would find time to stay with me for a day or two. It is a pity that the war in Afghanistan has blocked such an important link between Western Asia and Central Asian Muslim states. I am sure that once sanity prevails in

Afghanistan, it will become a very important route again.

It was again the hot and humid month of August when another German patient was brought to me.

This big, burly, bearded German was traveling in his Mercedes on the highway from Kabul to Pakistan when a truck suddenly appeared from a blind side-lane and hit the car with such terrible force that it was tossed into a dry ravine at some distance from the road. The German sustained numerous serious injuries such as a fractured femur and a broken neck. His right hand was completely chopped off. The truck driver ran off without trying to help his victim who was in real bad shape, trapped in the car lying in a depression and hardly visible from the road. The poor fellow lay there in his wrecked car with ants crawling all over his blood-soaked body. There was little chance of anyone noticing the wreckage in that wilderness and coming to his help. A senior Pakistani bureaucrat, who happened to be driving down that road with his wife and children, spotted the wreck somehow. He extricated the unconscious German out of the car, loaded him in the back seat of his own car and managed to bring him to our hospital at about midnight. He seemed an optimist and must have high hopes of the medical profession and retrieved the amputated hand as well.

It took us a couple of hours to revive the patient who had nearly bled to death. He was young and healthy, so he came around. I was also young, seeking an opportunity to do something I had never done before, something out of the ordinary, and something heroic. "Here is the opportunity, I told myself, replant the severed hand and earn a place in history." In those days re-plantation of limbs was not common. Only the Chinese had done a few successful replantation of severed hands. "Should I attempt to do it?" I asked myself again and again. More than eight hours had passed since the accident, there were ants still clinging to the amputated hand. I was not too sure that I could perform the operation with success and wavered between 'to do it or not to do it'. At last, I contacted my anesthetist, who, God bless his soul, came right away at about two o' clock in the morning. He encouraged me and pushed me into doing what would have been the most dramatic operation of my life. What with shock, a fractured and unstable cervical spine and other injuries, the patient was unfit for a general anesthesia. So, the anesthetist doped the patient, and I used regional anesthetic. It took me the whole night, or what remained of it, suturing together the arteries, the veins, and the tendons. By first light I had completed my most memorable operation, which I fondly hoped, would find a place in history books. Then we, my anesthetist and I sat by the patient watching the re-planted hand and guessing whether there was circulation in the fingernails or not. We gazed at my handicraft and wondered would it survive or not and if it did not, I wondered how much disappointment and guilty conscious I would suffer at the fascinating failure,

The German embassy soon got the wind about the accident, and in the next couple of days flew the German back home. The hand, to my dismay, did not survive but fortunately the patient did.

With the advent of operating microscopes these operations of re-plantation have become commonplace. I was in California in the mid-eighties when I read in the local paper about a certain Dr. Cheema who had re-implanted a severed arm. The familiar family name of the surgeon whom I had not met or known; and the laudable operation he performed, caught my attention. I located him in Fresno, famous for its vineyard, a town midway between Los Angeles and San Francisco. I visited him and stayed with him for a day or so to trace our tribal connections.

The severed arm was that of a Sikh young boy who had caught it in a machine that cleanly amputated it. This surgeon Cheema re-implanted the limb successfully, winning laurels and headlines in the media. The remarks of the father of the young Sikh, an old bearded typical Sikh Jat from Punjab were interesting. He said, "I have known of Cheema's breaking arms, this is the first Cheema who has re-planted it." And thank heavens; we have changed over to more useful pastimes than breaking bones.

I remember with what disdain the worthy judges of the superior court looked down upon the first Cheema who was elevated to the bench. They thought the right place for this man was not on the bench but in the dock.

What impressed me most during my service in the army was the gratitude of patients though sometimes I could not do for them as much as I wished to. While I was posted in the north of the country, one indebted patient, a tribal chief, invited me to his village somewhere on the border with Afghanistan. After enjoying the grand feast in the traditional Pathan style; when I was about to leave, he presented me two goats as a token of his gratitude, saying that it was their tradition and custom. I was at a loss what I would do with them, but despite my refusal, a couple of his servants dumped the bleating and vigorously protesting animals in the back seat of my car. I was left with little choice. I drove away feeling very uncomfortable with the two animals roaring their heads off.

My wife and my Batman always would take immense pains to keep our car immaculately clean. I wanted to give my back-seat companions as little time as possible to spoil the interior of the car; so, I took off at full throttle. Frightened as the animals were, they thoroughly wetted the carpets of the car and covered the seats with muck. The car soon began to smell like a barn. Standing behind my seat the two goats would from time to time turn their attention to me and sniff the back of my neck, try to pull off my hair or nibble my ears. I was racing home to avoid the embarrassing glances of amused people on the roadside. Suddenly I saw a little girl crossing the road chasing a goat. A big black dog followed her. I do not know what came in the head of one of the goats standing in my rear, but suddenly she tried to jump through the windscreen. She hit the windscreen, scratching it with her horns, then slumped on the steering wheel, and finally landed in my lap upside down while I desperately fought to gain control of the car. The hoofs of the goat, now bleating and struggling furiously to regain an upright position hit me repeatedly and rhythmically with full force under my chin and nose like punches of a boxer. In the process my glasses flew off. I applied brakes and the car screeched to a halt but not before it had hit the little girl. I rushed out to see the damage done.

The frightened little girl was lying on the road crying in pain. She had sustained a fracture of her femur. While I was about to pick up the girl, the black dog, growling with anger, came at me, grabbed my leg, and sank his teeth with dedicated venom in my calf. I jumped up and down trying to free my jerking, bleeding leg from the dog's vice-like jaws. The beast would not let go, the more I tried to free my leg, the deeper it dug its teeth in it. While I was hopping on one leg in pain, the Billy goat of the girl turned back and running at full tilt hit me from behind. He had timed the attack perfectly and struck me when both my feet were off the ground. The force of the blow sent me flying cartwheel in the air. When I came down, I landed on the poor girl who was already in great pain. This was adding insult to injury which made her let out a terrible blood-curdling shriek that brought a crowd of people rushing to the scene. They were furious at what I had done. Nobody seemed to be on my side. In situations like this it is always the driver of the car who is at fault. No one bothered to ask what the girl was doing on the road. Parents and relatives of the girl soon reached there and surrounded me, making all kinds of threatening noises and gestures. It was an ugly scene, and I feared being lynched by the angry mob. In the pandemonium that followed I tried to explain that I was a doctor and would take full responsibility to treat the little girl. Thank God, my plea helped to bring some sort of order to the mayhem. The girl's relatives after some deafening consultation among themselves, decided to allow me to take the girl to the hospital, treat her on the condition that I would bear all the expenses. The father of the girl picked her up and sat in the front seat of my car while two of his gorilla-like friends sat in the back with the solitary goat standing in the middle between them. One of the goats, taking advantage of the confusion had stepped outside the car and made good its escape. I was too bewildered and preoccupied to care for the runaway goat. In any case, I had had enough of this goat-business.

The cries of the girl made the matter look rather urgent. I therefore quickly got in the seat and slammed my foot on the accelerator. The two fierce-looking tribesmen, talking loudly in a language I could not understand, did not look very friendly. I drove as fast as I could. Fortunately, it was a holiday, and the roads were empty, but unfortunately the hospital was closed. I parked my car outside the Operation Theatre and went inside to fetch help. While I was inside, the remaining goat decided that it was the right time to make a move, and it jumped out of the car and disappeared. The attendants of the girl made no effort to stop her. They were too concerned about the well-being of the girl rather to look after my goat, and I don't blame them.

So, there I was left with the little girl with a broken leg and in place of my two goats in the back seat, three angry and ferocious looking men, a stinking car, and my torn and blood-soaked trouser that I had bought from Harrods of London and had reserved it for special occasions. I cursed myself for not declining the hospitality of the tribal chief. I did not know whether the dog that had bitten me was rabid or not, but at that point of time it was difficult to tell who was madder. The beast or the man, who instead of putting his feet up and relax over the weekend preferred to go on wild goat chase.

The screaming child was admitted in the hospital. I did my best to ensure the best medical help for the child and a very special treatment of her parents. During the next few days, they saw me in my uniform coming in and out of the ward where the child was admitted and acknowledging the salutes of the military staff. This impressed them and changed their hostile attitude toward me. At the time of her discharge from the hospital, the indebted Pathans were overwhelmed with gratitude, and they invited me to their village for a feast. I would have none of that as I had learnt my lesson. I politely but firmly declined, fearing that their hospitality would not allow them to let me come back without the traditional gift of goats.

While working as a surgeon in Peshawar, in the Northwest of the country in late sixties I used to be always in a spin. I would be called very frequently to see patients in the three hospitals varying from 20 to 100 miles away, whenever the local surgeons would either go on leave or would be under arrest! One of my class fellows a surgeon was being prosecuted for not being a good soldier. While he was under arrest, I had to cover surgical emergencies in his hospital as well about fifty miles away traveling on a tortuous and dangerous road. Several fatal road traffic accidents had occurred on that route. But it was Bannu the farthest outpost established during the Raj, where traveling since Rudyard Kipling's time was a nostalgic and sometimes a harrowing experience that I dreaded most. The distance was also much more and the terrain rough and it passed through the gun totting tribe's 'wild West,' FATA—where in a pass between the mountains one could buy from a machete to a missile, if one could haggle the price. It indeed was scary traveling through the free for all land during daylight and at night it could be very risky as the writ of the government there wore thin. So many vehicles and innocent people would be held hostage for extortion, ransom, and blackmailing.

The journey would bring me sad memories of that unfortunate British warrior slumped on his exhausted horse, exact replica of a painting in Red Indian Museum in Oklahoma. He was the only soldier left alive, presumably to deliver the painful message to his British superiors in first Anglo-Afghan war of 1840 the 'Auckland Folly.' Each one of over fifteen thousand soldiers and other personnel was butchered, massacred mercilessly. Half dead, the poor rider fell off his horse in front of gates of cantonment at Jalalabad fort; but lived to tell the horrific story of Afghans hunting British like prairie wolfs. Every soldier of that elite army of an Empire where the sun never used to set was brutally hacked to death. Dr. William Brydon like me was also a military surgeon!

About Afghanistan it is said (the Iron Amir—1840-1901) that one may conquer her, but no one can hold her; history of last two centuries has proved the point. The list of invaders is long. Afghanistan in practical terms means the capital Kabul, the rest of the country since its inception has been looked after by Allah! About the Pathans, it is narrated that "Afghans are brave people. They are not for sale, but you can always hire them!" And ever since the Maliks, (the tribal chiefs) are on the pay roll of the neighboring governments.

On either side of virtually nonexistent Pak Afghan divide over two thousand kilometer long, live the same fair, tall people-the Pushtoons or Pathans, ethnically not Dravidians, probably Israelites or Greek. Straddling the impossible and impassable mountains and caves like Tora Bora is a rugged terrain, over thirty thousand square kilometers, where there is little writ of any government. The lesson learnt by the British was not forgotten or ignored by Pakistan at the time of Partition of India in 1947; the Pathans were left alone! The area is run by tribal Maliks like in the medieval times of Islam. Every Pathan, furiously independent and ruggedly handsome grows a beard, has long flowing hair, wears same head gear, the *lungi*(a big turban) and always carries a loaded gun. It is difficult to tell them apart. All women wear a burka and it is difficult to tell them at all! The tribal justice here is crude but swift and women enjoy the safety and respect granted to them, not by the culture but by their religion; amply reported by Yvonne Ridley, the English women reporter of 'The Guardian' of England who was held captive in Kabul.

The desolate barren terrain is known as Federally Administered Tribal Area (FATA). This is a unique freak in the world politics. It is in Pakistan but still Government has little say in its governance. Time here has stood still since Alexander's days.

I had been to Bannu a couple of times during the day and did not really fancy be called again particularly at night. The journey was not safe, rather dangerous on windy roads over the hills and several people, including a couple of surgeons had already lost their lives on this route.

Their vehicles fell off the cliffs in road traffic accidents. During summer heat these hot rocks were like live coals. The mountains were rugged desolate and barren.

One hot and humid evening while I had just returned from Nowshera after operating on a gunshot wound through abdomen spending backbreaking hours on damage control, a call was waiting for me once I reached home. I was to travel to Bannu immediately to see an urgent surgical emergency. There were no other details available. Telephones those days were a rarity and the messages were sent through Morse's code and no one in the administration would take the trouble of asking for details. Once the central command passed a message there was not to reason why. In any case the clerks sitting in their offices would neither understand nor bother about the logistic difficulties faced by the specialists. They just passed on the orders.

Late in the evening a rickety jeep full of soldiers carrying guns arrived to take me to see this emergency. I looked at the Wily World War II vintage open jeep and wondered where I was supposed to sit. It was already carrying three soldiers and a driver. The soldiers were for my protection lest some terrible tribal abducted me as a hostage. Squashed amongst them I felt like a prisoner and the soldiers seemed there to ensure that I do not run away enroute! It was very hot and when the jeep started its clunk clan I really wondered if it would even reach the main road. The wind was still very hot. With soldiers sweating and smelling it was an uncomfortable journey on a bumpy half-metaled narrow road. Not a very long journey as crow flies but by road it could take hours getting there. We traveled most of the night and I was preparing myself to spend further few hours in the operation theatre repairing some damaged soldier, may be a gunshot chest.

I expected the hospital alive and bustling with feverish activity as last time when I was similarly called at an unearthly hour. An unfortunate Engineer in a suicidal attempt had shot himself in the head; the bullet traversing from one temple through his brain to the other. One could almost see through his head! In my imagination I could visualize the shining theatre lights crowded by the surgical team ready for the heroic surgery as last time.

Once we reached the hospital almost in the early hours of the morning, it was a different sight. Everything was quiet and serene, almost spooky. There was no activity at all in or outside the operation theatre. I cursed myself for taking so long to get there. I feared the worst. May be the injured person had bled to death waiting for me. It was with some difficulty that I located the 'emergency,' I was sent for, still in the surgical ward. The nurse on duty was busy with her crotchet, weaving a web under a solitary light with all the ceiling fans working full speed in a very empty ward where the few patients present were snoring heavily. The atmosphere was eerie, far from the battle cry I had in my mind. The nurse was not very sure why I was called, as all her patients were comfortable. With some difficulty she recollected a new admission passed on to her by the day staff that had some problem with his abdomen. That must be the patient that I had been sent for to see. She condescended to get up from her comfortable chair and took me to a patient, whose snoring was the loudest, reverberating and shaking the walls of the surgical ward. She thought this must be the patient I was supposed to see. I tried to wake him, and he let out a foul curse, as he did not like being disturbed at that unearthly hour. I looked at this big burly chap and started taking history. It was most frustrating to see that he had no problem, his abdomen was soft and there seemed not much the matter with him. He was disgustingly fit. I asked him why he was in hospital. The man was himself confused why was he in hospital as he was to drive his superior officer to Rawalpindi in the morning. He said he had not been to toilet for a couple of days and came to Reception of hospital to take some laxative pills when the duty doctor admitted him in the hospital. He was the driver of the most senior officer in the garrison and the duty medical officer was taking no chances.

An adolescent girl was brought to a hospital in a state of shock. She was the daughter of an officer who did not enjoy enviable reputation. The distraught mother kept wailing and howling trying to lead us towards a diagnosis of appendicitis. She was not forthcoming with detailed history and in her distress, it was difficult to trust her but not so difficult to smell fish. It was pointless wasting any time on her. When I examined the girl, she was ghastly pale, dehydrated, pulse-less and was gasping for breath. Her abdomen was enormously bloated. It was obvious she was about to die of Septic shock. After energetic resuscitation and heavy doses of antibiotics she was taken to Operation Theater for an exploratory laparotomy. This revealed a crude attempt at criminal abortion by someone very illiterate and ignorant. On opening her abdomen there was musty smell of a dead fetus lying in the peritoneal cavity with a ruptured uterus. It had delivered the wrong way. After doing the needful, to every one's surprise I in the end invaginated her appendix, to slough off. I had developed a very trustworthy surgical team and amongst us we beseeched that as in the papers the diagnosis of Appendicectomy will be adhered to. Illicit baby, and unwed mother in our set up can end up in honor killing.

We figured out that, that two half-truths when added can make one! Not a word was breathed of operative details to anyone including the father and our lips were sealed. The girl eventually survived. Years later, it gives me immense satisfaction to see her settled in life.

6

Doctors In Uniform

If military rules are followed in letter and spirit, a military surgeon should have little surgical work. A thorough medical examination at the time of induction in the army should ensure that only strong, healthy young men without any serious disorder are selected, and that no person who cannot bear the rigors of strenuous military training can get in. Regular medical examinations should weed out anyone who had managed to hoodwink the medical authorities at the time of recruitment. Any infirmities are exposed during the period of intense military training. So, unless there is a breakdown of the system, military surgeons should have little to do in peacetime apart from treating odd accidents. Prevention of diseases should be the hallmark of any good medical service. In the military, the stress should be on prevention of disease and accidents as it was in the past. During the British Raj, if an epidemic of infectious diseases broke out in a unit, the Commanding Officer would be lynched.

The families of the soldiers, however, are a different matter. Belonging to lower income groups they suffer all the ailments prevalent in the poorer section of our society. On the quality of the treatment provided to them depend on the morale of the soldiers who, working in far-flung areas, cannot themselves be present to look after their near and dear ones. They need an assurance that their families get the best treatment when they need it.

The repeated imposition of Martial Law in the country has changed the culture of the army. When generals took upon themselves to cleanse the country, the medical hierarchy in the army did not want to be left behind and decided to cure the world of diseases requiring tertiary care. Since the young soldiers did not have many health problems, the authorities started looking in other areas to find patients, under the impression that well-populated hospitals in peacetime are better than empty wards. In the army the top specialty should be trauma management and re-constructive surgery because that is what the soldiers of a dedicated striking force need both in times of war and peace.

The military should use its resources for projects relevant to its profession, for training in areas which are specific to the needs of armed forces rather to waste them on fancy projects like replacing heart valves, worn out joints, dentures, or kidneys. What terror can an edentulous force strike in the hearts of its enemies where the best facilities are reserved for patients who have weak hearts, immobile joints and wet their trousers!

I remember a story about the head of a socialist country, a military dictator who, while on a tour of the countryside, visited a school, a hospital, and a prison. He donated a small sum of money for the welfare of the students, and an equally paltry amount for welfare of the patients, but for the improvement of the facilities in the jail and for welfare of its inmates he announced quite a large grant. The allocation of this large sum for the prison surprised everyone. Someone complimented him on his concern for the well-being of the unfortunate inmates. The dictator seemed intuitive and explained that after he was thrown out of office, he might have to spend most of his remaining life in the prison; looks like the dictator was not the only one that farsighted.

An unenviable reckless event that I cannot forget and find most regrettable to this day is while I was seconded to Air Force and discovered 'the real person behind the persona,' the kind of chemicals I was made of; not much to feel proud about. Those were my early days as a young surgeon in blue uniform. One day I was busy in Operation theatre undertaking different kinds of surgeries. After operating on a couple of patients, I was scrubbing for the third case when a frantic call from the adjoining postoperative ward, alarmed me. The message simply said that the patient recently sent to the ward after surgery was dying. Leaving everything I dashed to the postoperative ward where the man in charge of the ward, a mild-mannered Master Warrant Officer (MWO), dressed in what looked like an emperor's regalia followed me dutifully on my heals.

The cyanosed patient was in a very serious condition: the way he was gasping for breath left no doubt in my mind that he was, indeed, on the verge of death. I immediately cleansed his mouth and throat. There was still a lot of fluid in him that I wanted to suck out. I asked the accompanying MWO to hurry and pull in the suction apparatus that was lying in the corridor. He quickly went out while I continued my struggle to save the patient. The patient in the meanwhile had a cardiac arrest. I worked frantically to revive the patient. My assistant, the emperor, was nowhere in sight and I desperately needed the suction machine. So I rushed out and dragged the suction machine into the ward and sucked the patient dry before inserting a tube in his throat. With fluid sucked and his airway clear, the resuscitated patient fortunately started to improve; and what a relief it was.

When we had things under control, in walked the MWO with a 'Laskar'(porter) in tow. I shouted at him, "Where the hell had you disappeared?" "I had gone to fetch the 'Laskar' to bring in the suction machine," he said. His reply set me on fire: A man is dying and this protocol-ridden buffoon instead of dragging the suction machine weighing hardly a few kilos, that too on the wheels, with his own hands goes in search of a subordinate to do the job! I could almost palpate a volcano erupting within. Unable to control myself, at his complete lack of realizing the gravity of the situation or was it the exultant snarl on his face that showed fire to the explosion; I barked at him and in a fit of temper slapped him. This knee-jerk violent reaction, when I stood bereft of all the norms that I attributed to my martial egotistical ancestry, may be okay in our feudal settings but cannot be acceptable in a disciplined force.

Now MWO is a very celebrated rank in the Air Force, like Subedar Major in the army, which one achieves at the zenith of life after decades of long colored service. No one in the forces, even senior officers would ever even envisage being disrespectful to, what to say of slapping a Master Warrant Officer; certainly not in public. It simply is not done. What I did was a cardinal sin and I felt sorry for what I did to the MWO, but I justified myself because of the dire nature of emergency and soon forgot all about it. The MWO, however did not, and reported the matter to higher authorities. One day I came to know that an inquiry was being conducted into the incident. The matter, which I thought to be just an unfortunate impulsive lapse on my part, seemed to have taken a grave turn.

After completion of the official proceedings of inquiry, we both were produced before the Base Commander. I recalled a story going around about military justice. A CO (Commanding Officer) was instructing his 2nd in command, who was appointed as president of a military court to try an erring soldier. "Give the bastard a fair trial and three months RI (rigorous imprisonment)," he instructed his subordinate officer.

The Base Commander despite his prefix was a very cultivated man. He later became Chief of Air Force. He greeted the MWO with a broad smile, "We have met before. Have we not?" He seemed to know him much better than he knew me who had just joined the service. "Yes sir, you visited us in Saudi Arabia on an inspection last year," answered the MWO who now looked more at ease than me. "Oh, yes," said the Base Commander, "You were working in Dhahran Air Force Hospital where I led an inspection team, and I remember commending you on the high quality of cleanliness in your ward." "Yes sir," said the MWO proudly, while I felt increasingly out of place. The Base Commander continued, "Yes, now I can recall vividly. I commended you for leading the troops with your personal example when you were sweeping the floor of the ward with a broom with your own hands." "Yes sir," beamed the JCO. The Base Commander's deft handling of an ugly situation impressed me and taught me a lesson that I cannot forget.

But this was not the only occasion when I skated on thin ice!

In 1971, just before the war with India over Bangladesh, the duty doctor admitted a young dashing Air Force pilot to the hospital with severe pain in the abdomen. I was asked to see him the following morning when most of his pain had disappeared. The routine investigations were negative except for a small speck over the kidney area, picked up by our over-observant Radiologist on x-ray of the abdomen. Further tests proved it; a pea size stone in one of the kidneys. Correlation of his pain with this concretion was debatable. Being pilot of a fighter aircraft one had to be very careful about his disposal, as this finding was dicey, like an inverted T wave in one odd lead of an Electrocardiogram. With these findings the decision to let them fly expensive aircraft becomes tricky. I know of a number of brilliant officers whose careers were marred by perfectionists on similar points. The stone was so small that I would not advise surgery which even if I did, I am sure the officer would have refused. There was nothing the matter with this pilot and he was itching to go.

Following morning yet another war with India started. The pilot now became very impatient. He pleaded to let him go, "These are the days for which our poor country invests so much on us and if I do not fight now, I will never be able to forgive myself. My colleagues will always taunt me for this act of cowardice." While in service I found these pilots quite an extraordinary breed; young, dashing, making split second decisions; wrong or right is another matter, always so close to death, like surgeons, yet so cheerful and ebullient. It was refreshing and a pleasure dealing with them. I had no choice but to relent under pressure of such patriotic fervor, in fact blackmail and discharged him from hospital, 'fit for flying.'

The pilot flew many successful missions in the next few days, was mentioned in dispatches and later was awarded a gallantry award as well for his courage and valor. When the war was over, head of Air Force Medical service, Air Cdr. (later Lieut. General) came for a visit to our hospital. Night before he stayed in the officer's mess. Early next morning while he was having breakfast in the dining hall, he could not help overhearing a few young fighter pilots, having breakfast at the next table, and bragging about their missions over India. The pilot with the stone in his kidney was proudly narrating how he got away from the clutches of a surgeon and flew such successful missions. The Air Cdr. heard that and called over this pilot on his table and he proudly narrated the whole incidence of being in hospital and then how he got away.

The Air Cdr. forgot his breakfast and drove straight to hospital where we were all lined up to receive him. The commanding officer started introducing the officers according to seniority and I was way down the line. Air Cdr. cut short the proceedings and angrily asked. "Where is the surgeon?" The name of surgeon woke me up and rang a bell about the incidence that I had nearly forgotten. He came straight for me. "You are a terrible chap!" he almost shouted. I feigned ignorance and innocently asked, "what have I done now, Sir? "You do not know what you have done?" He was furious. "Letting a pilot with a stone in the kidney fly a jet aircraft and you do not know what you have done. What if this pain had recurred over the Indian Territory?" I kept a poker face and coolly commented, "But it did not." And to press my point home I asked, "did it, Sir?"

Air Cdr. Khalil may God bless his soul, was a kind, fatherly figure and he meant no harm. "You are a terrible chap; I do not know when you will learn?" Exacerbated he said.

Our army keeps sending relief missions to friendly countries in the event of natural disasters and peace keeping ceremonial duties with UN forces and several of our personnel are exposed to international situations and are learning the need for change.

I have been a member of such teams in several such medical relief missions that are frequently sent to friendly countries in the event of a natural calamity.

Full field units with all their tents, pegs, poles and '*masalchis*' and of course the specialist doctors used to be packed in a transport plane and land in the middle of the disaster area, but often after the emergency was over.

It is a tardy affair. Once the orders are given for sending a mission, signals are sent to call the required personnel from all over the country. Their photographs are taken and passport requirements of a long list of unnecessary people are fulfilled. Tablets and injections are counted. Days are spent on lecturing, what is termed as 'briefing' and on other formalities. By the time the team is ready to leave most of the casualties are already cleared or buried and the relief teams of other countries are leaving the scene for home.

One of our medical missions reached an Arab country a full week after a natural disaster when there was no work left. By then most of the casualties had been dealt with and serious patients sent to main hospitals in the capital. To justify their presence the surgeon started performing circumcisions in the field hospital since he had nothing better to do. A month had elapsed after the disaster, but our team was still there. An assignment that was a mercy mission had become a paid holiday and a tourist excursion.

The Pakistani ambassador to that country visited the relief team many a time; and, finding that they had no work to do, suggested that they should return home; for our poor country could ill afford spending scarce foreign exchange on them for doing nothing. Each member of the more than one hundred strong mission was drawing hundreds of dollars a day for just camping there. Everyone got furious at the ill-mannered ambassador. When they chose to return to Pakistan, a red carpet was laid for the national heroes. All the important people were present to welcome them. They were even given the honor of having an audience with the head of the state. The ill-mannered ambassador was the main topic. After about a week the ambassador was recalled.

I knew this ambassador and his history well. He was thrown out of Pakistan Air Force for refusing his superiors, a shady errand. He was, however, selected to serve in the Foreign Service, perhaps to soften the blow of sudden, premature retirement from the Air Force. He was posted as a senior diplomat to Saudi Arabia. A well-meaning colleague gave him a piece of very useful advice, "You will have to understand and remember one thing while in the Foreign Service; you are no more in the armed forces. You will have to unlearn quite a few things." The gentleman never took the advice seriously. He was poor at unlearning that his upbringing had taught him; and because of this failing, had suffered a number of times in the past as well.

When one compares our medical relief missions with the European medical relief contingents, one finds stark difference in the logistics. Each European soldier is self-sufficient, carrying his paraphernalia himself. They reach the calamity-stricken area with lightning speed when they are really needed with supplies and equipment needed for emergencies, quickly get on with the job and then leave as quickly. In such dire emergencies, every minute counts as the victims are dying by the minute. In such circumstances one cannot have time to stand on ceremonies and for formalities. It is also unkind to ask any protocol or expect deluxe facilities from the host government as her resources are already stretched to the limits; the team must be self-sufficient as far as possible. The call is purely humanitarian, and members of the team should throw their heads down, get on with the job and do whatever they can, without being told or expect a pat on the back for every bit done.

It usually is the failure of the host government who cannot deploy such teams properly and profitably; but in the chaos of the sudden calamity, they are hard pressed, and their hands are full. Since presence of such teams is a mark of gracious gesture from friendly countries, these become sacred cows that the host country come what may, under no circumstances would wish to offend.

Fifty years after our independence we are still prisoners of colonial system of government. The only difference visible to common man is that bureaucrats with brown skin have occupied the chairs vacated by the white-skinned British. We forget that the British system of governance at home is quite different from that practiced in the colonies. The attitudes and procedures have not changed much. This was very much in evidence in East Pakistan, now Bangladesh, during the seventies when both the civil and military establishments treated that part of the country as a colony. It is time; our ruling classes learnt that in a free country people are citizens and not serfs.

Just before the birth of Bangladesh or amputation of East Pakistan I spent some time in the far-flung islands in the delta of the mighty Magna River. These islands are virtually under water in the rainy season of monsoon that the islanders accept with resignation as the normal course of events; but the real disaster descends when the cyclone strikes killing men and their cattle in great numbers. The floods just before the separation of East Pakistan in the seventies were widely publicized and politicized to gain political mileage. The Bengali leaders were whipping up the emotions of the local population into frenzy.

To appease the politicians, to blunt the edge of their propaganda, and counter the Indian's distortion of our army's role, hordes of doctors, specialists and paramedics were sent to East Pakistan. The separation looked inevitable because of the hate campaign against West Pakistan inspired and financed by the Indians. Religion was the only bond that could have kept us together, but the Bengali nationalism had by then become much stronger than the declining hold of the religion. It seemed our ways had finally parted. The writing was clearly on the wall.

The irony of the situation was that while the military commanders played politics, the politicians behaved like commanders. Political problems were being solved militarily and military, politically. It was obvious that unless a bold decision was taken quickly the events would overtake us. Such bold decisions come from statesmen of the stature of leaders like DeGale and Churchill. We had only shortsighted midgets; military commanders, who had taken over both military and civil authority in their hands: a perfect recipe for disaster. "Wars are far too dangerous to be left to the generals." Their disciplined way of life trains them as commanders not leaders. If a man has only a sledgehammer, he will use a sledgehammer, every time; even to swat a fly. If he has a gun, he will be trigger-happy. But if there is wisdom and foresight, the attitude of the leader will be quite different. Watching the going on, I had an opportunity to study the roles of the cream of the crop. The politicians were playing with people's passion; the bureaucrats and military brass being foot soldiers were busy doing a job. Right or wrong is a different matter. At such a juncture only, a visionary statesman could change the events and rewrite history; the time was right, to do the right thing rightly.

While a doctor treats one patient at a time, a politician has the opportunity of alleviating or compounding the misery of a group of people, while a leader, can change destiny of the entire nation. Looking back in history there were leaders who with their vision changed a lot of their nations and others who doomed their people by not rising to the occasion. We were most unfortunate not to have any visionary leader of that class at the helm of affairs that with altruism could see us through the crisis. Even a most naïve person could see the writing on the wall—that hell was about to break loose in my country.

The presence of the doctors was symbolic and more for political than professional reasons: they were there to help cool the local sentiments. There really was no need to send teams of surgeons and anesthetists to those god-forsaken islands where problem was, parochialism and poverty. We spent our time doing nothing that is nothing professional and felt that we were being wasted. Living amongst hostile, incensed Bengalis became an increasingly difficult predicament.

The senior most General, a distinguished officer, came for a visit to the island where we were stationed. Everybody took this opportunity to release the pent-up feelings by repeatedly asking him why were they there when there was no work? The General, a very unusual soldier, listened to all the emotional outbursts with great patience. He knew as much as we did that our presence there was politically motivated.

He answered all the questions very coolly. Finally pointing a finger towards the Bay of Bengal he said, "Over yonder is an island called Andaman. Condemned prisoners used to be sent there to serve life sentence. Then there is another island called Hawaii in the Pacific, also known as paradise. People spend a lot of money to go there on holidays. In this island where you are posted, you are being looked after as best as possible without being asked to do any work in return, and still, you feel so unhappy. All three are islands, and it is up to you what you make of this island, Andaman, or Hawaii. If there is no work, who is asking you to do any work. Enjoy yourself as if you were in Hawaii or keep sulking as if you were in Andaman. Life is what you make of it." He then left in his helicopter leaving us all dumbfounded.

The thoughts sounded familiar; I had heard it before some place. While he left the paradise, my thoughts drifted to my school days to another paradise, The Paradise Lost: -

"The mind is its own place, and in itself
Can make heaven of hell, a hell of heaven."

John Milton

After spending one month on this Island, I was asked to move to another, the second of three major Islands in the delta. The only means of transport was a steamer that came from Dacca and touched these Islands during the night. My friends helped me board the big ferry with my luggage, a box and a bed rolled in canvas. It was evening when we steamed-off. The ship was slow but the first-class quarters were comfortable. I was beginning to enjoy the deluxe comfort and soon dozed off. Around midnight I was woken up by an attendant and told that my destination had arrived. The engines of the ship were chugging in the middle of nowhere in the vast ocean. It was pitch dark and all one could feel, rather hear was the roar of the angry sea.

I descended the gangway touching the water along with an officer of the ship. In pitch darkness only light of the steamer shimmered on the waves of a fuming river or was it sea; it was difficult to tell the difference in the delta. Seeing no sign of life, I asked the officer where he expected me to go. He said there were small boats down under the stairs. I was still guessing what I was supposed to do now when the siren of the ship announced its departure. I remembered that the fellow who had carried my luggage down the stairway did not look very friendly. The Bengalis did not like the army and would not care to hide their feelings that could be plainly discerned on their sullen faces. Many unpleasant thoughts crossed my mind. Suddenly from nowhere in the dark something moved along the gangway. It was a contraption of some sort about which I was not quite sure; with a young boy holding a bamboo, standing on it. Apparently, he had brought his boat along expecting to find a customer. I was near the last step when the ship started moving. I had no choice but to step onto this thing, whatever it was. On close examination I found it to be a raftlike structure bobbing up and down on the waves generated by the departing ship.

The ship started moving, leaving behind a trail of agitated waters on which the small boat nearly capsized. The young lad, hardly ten years old and clad only in a loincloth, was my only companion and guide on that pitch-dark night. Many disagreeable, alarming thoughts invaded my mind. I suspected that this was a conspiracy to drown me in the sea without leaving any trace of the crime. My Lord, I pleaded, to die so young when I was just about ready to live. The makeshift raft, bamboo stems tied together with jute ropes, on which I stood with my luggage, was only inches above the water level. Through chinks in the bamboo poles water would well up, leave my shoes awash and drench the luggage. Soon it started to rain. The boy was not afraid of water at all while I wondered if this thing, I was sailing on sank what would become of me.

I could not help recalling a fable that I had read in my school days. An elderly learned scholar wrapped in academic cloak approached a boatman for crossing a river. The young boatman, a peasant paddled hard to keep the boat on course as a storm was brewing up on the horizon. The scholar started a conversation and asked the sailor, "Have you read Shakespeare?' The ignorant man had never heard of the name. The scholar was surprised and checked up, "Can you read at all?" The illiterate boatman replied in the negative. The scholar felt sorry for the poor man and admonished him. "You have wasted half of your life, son." Soon the storm caught up and when the boat reached in the middle of the river, blustery winds capsized the boat. The boatman was an expert swimmer and started his swim to shore, when he saw the scholar gulping water and drowning. He asked the scholar, "Can you not swim?" Coughing furiously and bobbing up and down in the turbulent water, the scholar shook his head. "Looks like you have wasted all your life!" lamented the sailor.

Many years on when I visited the prestigious Harvard University I was intrigued to know; that the only precondition the benefactors of the main library had decreed for the use of the facility was, that the reader of the books——should be able to swim! Presumably in the memory of some of their dear departed who drowned in the Titanic. Looks like they had also read the fable of the scholar and the peasant!

I remembered an uncle of mine, a sports-goods manufacturer who, while ferrying timber for his factory many years ago, was drowned in the Ganges. No trace of him was ever found. I had little doubt that history was about to repeat itself and that 1 would soon be joining him in heaven. My thoughts went to my mother, brothers and sisters who were so proud of me, to my wife and a little daughter who would never see me again. All the efforts and expenses of my parents to educate me in Pakistan and abroad, I believed, would soon drown in the dark, deep, boundless ocean.

So, there I was, a FRCS surgeon, a Major in Pakistan Army at the mercy of a young urchin somewhere in the Bay of Bengal.

In those few minutes, while the lights of the ship were fading away in the distance, my entire life flashed before my eyes like a motion picture. I remembered the joy that the completion of my fellowship brought to my family. They had not communicated to me the death of my father, fearing that the news might cause me a nervous breakdown in a foreign land. I was in a trance, and I prepared myself to meet my creator. Even in that grim hour I remembered Sir Winston Churchill's quip about death on his 75th birthday: "I am ready to meet my Maker, whether my Maker is prepared for the great ordeal of meeting me is another matter."

I was jolted out of my memories when a big wave shook the raft and nearly capsized it. The first thing I noticed was that I was drenched with water, and the little boy with his bamboo was working very hard to keep the raft on course. I was not sure which way the raft was heading as in that pitch-dark night there were not even stars to help the boy find his way and I was in a state where I really did not care; my mind was busy drafting an obituary—my own. The young lad paddled for a long time and then suddenly said something in Bengali and pointed towards a dim light flickering at a distance. First, I thought I was hallucinating but the boy said that was the island we are heading for. He had his bearings right and paddled and pushed the raft to a lagoon that had a jetty where a bearded skinny man with a hurricane lantern stood waiting for us. He was, I learned, the boy's father. I got off the raft, squelched to the safety of dry land and as a token of my gratitude stuffed in my savior's loincloth whatever cash I was carrying in my pockets. The boy was surprised at the generous tip for a short journey. Little did he know how far I had traveled in my imagination! To eternity and back!

The island I was posted was a desolate place, barren and bleak. There was no mode of transport except cycle rickshaws on the dirt tracks along which were strewn hamlets of nearly naked lean Bengalese with numerous children. The island was really a great heap of sand in the delta with water all round cutting creeks into its shores. I was to live and work in a deserted primary school consisting of couple of rooms. There were a few medical supplies which I dished out freely to whosever came to me for treatment, amongst them the young lad who had ferried me in his raft. He had a large family and lived in a hamlet in subhuman conditions with his parents and grandparents and multiple brothers and sisters. Most of my patients had pulmonary tuberculosis and suffered from malnutrition where I as a qualified surgeon could make little contribution. I suppose my patients must be grateful to me for whatever I was doing, but the general attitude against a Punjabi military officer was sullen and hostile and I could feel the palpable hate campaign. My young raft friend in his broken Urdu kept me posted.

One day he informed me that a mob of incensed locals was brewing up and might raid my premises at night. I was getting quite scared by the hostile attitude of the islanders, but there was little I could do. The law-and-order situation had completely broken down, the Bengalis thronged in strength and I had no contact with any other military personnel. There were no means of communication left due to repeated strikes and processions of Bengalis in the mainland. I could occasionally listen to BBC, huddled on the floor at night from my transistor with its battery dying by the hour till it became silent. The streamer I had traveled had stopped its service due to riots and I was at the mercy of the inhospitable local population. One night while I had gone to the shore to wash my clothes, on return I found a harrowing scene. My 'home' had been ransacked and a few belongings I had, looted, or thrown all over the place. I could well imagine what was coming next. I had lost all hope and even the fear of death, and I just did not care. Today was no different from yesterday and tomorrow was no worse than dying any other day. With no communication or any means of escape my fate was like that of a rudderless ship at the mercy of the waves of sea. Only a miracle could save my life.

Living amongst surly Bengalis I used to wonder at night what madness must be like. People had nervous breakdown when they felt utterly bereft and not been able to communicate or do anything of their choice. The rest of the world becomes like Mars and the utter sense of despair and helplessness drive people crazy.

Next day in the afternoon while I was deep in a reverie, I heard a noise overhead. Fearing the worst, I came out in the open and instead saw a helicopter hovering over the island. I thought I was daydreaming. I never gave myself airs that Pakistan army had sent it to evacuate me, a measly Major. In fact, the lines of communications were so uprooted that I wondered if any of my high ups even knew where I was. There was utter chaos and confusion all round; everybody on his own fending for himself.

As a humanitarian gesture for the cyclone all sorts of aid had poured in East Pakistan from the Western world. Since there were no means of transport left, helicopter was the only way of reaching the needy population. This helicopter had Luftwaffe markings on its body and had come to drop some supplies for the islanders. I was not sure what to make of it. Was it a miracle I had been dreaming of? But this was a German army helicopter. What of the rules and regulations of the armies, I was not very sure. While the helicopter was being unloaded, timidly I approached the crew and introduced myself and mustered enough courage to request the pilot if he could give me a lift to the mainland. Mercifully the German agreed. He flew over from delta to Dacca over most of what was to be Bangla Desh and we landed at the airport in the evening. Throughout the flight while I peered through the porthole at the monotonous landscape down below, the emotions ran high as to what was to become of my country, where people had gone mad.

****

I had completed nearly seven years of service in the Army, and the itch to move again was already beginning to assert itself. My stay in Sargodha where I worked in the Air Force Hospital was a fruitful period of my life, and it helped me discover my roots again. Having spent all my life in hostels and hospitals abroad, I was completely cut off from my clan. In Sargodha, I discovered that there was hardly a village where I did not have relatives.

I had many relatives in the area around Sargodha, and I soon came to know about them; but I hardly imagined that I would have a full clan of relatives, both close and distant in the district. Most of the private patients who came to me were the people I had never heard of before, but they would claim some sort of tribal relationship with me, actual or imagined. I had no time to verify these remote connections, but I always looked after them and did the best I could for them and for their ailments. This was the reason that I would find complete strangers on my doorstep almost daily. Many had a patient in a car, a hired van, a 'tonga'—horse driven buggy or a tractor trolley waiting outside. Lost kith and kin were rediscovered. The result was that I had a very busy social life. I found all my relations very decent folks. Most of them were sons of the soil, not very well educated but very friendly and hospitable. Some of them owned farms but most of them eked out an uncertain living by tilling small pieces of land. I would not charge them any fee for any minor procedure or medical advice. They would insist on paying for my services, as these people had a very sensitive ego in such matters; and they did pay me mostly in kind as they could not afford cash. I had to accept whatever they offered as a token of goodwill rather than a fee, for I did not want to offend them by hurting their sense of pride.

It became difficult to refuse the hospitality of grateful but poor relations. I feared that refusal to accept their gifts and invitations would be construed as arrogance. One day as I was about to drive from hospital at the end of a busy day, an old patient from a village arrived with about a dozen chickens. He motioned me to stop the car. As I stopped the car, without giving me a chance to refuse, he dumped the birds in the car. The hens, very frightened and confused in the new surroundings, began making all sorts of noises and started jumping in all directions. Mistaken by the transparent glass windows, they would fly into them again and again or would try to land on my cap making a mess of my uniform in the process. The little foolish creatures did not know that the P in P cap stood for peak, and not for pee. To hide my embarrassment from the other uniformed personnel around I drove off at full speed.

When I reached the barrier before the cantonment, I lowered the glass of my window for the corporal on duty to recognize me and lift the barrier. Just at that moment another car full of young children came and stopped parallel to mine. The children seeing the birds, one of which perched on my shoulder, started clapping which frightened the already agitated chickens, and they started fluttering in all directions. In a frantic effort to evade their assaults I had to duck my head almost every moment; and this frantic ducking and dodging of an officer in uniform provided additional amusement to the clapping children in the next car. It was difficult for me to keep a straight face.

The corporal looked astonished at the noise and fluttering of the birds in my car. When he stuck his head inside to see what was happening, one of the birds flew in his face causing abrasions. The hens must have thought that I had lowered the glass for their exit; so, they took off instantly. The corporal who was about to raise the barrier saw that. He thought that he could not let his superior officer incur financial loss. Forgetting his duty at the barrier, he dashed after the fleeing birds. With great difficulty and after a hot pursuit, which involved some crawling exercises under the bushes, he managed to grab a couple of birds while the others succeeded to escape into the roadside plantation. The bleeding corporal, in disarray with his uniform in a mess, very proudly marched towards me. He saluted me with one hand and with the other presented me the recaptured birds. I was considering the propriety of handing the birds back to him as a gesture of appreciation for his loyalty to the corps and the service, and the country. The clapping of children and the screeching of brakes behind my car forced me to slam on the throttle.

During my stay in Sargodha, I do not recall any occasion when I had to buy any eatables. Because of this barter system my stores of vegetables, fruits, rice, and wheat were always full. There was never any dearth of chickens or sheep, alive or slaughtered.

7

Seven Year Itch

Those were blissful years I spent at Sargodha. I had all I could have asked for. Yet I always had that nagging feeling that I should have worked a bit longer in English hospitals after FRCS to gain more experience, when I had no worries about my examinations. Those were the days when after your surgical fellowship, the consultants would put faith in you, give you a free hand and let you work on your own. The words of that British surgeon, who failed me in operative surgery in my maiden attempt at fellowship examination, still echoed in my ears, "Obviously you have not done much surgery yet."

So, I was all along on the lookout for such an opportunity, as the old connections in UK were still fresh which would be useful. Having worked for seven years in different military hospitals as an independent surgeon, I had gained enough experience and polished my surgical repertoire. I therefore, applied for two years' sabbatical. I thought having worked long enough as a general surgeon, doing hernias and appendices, it was time to move to my chosen specialty, orthopedics.

People around me did not like my decision to go on leave: they thought it was a stupid thing to do. But then I had done such things before. When in the sixties I left Hammersmith hospital in London abruptly in the middle of my tenure, my consultant had serious doubts about my sanity and thought that I needed to have my head examined.

I had to make some effort to get leave, but finally I succeeded in obtaining two years' leave without pay and was free to go and update my professional knowledge.

I had by now enough contacts in the Air force to get a free ride in one of the transport planes. One day in early seventies we, my family and I, boarded a plane going to France. The route was via Saudi Arabia, Egypt, and Libya. It was a C-130, a huge Hercules monster carrying enormous loads. My small family and a few other passengers, including a young lad in his teens, son of Pakistan's military attaché in Paris, were huddled in between the big boxes. One advantage of traveling in the military plane was that all its stopovers were to be at the military bases where getting accommodation was no problem.

My wife had visited the Holy Land umpteen times for *Hajj* and *Umra*, yet her desire to go there again and again was insatiable. She was thrilled at the opportunity of visiting the Holy Land once again. She had managed to convert me also into half a Muslim. In any case, every Pakistani traveler, be he a devoted Muslim or a half-hearted one, feels it mandatory to visit the holy places even when his plane lands in Saudi Arabia for a stopover to the great annoyance of the Saudis.

So, after visiting the holy shrines in the Holy Land we left for Libya where a good old friend of my elder brother looked after us with great affection during the stopover. Colonel Gaddafi had by then packed off the Americans from the Wheeler base that was now deserted. We were housed in a recently vacated house. It was bitterly cold and with howling winds tearing we spent the whole night in the big house keeping ourselves warm. For sightseeing we were taken around Tripoli during the night. It was a very chilly and windy night, and no one would dare get out of the cozy car. Tripoli, having been built under Italian influence was a mixture of the Roman and the Arab architectures. The grandeur, the sights, sounds and smell of place reminded one the saturated memories of patrician life the city had once seen. It was a pity that the intense cold and blustery winds denied us the opportunity of wandering around in the city, but I still have fond reminiscences of that short stay.

Our last stop was at Biarritz, a beautiful, spotlessly clean, out of this world town in the Pyrenees Mountain range on the border between France and Spain.

The customs and immigration clearance were only perfunctory, no more than a simple formality in comparison to thorough, even humiliating procedures of today. In military bases due respect was shown to all uniformed personnel.

There we came across an old friend and had lunch with his little family. They very generously invited us to spend the night with them although their apartment was very small. We did need a good night's sleep after so many sleepless nights. We appreciated their gracious, heart-warming hospitality but we did not want to inconvenience them. Members of the forces develop a unique kind of comradeship, a deep sense of belonging to an extended family. They may not be rich, but that would not deter them from being generous to their fellows. Even when their pockets are empty, their hearts are brimming with warm feelings. I used to marvel at the enthusiasm of the long lines of blood donors waiting patiently to give blood for an injured soldier unknown to them, but just because he wore a similar belt.

We took leave of our host and boarded the night train that went to Paris via Bordeaux and Toulouse. The coupe we occupied had four berths and we had tickets for three. The fourth berth was unoccupied, and I hoped, rather selfishly, that it would remain unoccupied, so we spread our beddings on all the berths. However, as the train was about to steam off out of Bordeaux, in came a pretty young French lady wrapped in a long fur coat to ward off the intense cold outside. I was standing in the middle of the compartment re-arranging our luggage and children on different berths to make room for her when she began putting her few little packets on the rack above her head. Suddenly I felt something warm and moist licking my cheek and nibbling at my ears. I had heard of French promiscuity, but this show of affection right before my wife and small children, I thought, was a bit too much, even by French standards. Paris after all was a whole night away! As I turned around to look at the lady, hoping not to catch my wife's eye, I saw two button-like things peering at me from within the collars of her coat. They were the bright, round eyes of a small dog, the smallest that I had ever seen. It had managed to pop its head out of the lady's fur coat under her chin and was slobbering my face. The lady had it tucked snugly at rather an unusual place I guess, to protect the little delicate thing from the freezing cold. The color of the fur coat and that of the dog were so similar that it was difficult for me to differentiate as to who was nibbling at my ear.

The train reached Paris early the next morning. Thanks to the young lad's father, an embassy car was there to receive us. The hospitality of the military attaché was unforgettable. He lent us his car in which we wandered around Paris the whole day. I had many years earlier hitchhiked in Paris when I was studying in England, but to see Paris in the comfort of a chauffeur-driven car was indeed a different experience. It was a pity though that my wife was too exhausted after the long journey to enjoy the trip, and the children soon fell asleep.

Again, we decided not to burden the military attaché for the night and decided to take the night train to London. He bade us farewell at the Railway station. Once we had got on the train, I thought my loading and unloading of luggage and children was over. However, in the middle of the night, we were asked to get off the train and walk up to the ferry. My wife, a typical Pakistani housewife considers it a sin to travel light. So, she had packed three suitcases to the brim and, to ensure that no one misses our Pakistani origin, had also brought along a '*razai*', a quilt of carded cotton that she thought would be useful in the cold winter of London.

This reminds me of an incident in the London underground many years ago, when a Pakistani laborer carrying a *razai* entered the tube last of all. The tube was jam-packed, and he stood next to the sliding door. He was carrying a lot of luggage in addition to the *razai*. The automatic door would slide to close itself but finding his *razai* in the way would stop and slide back. It would try again but sensing the obstruction would return to the open position. The train would not move until the door was closed. Finally, the guard of the train got out on to the platform to investigate the trouble with the doors. After some time, he found out the offending object and politely but firmly admonished the Pakistani, while the whole trainload of passengers looked daggers at the poor fellow. I did not want our *razai* to involve me in any such trouble.

I woke up the sleepy children and dragged them out. They were so tired that it required some effort to wake them up from their sound sleep. I carried the two heavy boxes, wondering how my wife could manage to stuff so much in them. She picked up our son and remaining odd bits of our luggage, and our little daughter balanced the *razai* on her head; and, like a family of poor gypsies carrying all their possessions on their heads, trudged towards the ferry in the dark. The two heavy boxes exerted an almost unbearable strain on my shoulder, elbow, and wrist joints. Now, like all hardworking orthopedic surgeons, I have strong arms and shoulders with well-developed muscles. Most people think that I have acquired these strong muscles by working hard in the operation theatre, but I know the credit for giving me such firm muscles goes to my wife who has made me carry deceptively ordinary but hellishly heavy suitcases all around the world.

A railway worker noticing the plight of my little daughter carrying her *razai* on her head stopped his funny looking vehicle; picked her up and put her on board his jalopy. She kept on clutching the *razai* as her family duty and would not let go even when he asked her to place it on the floor of the vehicle. Being a decent man, he also asked my wife to sit on this contraption and taking no notice of my puffing and panting drove off towards the ferry.

We reached Dover early in the morning. I wanted to catch the next train to London, but my wife looked awfully pale and exhausted. Almost a week's traveling in a noisy and vibrating transport plane and sleepless nights in different countries had disturbed the equilibrium system in her ears. She would sway and feel nauseated every time she tried to stand up. I realized that she could take no more punishment. Long flights never suited her. The longest non-stop journey that we ever undertook was from Los Angeles to Tokyo. All the comforts of the elite class of the Japan Airlines could not keep her in good spirits. In fact for all the passengers the long journey soon became a dreary experience. For hours on end all you could see was sky above and sea below. This droves everyone nearly crazy and once the plane touched down at Tokyo Narita airport, all the passengers stood up in their seats cheering and clapping lustily at the end of what seemed an endless flight. On our next tour on this route we, therefore, decided to break our journey in Hawaii, the paradise the Americans are crazy about. My wife unfortunately had the same airsickness and does not have very fond memories of that beautiful island and its capital, Honolulu.

So, to give her time to recover, we stopped over in Dover and took a hotel suite facing the English Channel. The rooms were warm and comfortable. I do not know for how long we slept but when I woke up it was close to midnight. We had slept the whole day and were very hungry. The hotel kitchen had closed, so I went out to find something to eat. Luckily a Kentucky chicken shop was open. I asked the attendant to pack two steaming chickens and rushed back to the hotel, my mouth watering. I sat my children round the table and took out a plate and unpacked the chicken. We were all set to enjoy a hearty meal. My wife, who despite her vertigo was offering her prayers, looked rather dolefully at us sitting around the steaming chicken, and said, "But this is not halal meat." Last time when I was in England as a resident doctor, I ate in the doctors' mess. I would not touch pork but ate the other dishes convincing myself that the English were Christians and Christians like Jews were 'People of the Book'. I now tried the same argument with my wife. She would have none of that despite her ill health. I had no choice but to throw the chicken in the garbage bin, of course very reluctantly. I went out again on the food-hunting errand. All the shops were closed. One fish and chip shopkeeper was pulling his shutters down. I bought a handful of fish and chips. I was sure my wife would find them quite in order. Back in the hotel room when I opened the packet, she again objected, "How do you know they have not fried this fish in lard?" I was so hungry that I retorted, "Look lady, in the state that we are in anything is permissible." For the next two years that we were in England she spoiled most of my weekends by making me travel hundreds of kilometers to far off places for halal meat.

We left Dover the next day; she was still shaken and dizzy. We spent the next few days in a place called Southal. A friend had arranged a flat right in the middle of 'Little India'. There are two places in England, which are densely inhabited by the Asian immigrants, Southal, London and most of Bradford in the north. In Bradford even the signboards are in Urdu. The Asians have purchased vast real estate in these two places, though in other parts of big cities like Birmingham, Leicester and other towns in the midlands there are substantial Asian colonies. The number of Asians increased tremendously after their exodus from Kenya and Uganda. If one goes to any Pakistani or Indian restaurant, the Tunduri, of which now there are many even in the posh areas of London, he would find more Europeans than the Asians eating spicy, zesty food; and sweating and soon looking for fire extinguishers! They like the Asian food; it is the smell of curries they detest. Sometimes the curry smell from the neighboring houses of Asian families would drive the English residents with more sensitive noses to sell their houses to affluent Asians at rather cheap prices, and shift to 'cleaner' districts. Now in almost all the lanes of Southall there are rows and rows of houses owned by the Asians. There are hardly a few European left in Southal.

We spent quite some time in this place before I found a job. More than ten days had passed since our arrival, but still I was jobless, unlike my first visit in the sixties when within three days of my arrival I had three offers. I appeared for one interview after the other but no luck. I was getting impatient, and my wife must be giving different explanations to the children as to where their father disappeared every few days.

An Asian family owned the apartment and lived downstairs. They like us had small kids. Every day the ding-dong music of the Ice cream van would bring children rushing out on the street. My little daughter would watch them wistfully. She would not ask even her mother that she wanted ice cream. She was hardly five years, but somehow, she knew that I had not yet found a job. When the children in the next-door flat would offer her a bite she would think it was below her dignity to accept it, and say, "I will also buy ice cream once my father gets a job." I was really touched when I came to know of it. Daughters are certainly more understanding than sons; and their attachment to their parents does not ever diminish as the proverb says: A son is a son till he gets a wife while a daughter is a daughter for the whole life.

Our son, hardly four years old at the time, would go out of control, whenever we used to visit a supermarket for shopping on weekends. During Christmas time the stores were tastefully decorated and filled with all kinds of goods in that shopping season, including a vast range of fancy, expensive toys that child would find irresistible. During one of these visits my son found his way to the toy section of the store despite our attempts to divert his attention. He insisted we buy him a toy he had fancied. I asked the price. It was staggering, much more than I thought I could afford. I tried to get him interested in some cheaper toys but he remained adamant. I spoke to him in Urdu, so that the people present in the store would not understand what the row was about. The little blighter would, however, shout at the top of his voice in perfect English, "You don't buy me anything, you don't buy me anything." It became quite embarrassing to face the stares of the onlookers. There was no mistaking where their sympathies were. The shoppers, and there was quite a crowd of them, looked at us in disgust. We dragged the bawling kid out of the store, still shouting, "You won't buy me anything, you won't buy me anything."

On the other hand, when we did not buy a cheaper toy for our little daughter she said, "All right, if you cannot buy it for me, please buy it for my brother and I will share it with him." I was really hurt to realize what she thought about us, for so far as I knew we never gave preference to any one of them over the other. In fact, I had always remembered that classic song from Gigi, "Thank Heaven for Little Girls," but obviously she thought otherwise. It hurts me even today to recall her words; maybe I had slipped somewhere to give her the impression that we cared more for her brother. Since then, I have tried very hard to avoid any hint of discriminating between the two.

I soon got a senior post in orthopedics and worked for two years in a lovely hospital doing all the orthopedic work I wanted to do. I learnt so much in those two years, as I had not done in the previous five years. In addition to my work in the hospital, there were two weekly visits to neighboring towns where some of our patients were sent after surgery. One of them was a mental asylum located in a beautiful scenic wood. The inmates of the asylum after falls were brought to our hospital when they needed orthopedic treatment. As it was difficult for us to look after them and give them specialized treatment for their mental ailments, we used to send them back after fixing their broken hips and limbs. This hospital was a bleak place, with a labyrinth of dark cavernous corridors where one could easily get lost. The walls of the rooms were well padded, and the doors were kept locked. There was a smell of heavy thick despair in the air. The patients were monitored through keyhole-like small glass slits in the doors. Every Wednesday morning, come rain or sunshine, exactly at ten o'clock on the dot, the matron of the hospital along with her entourage including a physiotherapist, a dresser, and several nurses of all descriptions would wait for me in front of the porch. Since she was never late by even a minute, I also ensured I did not keep them waiting.

The asylum was at about an hour's drive from my place. My wife after escorting the children to school usually did not have much to do, so sometimes she would accompany me. It was a lovely drive on an old Roman road through beautiful countryside. I would drop her in a superstore, go to the asylum, do what was needed, and then on my way back pick her up after her heart was full and pockets empty.

The protocol the matron of the mental hospital gave to me would have satisfied even a professor, but it embarrassed me, for I was years away from joining that select class. She would take me around in style, like they do in a teaching hospital. I was convinced though that she knew much more about patientcare and medicine than I did and that she was only trying to humor me and make me feel taller than I was. At the end of the round, she would invite me to her office overlooking an idyllic piece of landscape and serve hot coffee. She would then very courteously see me off at the hospital porch. The matron's exaggerated though sincere courtesies made me feel rather small before her. Sometimes, however, the ritual became unnecessary: as on my arrival she would give me a subdued smile and say, "Sir, all your patients have died!" Then she would lead me straight to her office for the coffee that would feel like a lump in the throat, and I would swallow it rather uncomfortably feeling responsible for those deaths.

The two years spent in England proved to be very fruitful both for me and my family: I acquired the skills I needed for becoming an orthopedic surgeon, my children started their education in good English schools, and we traveled a lot to explore the English countryside.

The journeys to and back from England were memorable. We had traveled to England in a military transport aircraft; now we decided to return home by car driving through Europe and Middle East. And this is what we did and performed *Hajj*. It was a journey to remember and howsoever try I may, I can never forget for several reasons.

8

Road To Medina

For this trans-European journey to Saudi Arabia, I had bought a new car. My family accompanied me to London for collecting it. My first ride in it is still vivid in my memory. It was a rainy day when I took delivery of the car and, along with my family and a young brother-in-law whom I had specially invited from Pakistan for the trip, set off for Lincoln. Not yet being conversant with the various air conditioning controls of the new car, I sometime warmed it so much that the windscreen would become foggy. Then I would put the fan on but it would make matters worse. The already foggy windscreen would become completely opaque. I would switch on the AC to clear the windscreen. The maneuver would work: the windscreen would clear, but the children would shiver with cold and complain bitterly.

I kept playing with different buttons and switches while driving on the motorway. At Grantham, hometown of Lady Thatcher I had to exit motorway. Going to Lincoln was a simple affair. All I had to do was to get off the motorway, climb on the C curve to the bridge over the motorway that was the road that went straight to Lincoln Before the bridge I slowed down and entered the exit after the bridge and climbed on the C bend to merge into the lane which led to my destination. My experimenting with the temperature controls and the foggy windscreen had by now mystified my mind so much that after negotiating the C bend I lost all sense of direction. At the end of C bend, when this road merged with the lane going to Lincoln I instead crossed it at right angle, drove over the green median that separated the two one-way lanes, and then crossed the other lane. In doing so I missed a long trailer hurling down the road at a tremendous speed by a hair's breadth and somehow managed to stop the car on the grassy lay by; the car now facing Grantham. The traffic was thick and fast on both the lanes, and I still had not figured out how I had managed to cross the double road. As to missing the long trailer, I must confess that I had no hand in avoiding a collision; it was the trailer driver who hit the brakes, wrenched his steering wheel to the right at the right moment, overrunning the green median and to let me cross the road. If he had delayed his action by a split second neither I nor anyone else traveling with me would be here to tell the story. Utterly confused and disorientated I sat in the stalled car as in a trance staring blindly at the thundering trailers rolling by. I am sure even Schumacher could not have done what I had managed to do; dart through two fast lanes of long monstrous vehicles moving in the opposite direction.

The driver of the trailer stopped his vehicle at the lay by, got off, and started walking towards my car. I was still trying to figure out what had happened and how it had happened in that fraction of a minute. My bother-in-law, seeing the big burly driver sauntering towards us, warned me of the impending trouble. I rolled down the window on my side. The driver came to me and said, "Which way are you heading mate?" "To Lincoln," I replied. While talking to me, he stuck his head inside the car, saw my frightened children and dazed wife. I think he wanted to smell whether I was drunk. No one with a grain of road sense would have made such a suicidal blunder. He shuffled in his shorts, "but Lincoln is that way," he said pointed towards the direction the trailer was coming from, "This road goes to Grantham. You ought to go in the opposite direction." Then he stood still, thought for a moment, and then suddenly said, "I will tell you what, I am in no great hurry I will turn my trailer and you follow me." Before I could open my mouth, he had walked away to his trailer and climbed up into the driver's seat.

As he was coming from Lincoln, he had to maneuver his trailer in a U turn that he did with professional skill and set off towards Lincoln. I followed him for a few miles. He stopped by the roadside sign "Welcome to Lincoln" and, pointing to the signboard, waived me good-bye. He then turned his trailer and went his way, leaving me drenched in sweat, despite the freezing cold outside, without giving me time to express my gratitude to him. May God bless him. I was totally shattered. I had nearly killed everyone in my car. His kind behavior made me hang my head in shame. Later I realized that his purpose in escorting us for so many miles was to assure himself that after that close brush with death I was in the right frame of mind to drive.

This reminds me of the time when I was in Edinburgh after Christmas. It was a very cold January of an unusually bleak winter with heavy rain and snow. The sun had not been seen for days. A blanket of fog would envelope Edinburgh in the morning and evening.

The schools had just opened after New Year holidays. Early one morning, a group of school children was walking in the infamous Edinburgh fog to their school with satchel-like haversacks strapped on their backs. They walked in a single file on a pavement. It was difficult to see anything beyond a couple of yards in the thick fog. A double-decker bus groping its way in the almost dark street skidded to the kerb while negotiating a bend, and then on to the pavement where the school children were walking in a file. The driver could not see the children, and all five of them were trampled under the big wheels before the driver could stop the bus.

It was a terrible, gruesome accident. A pall of grief fell upon the whole town, more oppressive and benumbing than the fog. The driver of the bus, realizing what he had done, felt so utterly bereft that he had to be taken to a hospital. As his condition worsened over the next few days he was transferred to a mental asylum and put under the care of psychiatrists. But nothing seemed to lessen his sense of guilt, and he went from bad to worse. The parents of the five dead children got together, decided to bury their intense personal grief for a while and prayed that the driver does not suffer. They visited him in the mental hospital. They tried to console him as best as they could. "It was not your fault, you could not see anything," they said.

My condition after the narrow escape on the road to Lincoln was not much different from that poor devastated driver though we had escaped unhurt.

In the long journey back to Pakistan my wife's cousin Nasim and her husband Irshad with their little son, *Munnoo*, accompanied us in their car. Traveling across Europe was a pleasant experience. I enjoyed driving on the busy roads of the continent. The Middle East was developing fast thanks to the oil boom. There used to be bumper-to-bumper traffic of the long trailers on the highways leading to oil-rich countries of the Middle East. I remember seeing trucks and trailers of all descriptions moving slowly in an endless chain on most of the roads we traveled. On the Bulgarian-Turkish border we came across a seventeen-mile-long caravan waiting for clearance to enter Turkey. There was a similar scene on the Syrian Jordanian border, long queues of trailers blocking the road at the checkpoint.

It was always an ordeal for me to overtake those long convoys of heavily laden slow-moving vehicles. My son, during one of these journeys when I had overtaken a few long trailers with a lot of difficulty and almost risking my life, asked me to stop the car because he wanted to pass water. My wife supported his demand without realizing my plight. If I stopped, the line of long trailers would move ahead, and I would have to go through the hazardous process of overtaking them once again; and that was what I hated most at that moment. So, I lost my temper: Why should the little blighter feel the necessity of passing water at that very moment when I had managed to overtake the infernal convoy? I know I behaved unreasonably: the intense pressure of weeks of driving was telling upon me, and I took my anger out on the poor kid. Anyway, the crisis was resolved when I asked him to use one of my spare shoes to relieve himself.

Passing through Damascus at night we got lost in the labyrinth of streets. We kept on driving in circles and could not find our way out. We asked a taxi driver to get us out of the city and on to the road to Jordan. He was a poor man, who probably had had no customer the whole day. He set a price on taking us out of the labyrinth. Had he waited till we had got on to the main road, I would have tipped him anyway.

During these travels we learnt a practical lesson; useful for those traveling by road. For spending the night in a big city, do not try to drive to the middle of a town. A few miles short of a big town, or past it, look around for a small inn, motel or a country guest house in the suburbs. Disembark and spend the night out in the woods or at least away from the pollution and the traffic jams of big cities. If you want to visit the historical or interesting places of the town, do not drive your car. Use public transport. The advantages are many. All five-star hotels in big metropolitan towns are alike; may be in Singapore, Melbourne, Islamabad or London. Even the lay out is identical; a square bedroom out of which a bathroom has been cut out in one corner. Even the furniture is so identical; everything is so stereotype. There is no local taste and culture. All starred big hotels look the same. What you have traveled so far away from home is to see the country, the people, and their living. People in small places will be more native, hospitable, and helpful and the stay will not only be more enjoyable, memorable but also lot cheaper.

As we traveled from Europe to Pakistan through Middle East, we found the level of corruption and inefficiency of the customs and immigration officials increasing progressively. At the Jordan border the local officials demanded a bribe, which we refused to offer, and they delayed us for some time on one pretext or the other. My wife's cousin reminded them of Pakistan's intimate connection with Jordan's royal family. Fearing that we may be related to, or at least acquainted with, the Crown Prince's wife, they relented and raised the barrier in a flash.

Three weeks after leaving London and driving through almost the whole of Europe, stopping when and where we liked and seeing places that probably we would never see again, we entered Saudi Arabia early in the morning. Seeing a mosque at the border we drove straight to it and with a sigh of relief and sense of gratitude to Allah, we offered the Fajr prayers. We thanked God for having made it to the Holy Land before the borders were to be sealed that day for the *Hajj*. We offered our prayers at peace with ourselves and were most grateful for this wonderful journey at the end of which we were to perform *Hajj*. We hoped to be in Medina by lunch, but what the fate had in store for us, we did not have the slightest clue.

It was to be the last day when the family of my wife's cousin was to travel with us. They planned to stay in Medina where her parents had arrived earlier to perform *Hajj*. We, i.e., my wife, two children and their young uncle, would travel on to Mecca, where I was to join the medical mission from Pakistan. After a hurried breakfast we set off towards Tabuk on the last leg of our journey together.

It was early in the morning; the road was straight and empty. One could see for miles ahead and there was not a man or a vehicle in sight. Completely at peace with myself for having kept the schedule I started appreciating my surroundings, the glorious beauty of the desert in the calm of the morning.

The car of my wife's cousin had followed our car all through Europe, to ensure that we keep together and do not get lost. Seeing the empty straight road, Irshad, our cousin's husband remarked, "Even a fool cannot lose his way on this straight road." So he decided to lead the way. While he drove, his wife sat next to him and their young son *Munnoo*, was in the rear seat squeezed in between heaps of luggage. My brother-in-law, who had been relieving Irshad and me off and on, took the wheel of my car while I dozed off in the rear.

The sudden screeching of the brakes of our car woke me up. My bother-in-law had stopped the car behind an overturned truck. I, still half-asleep, got out of the car to find what had happened, and there, before my eyes was a nightmare that I can never forget. It was the most harrowing scene I have ever witnessed. There was a huge truck loaded with apples, leaning on the car of our cousin, which lay crushed under its weight. My wife was reciting aloud verses from the Holy Qur'an. I rushed towards the driver's seat and saw Irshad slumped on the steering wheel without a sign of life. There was broken glass and apples all around. Our cousin trapped in the crushed front of the car and bathed in blood, wailed in agony. There was no sign of life on the rear seat where luggage lay crushed and scattered. It was a heart-rending sight. In a split second two persons had been obliterated, one cut down in the prime of his life, the other snuffed out in the early years of boyhood; and the third, her life shattered, left to the life-long ordeal of remembering and mourning. Standing there at the scene of the accident in the middle of a desert I realized how utterly helpless man could be. Here I was, a trauma surgeon proud of my skills acquired by many years' hard work in the best hospitals of Britain, feeling helplessly inadequate in the situation that confronted me.

We, the surgeons seldom see such severe accidents. The casualties are wheeled on trolleys to the emergency room for us to treat. I had always treated the victims of accidents in the security of my operation theatre; but here I was required to do at the scene of accident what others, like fire brigade and rescue teams did; but with bare hands there was little I could do. We tried frantically to extricate the poor battered lady, who, by now had realized how in one moment her life had changed forever. It was not her injuries, I guessed, that made her cry, but the sudden awareness of the destruction of her life. Despite all our efforts, my brother-in-law and I could not pry open the jammed doors of the battered car. The screams of the poor lady were getting more and more doleful and desperate.

The magnitude of the tragedy had by now dawned on all of us. My two children were in a state of shock. I realized that if we do not get the lady out of that mangled steel heap she might die as well. So, we tried again to force the doors of the car open, but all our desperate banging, pulling, and pushing would not open them. I was utterly devastated. The driver of the truck, seeing the extent of the damage, had gone berserk. Wailing loudly in Arabic he ran off and disappeared in the vast desert.

When we had lost all hope of rescuing the trapped lady, out of nowhere appeared a bus, braked to a stop at the scene of the accident, and out came a group of Turk pilgrims bound for Medina reciting aloud holy verses. The driver of the bus produced a tow chain. Tying it to the door of the car, the busload of pilgrims pulled open the door. And we got the badly battered and broken-down lady out of that wreck. I do not know how the police received the report of the accident, but it did arrive at the scene and started its painful proceedings. At that time, I had only one concern—-to take the seriously injured lady, as fast as was possible, to a hospital where she could get immediate treatment. Even a few minutes' delay might cause her death. I tried to argue in my scanty Arabic with the police as best as I could, because that was the only language they spoke and convince them that the lady needed immediate medical attention and that they could complete their legal formalities after they had taken her to a hospital. They could not understand my English punctuated with a few Arabic words I knew. It was a frustrating experience; but thank God, they recognized the urgency of the situation and after a few minutes, although at the time it seemed an eternity, we were heading towards Tabuk, the nearest town in that wilderness, the very town we had just passed earlier on.

The magnitude of the tragedy had shattered me completely. A thousand thoughts and questions, confusion and chaos invaded my mind. Sometimes I thought that what had happened was only a bad dream that would end as soon as I opened my eyes, but then I realized that my eyes were wide open. Suffering from delusions of reprieve, I clung on to shreds of hope and to the last moment hoped against hope, that it would not turn to be so bad; in fact, it was worse. I could not figure out where I had gone wrong and what I had done to deserve all this suffering, and what the dead man and his son had done to invite this terrible fate upon them, and what the seriously injured woman had done to suffer lifelong distress. I was very confused and my feelings and relations with my deity seemed at very low ebb; quite the opposite of what this journey-the pilgrimage, was supposed to be for.

At last, we reached the district hospital at Tabuk. The dead bodies were deposited in the mortuary. A local doctor mentioned to me about the presence of a contingent of Pakistani military mission in the town. We rushed the injured lady to the military hospital. My relief was beyond description when I saw the face of an old friend, Brig. Bashir Rathore, a senior surgeon in the Pakistan Army, then on deputation with the Saudi Army. He was a noble soul. Tears rolled down his cheeks as he saw the injured lady and realized our predicament. From then on he took charge of all our affairs. When all doors close and it is pitch dark, somewhere He opens a window; I tried to soothe myself.

The battered lady was admitted in the military hospital. She had multiple fractures and was in a state of severe shock. Being a surgeon, I could foresee that from physical shock, she would recover; but what psychological upheavals the poor lady would suffer for the rest of her life, I dreaded to envisage. Why in a fraction of a second, her lot had changed forever was beyond me. It seemed that for the last three weeks, we were racing to that point to meet the destiny waiting for us. We did not know but it was to be a date with the fate, and we were being driven inexorably by the Divine will to keep the appointment at the time and place set for it. Allah has His own ways that we mortals with our limited vision do not always comprehend. We must submit and accept; I philosophized.

My friend, the surgeon in charge, not only admitted the injured lady in the military hospital, but to personally supervise her treatment, cancelled his program for performing *Hajj*. When I protested, he dismissed my pleas by saying, "Tell me, what will please Allah more;

traveling to Mecca or comforting this lady?" He persuaded us to continue our journey for *Hajj* for which we had traveled all the way from England. The poor lady, he said, would be in the hospital for a while anyway and he was there to look after her. She, on her part, was not much worried about her injuries, but entrusted us to arrange the burial of her deceased husband and son in 'Jannat ul Baq'i'(revered cemetery) in Medina, the city of the Prophet. After the death Muslims the world over long for burial in that venerated site.

The connections of my friends with the Saudi military helped us in obtaining clearance for transporting the dead bodies to Medina. In Saudi Arabian culture, which is in fact, in complete conformity with Shariah, the dead must be buried as soon as possible, preferably on the day of their death without any delay, there and then. There is a lot of wisdom in this custom, because the chains of events leading to acceptance of the inevitable starts only after the dead have been buried in the graves. Instead of sticking to this tried and tested ordained concept, unfortunately the Saudis have also started pickling their dead now, by delay prolonging the misery of next of kin. With two dead bodies in shrouds in the rear and my small family perched behind the driver of the van we started our long painful sad journey in the blazing sun towards Medina.

We reached Medina late in the night. Another friend in Medina took charge of arranging the *Janaza* (burial) after the Fajr (morning) prayers early next morning. The *Janaza* prayer was attended by hundreds of thousands of pilgrims present in the mosque. Ironically, the parents of our cousin attended the *Namaz-e-Janaza* (funeral prayers) without knowing that they were seeing off their own son-in-law and grandson and invoking Allah's mercy for them. We had not been able to trace them and inform them of the tragedy yet.

When we did locate them, we did not know how to break the terrible news. It was an ordeal, but we, somehow, went through it. I have neither the words nor the heart to describe their condition on hearing the news.

During that period, I came across several friends and acquaintances whose kindness restored my faith in the human race. It was amazing to see how sincerely people could share our grief and do all in their power to help us. To this day, we are deeply indebted to all the Pakistani doctors, particularly Brig. Bashir Rathore and Wing Commander Abdi. May God bless them all for looking after our cousin with such noble dedication and helping us in that sad hour.

My brother-in-law, who was accompanying us, was only a raw student and many years younger than me, but his courage, his mature advice at every stage in those awful days helped me greatly and saved me from complete breakdown. I do not know how I, utterly depressed, devastated, and helpless as I felt, could have coped with the catastrophe that overtook us on that fateful day but for his support. At that tender age, he had nerves of steel and a very sane head on his green shoulders. His presence, I am sure was God sent; as I tried hard to shore up my fledgling faith.

9

Cultural Crossings

"East is East, and the West is West, and the twin shall never meet." Those words were uttered perhaps during the days when animals on land and rafts on sea used to be the only mode of traveling and the messages used to be sent through homing pigeons. In addition to the population explosion the other explosion today is in the field of communication. More and more people are traveling; faster and longer and the airports are cluttered due to traffic jams. The planes are becoming bigger, faster and the traveling today has reached within the grasp of an average income group. The stratosphere is inundated with people talking to each another all the time. The number of cell phones has multiplied by unbelievable exponential; soon every man, woman and a child will have one if not more. The TV screens in our bedrooms are showing live the events that are happening anywhere in the world, sometimes even before these are about to happen! Prying nosy paparazzi have played havoc with the privacy of people with their candid cameras.

The world they used to say a global village has shrunk further into a parish. Every fourth person on the globe today is either a Chinese, Christian, Hindu or a Muslim; being over a billion each. Walking through the streets of Southal or Bradford one has difficulty telling whether one is in London or Punjab. The China towns in American and other countries can be confusing as if one were in Mainland China. The Chinese products have taken the world market by storm. The economy of the East will soon surpass that of the West. Most people today are better informed, have traveled the world and the dividing gulfs are fast shrinking. The hold of religions is loosening as the economics become more important than other considerations. Immigrants are jumping over the fences and the world today stands very muddled and mixed. Due to changes in eating habits the foods have become universal. While the steaming hot curry is a favorite with snobbish English, Spaghetti and noodles are popular all over the world. Europeans and Americans eat Pizza with relish with their fingers and the far Easterners use chopsticks to pick up each grain of rice and bean. The etiquette and protocols of the snobbish Westerners are thinning out; and they work relaxed in jeans and scrubs. The Asians and the Africans on the other hand are wearing three-piece tuxedos despite the stifling humidity and boiling temperatures and feel high-hat to eat with fork and knife. People today are very mixed and varied and the world has changed beyond recognition.

The color of local culture is quite strongly reflected in our daily life in Pakistan. Our marriage rites, for instance, are deeply influenced by the Hindu culture as portrayed and glamorized by Indian films. All the rituals and customs we so fondly observe on this occasion have nothing to do with Islam, the religion we proudly claim to profess. In the Middle East I have seen the attitude of Arabs towards death as long as a patient was alive they would look after him with extreme affection. But when he breathed his last, they almost instantaneously reconcile with the loss, for death for them is only a transition from one state of being to another, and not something to wail about. We, the Muslims of Pakistan, are in the grip of a deep cultural crisis, and are therefore, very confused about our identity. We call ourselves Muslims, live like Europeans and follow the Hindu culture. We are not sure who we are and which way are we heading. Sometimes we, at least our affluent classes, seem to be ashamed of our own heritage. We prefer to send our children to convents and English medium schools at great expense.

Pakistanis are certainly more 'international' than any other nation. The very word 'International' mesmerizes us. One is amazed to see the number of 'International' business establishments in almost every corner of the country —from airlines to small one-room English medium schools, from hospitals to tiny 'niswar' shops. Anything that comes from a foreign land or has a foreign name casts a spell on us. Give any kind of junk food a foreign prefix, and the whole city will make a beeline for it. American chicken, French-fries, Russian salads, Italian pizzas, multinational burgers have taken us by storm. It appears that our craze for foreign names has completely blinded us to all aspects of our culture.

The natives rightly label the rising generation of Pakistanis being brought up outside Pakistan, North America or in Britain as ABCD, American Born Confused Desis, or BBCD. One may sympathize with these unfortunate teenagers caught up in conflicting cultures at an age when all that glitters is accepted as pure gold. The circumstances in which they find themselves that leave them little choice. But what excuse do we have for providing every opportunity to our children born here in Pakistan to become willing prisoners of cultures, inimical to all that we claim to value and cherish.

There seems a strange dichotomy of thought in our confused minds. Recently I went to America and met several Pakistani immigrant families. At a great cost most of them had set up private Islamic schools. And with even greater effort the parents stole a few hours of their very busy time to escort their children to and fro from such schools. While in Pakistan the same parents used to hunt for English medium or American schools for their children!

Under the impact of Western cultural influences our souls are slowly shriveling. We are letting ourselves be led away from our erstwhile belief that an improvement in living standard should but be a means to improve worldly and spiritual perception. If we accept progress as a means and not an end, we may not only retain our own inner freedom but also perhaps pass on to the West the lost secret of life's sweetness.

By adopting modern methods of science and technology we are doing nothing more than following the evolutionary instincts, which causes man to avail other men's experiences.

Most of us Pakistanis, I think, love to travel. Far-off lands do fascinate us, but the real and imagined economic opportunities abroad exercise a greater attraction. Small minorities of the affluent Pakistanis have the means and time to go to foreign lands in search of pleasure and adventure. But most of the Pakistanis one meets in all parts of the world are manual workers, skilled and unskilled, separated from their parents, wives, and children by their dreams of a better future in monetary terms. This class of immigrants, driving heavy trucks and operating all kinds of machinery under the red-hot sun in the Arabian deserts, working day and night to earn as much as they can, perhaps find little time to think about the price they are paying for every dollar they earn. But their wives back home do sometimes wonder whether a color TV, a 12foot refrigerator and a hi-fi stereo system are fair compensation for what they must suffer in the absence of their husbands single-handedly—single parent family running a household and bringing up, also trying to discipline the children who have little idea of how the bank draft which arrives every few months is earned. They, or at least most of them, tend to waste the opportunity given to them by their parents by falling in bad company, acquiring wayward tastes, and 'enjoying' life in the fond hope that the fountain from which dollars, pounds and Dinars gush out will never run dry.

Sometimes one feels that every Pakistani is on the lookout for an opportunity to get out of his homeland and go wherever circumstances take him—to the American paradise or the dark side of the moon or some remote corner of hell. Unfortunately, the measure of success has become as to how further from home one can exile oneself. The result is that wherever you go in the world you will find a sizeable number of Pakistanis, even in the less known and not very affluent countries of South America. Some have settled there and all but forgotten their roots. Some still remember their origin and come back to visit their families when circumstances demand. Some nobler souls, even after acquiring foreign nationality, remain Pakistanis at heart, and visit their ancestral land regularly and do everything they can to share prosperity with their people.

Airports are exciting places. Pakistan has a large immigrant working class in Middle East and European countries that keep the airports busy in all seasons. In the Arrival lounge one witnesses the happy side of human nature expressed in warm handshakes and emotional embraces of long-separated friends and relatives. In the Departure lounge on the other hand sights are quite different. Sad melancholy faces, tears in abundance. Seeing off their near and dear ones not knowing when they will return, a year or may be two which right now seem light years away.

Unfortunately, we Pakistanis have earned such a poor reputation as a nation that customs and immigration officials all over the world suspect that every person with a green passport is either a drug peddler or an illegal immigrant trying to sneak into the Western paradise. It was not so, in the good old days. The first time I drove through Europe in early sixties there were no visa restrictions for a Pakistani passport holder; one had to just wave the document through the car window at checkpoints to cross the borders.

Those were the days when Ayub Khan was at the helm of affairs in Pakistan, and he, despite seizing power through a military coup, enjoyed great reputation in the West as a valuable ally of the democratic 'free world'; and Pakistanis were considered ordinary human beings, no worse and no better than the people of other nationalities.

I was a Resident in Bristol Royal Infirmary when a Commonwealth Conference was being hosted in England. We the doctors, mostly

British, were watching the proceedings on the TV set in our retiring room. We watched the heads of the Commonwealth countries enter the conference hall one by one with some sort of curiosity without registering any emotional reaction. And then, a tall, fair, handsome, graceful man with a beaming, captivating smile wearing an immaculate suit and a Jinnah cap entered the scene. All the doctors present held their breath in admiration waiting rather impatiently for the announcement of his name. They could not believe their eyes and ears when it was announced that this man was Ayub Khan, the President of Pakistan. "But he looks more of a European!" was the involuntary but unanimous exclamation of disbelief and admiration. One of the English doctors sitting next to me looked at the TV screen and then at my haggard face and dug his elbow in my ribs and commented, "He does not look like a Pakistani."

Those were heady days when the country was progressing at a tremendous pace in every field in a very organized way; in fact, poised to become an Asian tiger while Middle East was a desolate desert. Flying to America President Ayub Khan had once a brief stop-over in couple of now oil rich, then dirt poor Middle Eastern Sheikhdoms to meet the Pakistani immigrant community. The cheering patriotic workers wildly greeted him and at both the places he was asked to open Embassies as the Indians had done so already. Annoyed by the repeated demand he lost his cool and admonished his compatriots, "Pakistan is a great country, and you don't expect me to open an Embassy at every gas station!"

The relations between the countries are no different than amongst the individuals; the not so well off become like poor relations.

Ayub Khan's visit to the United States in the mid-sixties was a resounding success. I remember that in the official reception at the White House his towering personality and graceful manners overshadowed everyone else. He received favorable press and won headlines. The average American would say about Pakistan, "Pakistan is a friendly country whose friendship we value." Indeed, in those days when Pakistan and America were very close, so close that a Pakistani camel driver from

Karachi, Bashir by name, was invited by no less a person than the US Vice President Lyndon Johnson to America and received in the White House.

The warmth between the two allies, however, did not last for long, and even Ayub Khan had to look eastward for friends. He gave vent to his disillusionment with American friendship in his book 'Friends, Not Masters.' While most heads of states write their memoirs after retirement, the dictators are not so sure what is going to happen to them tomorrow and write theirs while in power. The true and factual half of unbiased biography is however written by historians and obituary writers once they are booted out. They know far too well what is going to happen to them once they are ousted from power. They are riding a tiger and one reason they do not want to part with power is that the moment they dismount, the tiger will eat them up.

But what sort of friendship can there be with a superpower? Without any legitimacy, a dictator with a begging bowl in his hands, when meets a leader of a superpower, there is nothing to reciprocate except barter his country's national interests. After a couple of photo sessions in the white house, most dictators get into their heads the notion that they are now buddies for life. The friendship amongst unequal's is like seeing your reflection in a looking glass. You can see yourself when standing in front of it and when you leave; the mirror has no memory.

While living in a jungle a mouse and an elephant became friends. One hot summer day the elephant was having a dip in the cool water of the river when his friend Jerry came on the bank and asked the jumbo to come out of water for a minute. Thinking it important the elephant obliged and with some effort climbed out of water. When he came out near the mouse, the mouse told him that now he can go back in the river. Annoyed, the jumbo asked his friend, "What is the big deal? First you get me out of river and then tell me to go back." The mouse said, "I have lost my swim shorts and was looking for it. Not being able to find it, I thought maybe you may have worn it by mistake!"

The wavering of the relations between our two countries have been perplexing; beyond most Pakistanis. How can a world power be so fickle in its international behavior? Whenever the Americans needed us, like for China or in Afghanistan they would embrace even a brazen faced dictator as their ally and whenever we need their help, which unfortunately is very often they would deliver sermons about the democracy and the human rights and signal IMF and the World Bank to twist our arm as fundamentalists.

I do not propose to discuss Ayub Khan's successes and failures, nor the history of Pak-US relations, all I wish to say is in that period Pakistan was not considered one of the most corrupt countries of the world and nor was every Pakistani passport holder treated as a leper.

Once, I along with my family, that is my wife and two small children, were passing through London Heathrow. I asked them to wait for me at a certain point and left them, to sort out our schedule for going on to USA next week. We were to spend a few days in London.

When, a little later I returned to collect them at the rendezvous point, they were not there. I looked around in all directions, but there was no sign of them. So I stood where I had left them, thinking that they might have gone somewhere nearby for some reason and would return in a few minutes; I waited and waited but none of them turned up. Now I was gradually getting worried. All sorts of dark thoughts started invading my mind: Has somebody abducted them? Or has something even worse overtaken them? Then I consoled myself with the thought that this was not Nigeria or the Wild West, not even Pakistan, so this sort of thing could not happen in a busy airport of capital London, in the heart of the civilized world. But as time passed my anxiety had turned into panic. I ran upstairs, downstairs, to the public utilities and from one air terminal to the other, Heathrow being such a sprawling airport.

I was exhausted with fear and exertion, when I suddenly saw a kind looking, portly English policeman leisurely pacing the immaculately clean floor of the airport. Being an organized and peaceful airport, he was seldom called upon to do anything. I had worked in England for a long time and knew that these police officers, affectionately known as 'Bobbies' were famous for their helpful demeanor. Short of breath and dry mouthed as I was, I ran to the bobby, and with great effort, could only croak. "Officer, I have lost my wife." My panting did not let me say more. The police officer stopped, looked at me benevolently and then with a twinkle in his eyes said, "Aren't you lucky Guvernor?" I looked at him in utter disbelief. I had heard so much about the helpful attitude of English police but here before me was this plump insensitive fellow indulging in crude, mistimed humor without realizing the plight I was in. I caught my breath and tried again, "Officer, I am serious." "So am I sir; so am I." he repeated in his typical cockney accent. This, I thought, was too much, but he did not stop at that, and gave me another piece of advice, "If I were you sir, I will run. Catch the first flight home before she finds you."

While traveling abroad the most important piece of travel is your passport and you are no body, just a robot carrying it and it usually gets all the attention and protocol, but not always.

One of my friends went on a business trip to London. He was also to visit Ireland to attend a day seminar in connection with his business. Mixing business with pleasure he took his wife along. The morning he was to fly to Ireland from London he overslept. A glance on the clock made him panicky, as he had to travel first by tube to Heathrow. Seeing that it was nearly flight time he quickly got up, washed his face, did not disturb his sleeping wife, grabbed his passport and his briefcase and ran to tube station. It was only a day trip as he would be back in the evening he thought. He reached airport in the nick of time and was lucky to board the plane. Relaxed, after catching the flight he dozed off. Landing at Dublin airport he was pleased with himself that he did not miss the flight and was just in time to attend the conference for which he had come so far from home. At the immigration desk he presented his passport, picked up his brief case ready to leave the counter when the immigration officer peering at his passport casually mused, "You have changed a bit sir." "Yes," replied my friend in the same tone, "who is getting younger?" "No sir, you have changed quite a bit and do not look like your photograph." "Yes," my friend again said, "I have put on some extra pounds lately and am working very hard to shed them." Getting bit irritated at the unnecessary delay my friend was building up steam. "No sir it is not that, you look quite different," said the immigration officer. "Oh yes," my friend remembered, "I now wear glasses which I did not when this picture was taken." Despite holding a Pakistani passport and used to such insults my friend was reaching his flash point. The immigration officer said, "But sir, even your sex has changed since." My friend now lost his temper and was about to blow up when the immigration officer showed him the passport he was holding: his wife's passport!

It went to his credit though that he let in my friend despite leaving his own passport back in London.

We Muslims have made it mandatory upon ourselves to stop over in Saudi Arabia to perform *Umra* whenever we fly past, or even close, to the Holy Land to the great annoyance of Saudis who at times get fed up with flocks of the faithful who swarm there in all seasons. My wife would not either let me miss any such opportunity. I have lost count of her *Umras* and *Hajjs*. Now when we were going back after holidays in Pakistan, we had chartered our route to Lagos via Saudi Arabia, Ethiopia, and Kenya.

It was my most cherished desire, nurtured over the years, to visit the ancient civilization of Yemen, the land of Queen of Sheba mentioned in the Holy Koran. Incidentally my brother was the Head of Pakistan Chancellery at Sana'a. I would not miss this God-sent opportunity to spend some time in that ancient country. So after performing *Umra*, we broke our journey at Sana'a and stayed there for a fortnight. It turned out to be quite a different country from what I had imagined it.

There were two Yemen, the socialist Yemen and the capitalist Yemen supported by the two superpowers. The Yemenis, divided as they are politically, and dirt poor as compared to Saudis remain an arrogant and defiant nation take pride in their magnificent ancient history. They look upon the Saudis, without concealing their contempt, as upstarts and novae riche. The country, which must have been green and fertile in the past, has become a waste land without any trace of the extensive woods and large fruit gardens mentioned in the Koran. Now the country has no resources worth the name, and most of the population has no regular source of income. The country is almost totally dependent on remittances from immigrant Yemenis working in Saudi Arabia, and some aid from the Saudi monarch. The Sana'a airport was no better than a flying club back home. The fabulously rich ancient history and culture attract a handful of tourists for whom a couple of five-star hotels have been built. During our stay we visited several historical places. The trip was, in fact, a journey into ancient history. After spending a rewarding fortnight in Sana'a, we left for Addis Ababa on way to Nairobi and Lagos.

Since there was a layover in Addis Ababa on way to Nairobi, the airline booked us in the local Hilton for the night. Perhaps the best, most enjoyable part of air travel is the stopover at the airline's expense in expensive five-star hotels. We had already enjoyed this luxury at Amsterdam, Hawaii, Tokyo and Geneva thanks to KLM, the Scandinavian airline SAS, Japan Air and Swiss Air. There is some piquancy in the gratis food and shelter. We were therefore looking forward to a comfortable night in the Ethiopian capital.

Ethiopia was, at the time, experimenting with socialism and making mess of the country. The socialist influence was very much visible as we alighted from the plane, and the first thing that caught our eyes was the life-size posters of Lenin and Stalin. The local population hardly knew anything about these white men and what they were doing in black Africa; only pictures of sickle and hammer seemed indigenous.

The small Russian plane of Yemen Airline dropped us at Addis Ababa airport in the night. The hassle for overnight stay at the airport was unbelievable, and I started wondering if this stopover was worth it. The African inefficiency was bad enough, but now, fortified with a heavy dose of nationalism and socialism, it had deteriorated into a corrupt, arrogant, unbearable disorganization. All the currency and traveler's cheques brought into the country were counted, recounted, recorded, and re-recorded. By the time we left the airport we were utterly exhausted. It was middle of the night, and I was looking forward to a sound sleep in a plush bed of the Hilton. We boarded the airline bus, with a fat, suspicious-looking character in charge, which was to take us to the town. I handed him my booking at the Hilton hotel. It did not make any impression on him, and he kept staring at me, which I guess was his manner of indicating that my papers were not complete, and he expected something more. Since I was exhausted, I did not take any notice of his stare. My wife was visibly frightened. Then I noticed some passengers, who appeared to be businessmen and I guessed, had been to Addis Ababa before, putting a few dollars in the pocket of the fat man. At first, I did not understand the meaning of this transaction. I might have tipped the man on leaving the bus as was customary in capitalistic countries; but the significance of this exchange of money inside the moving vehicle did not dawn on me. However, I found out later that the ground staff in collusion with hotel staff would charge the airline the rental of a 5- star hotel, but dump the simple, rustic passengers in cheap hotels, and pocket the difference. If you had a booking at a five-star hotel and wanted to stay at a five-star hotel, you had to put a few dollars in the pocket of your escort; otherwise, he would deposit you in a cheap, filthy hole of a hotel.

It had become too dark to see the city. The passengers who had greased the palm of the fat man were dropped in what appeared to be decent areas, while we were asked to get off the bus at a rather dingy place. I thought this must be the back of the Hilton. The bus left and we walked into the hotel that proved to be the filthiest I had ever seen. It was past midnight, and there was no one to whom I could complain. The only person around at that hour was the sleepy doorman of the hotel and it was useless to register my protest with him. The place was eerie and spooky and foul smelling. The room we were shown into was infested with cockroaches and mosquitoes. My wife and I spent the night walking from the room to the terrace and from the terrace to the room in a vain attempt to escape the obnoxious stink and equally vicious mosquitoes and picking on each another for no reason at all. It seemed that the spooky atmosphere of that God-forsaken place had got on our nerves. I remember ticking off my sweet little chubby daughter for her puppy fat, which she has not forgotten to this day.

My wife was very upset, and I had to bear the brunt of her anger on this disastrous stopover. She scolded me and tried to convince me that I was very careless in planning tours and keeping money safe and that I was becoming absent-minded. She was in that state of mind in which everything looks suspicious, and everybody seems a crook. She declared that from then on, she would carry all the money, for it would be safer in her custody. So, after much debate, characterized by recriminations and counter-recriminations, we made lots of vows that night, one of which was that in future we would not make unnecessary detours from the straight path between the point of departure and the point of arrival, and would not opt for needless stopovers in the hope of enjoying the luxury of a 5-star hotel especially in Africa.

Somehow the night came to an end and with a sigh of relief we set off for the airport. Boarding the airplane was again an ordeal: our entire luggage was searched once again. My wife, who had volunteered to carry all our money, was taken to the ladies' counter, while I along with the children headed for the lounge. As she did not join us for quite some time, I got worried. Then the departure of the flight was announced, and I became quite panicky, and rushed to the lady's counter. My wife was standing there looking pale, shaken, and close to tears. She had put all the cash she had on the table, down to pence and cent. The customs lady wanted to know where the ten dollars had vanished for which we had no receipt. My wife, a deeply religious, upright, honest lady did not understand what all the fuss was about when everything was in order. She must have counted the money many times over but failed to satisfy the scrupulous lady at the counter. I had learnt my lesson last night and as the departure of the flight was being announced again, I realized that there was no time for argument. So, I wrapped up all our wealth, stuffed it into in my wife's purse, then took out ten dollars and put it in the pocket of the woman saying, 'Here are the missing ten dollars.' As we turned to leave, the fat lady despite her girth managed to bow in courtesy and almost touched my feet. When we had comfortably settled in the plane and my wife had recovered her composure, she quietly slipped all the money and traveler's checks back into my briefcase! She, too, had learnt her lesson.

Nairobi was the next stop. The airport was well designed but nothing was in working order. Unfortunately, in all the developing countries, things instead of improving are rapidly getting worse after their freedom. Nairobi was once the jewel of East Africa. Now everything was in shambles. Lots of people from the Indo-Pak sub-continent had come and settled in Kenya and the neighboring Uganda during the British Raj and contributed so much to the development of the local economy. They were hard-working people, well versed in business practices, and had gradually acquired a strong hold on the economy of the country, adopting the attitudes of their white colonial masters and attracting the jealousy and mistrust of the natives.

President Idi Amin very generously offered them local citizenship, but they opted for a sort of British passport that did not entitle them to enter Britain without a visa. His advice to the Asians was, "You sometimes need to feed the cow you milk." After giving them a long rope, he threw them out. They were stuck in the throat of their colonial masters who could neither swallow nor spit them out. Following a long struggle, they finally got admitted in Britain where they are trying hard for integration. Assimilation in the society, only time will tell.

Once, when in England, I asked an old friend, an elderly businessman of Indian origin, "First you left your homeland in the subcontinent and settled in Kenya, then you were thrown out of Kenya, then from Uganda, and now you are in Britain, refugees for the third time. If you are thrown out of Britain now, where will you head for next?" His answer expressed his faith in the urbane society of Britain and his confidence in the British system. He was not a very literate man, but a businessman with a lot of horse sense: "If British slay us," he said benevolently, "they will, I am sure, throw us in the shade." This confidence in the system despite Enoch Powell's slogan 'Keep Britain white' has made England a multiethnic country. His body must be turning in the grave casting a glance at 10 Downing Street these days!

Nairobi is a scenic place with plenty of wildlife and parks. Several foreign animal lovers have settled in different parts of Kenya and are helping a lot in the preservation of wildlife, particularly the elephants, which was once at the verge of extinction. Because of its tusks the poor animal is hounded and killed mercilessly.

When we left Nigeria, we still had a few thousand in local currency that we wanted to spend on buying some souvenirs as a remembrance of our visit. Against my wishes my wife bought a couple of tusks. I was amazed at their price. Perhaps it was the price that made her buy those remains of dead animals.

When we sent our entire luggage by air to Pakistan, she, without my knowledge, did not part with the tusks and somehow managed to pack them in the luggage that we carried as personal baggage around the world, checking in and out of at least two-dozen airports in three continents. God bless all the custom officials who seeing my little children clutching to their belongings did not want to delay us and just waved us on. Ignorance is indeed bliss. Had I known that I was carrying these banned items, I would not have been able to go through the customs without feeling a sense of guilt in my shaky legs and showing it on my face also. In busy western airports, the customs officials cannot possibly search the entire jumbo load of luggage belonging to five hundred odd passengers; so, they look at your face for telltale signs of guilt or tension and at your passport to confirm their suspicion before deciding to look inside your suitcases.

My wife never trusted anyone with our expensive possessions. Instead of booking these items as unaccompanied cargo, she would stuff everything in our four suitcases of accompanied baggage. Carrying these infernally heavy suitcases around the world, my arms would have gained a couple of inches in length, and the lower limbs must have lost a few inches under their crushing weight. She was right, though, in her insistence on always keeping our luggage with us. Once when we arrived home after booking our excess luggage to follow us, her point was amply proved. When all the twelve cartons we had booked on our national airline arrived, we heaved a sigh of relief that none was lost in transit. The big stickers "Great people to fly with" pasted onto the two canvas cases looked good showing the marketing gimmicks of our airline. But, alas, our relief on receiving our luggage and our appreciation for our national airline were short-lived. When we opened the two suitcases, we were shocked to find that several very expensive and sentimental souvenirs bought in different parts of the world were missing. Someone had neatly slit open the top of each bag with a blade and then pasted the sticker to hide the incision. Disappointed as we were at the loss, I still consoled myself with the thought that the sturdy wooden crates with strong locks that I had had specially made to withstand tampering would be safe, but obviously I underestimated the skills of 'The great people to fly with.' When we opened the cases, we found that many costly things were not there. They had tampered with the locks of the cases, stolen what caught their fancy, and then, very thoughtfully, stuffed in pieces of good packing material to protect the remaining items from damage by knocking against one another.

I have noticed that the airline has given up using this famous slogan, and I guess they must have a good reason for doing so; but I do not know if the great people have given up other things that made them notorious.

Malpractice of many kinds are common in the airlines of almost all the countries that were once labeled as developing countries though

I doubt the relevance of the epithet now when the promise they once showed for development is no more in evidence. My brother-in-law, an economist in an international organization went to attend a conference in one of the Central Asian Republics. After the meeting while he was checking in at the airport, he put his brief case on the conveyor belt for inspection by the scanning machine. The brief case contained all his traveling documents. The briefcase disappeared into the machine but never came out on the other end. When questioned, the attendant of the machine feigned complete ignorance. My brother-in-law could not leave without his briefcase. He made a lot of hue and cry. The protocol officer who was seeing off the delegates arrived at the scene. He spoke to the attendants of the machine in the language they understood and told them that the delegates were very important people. The operator without showing the slightest indication of shame at his abortive attempt to cheat soon produced the briefcase.

I had heard so much about the international court of Justice at The Hague that I had been looking for an opportunity to see the place. There were two reasons for my interest, first the name of the town fascinated me; why should there be a 'The' before the name of a town and secondly, Pakistan had the unique honor that in the sixties one of its illustrious son, Sir Zafarullah Khan, a family friend hailing from my place had been the Judge and later President of the court. While we were traveling from Geneva to London via Amsterdam, the stopover and change of planes gave us a few hours to do what we pleased. I thought that it was the opportunity I was waiting for. So I left my wife and daughter in the vast duty free area at the Schiphol airport to see the place to their heart's content; taking my young son with me, in order to free the ladies from the responsibility of looking after him. We left for The Hague by train. I calculated that it would take us half an hour to reach the city and another half an hour to come back. That would give us at least one hour or so for wandering in the town of The Hague and still leave us some time to spare.

The train was fast and comfortable. I heard some passengers talking about some industrial action by the railway workers to press their demands. When we got down at the railway station of The Hague, I saw some posters on the platform announcing an industrial action (strike) by the railway workers starting the same day.

My heart sank and a cold chill ran down my spine at the thought of being stranded in The Hague. What would my wife and daughter do if I did not reach the Schiphol airport in time for onward journey to London? I thought of canceling the trip to the international court of Justice, taking a taxi and going back, but I was not sure that the taxi could get me back to Schiphol before the departure of our flight. Then I thought that I should consult the stationmaster about the severity of the strike and possible interruption of train services. He told me that the strike of the railway workers was on. "But I see the trains plying up and down." I said pointing to the trains moving in and out of the station. "The strike is on", he told me again, "Don't you see that all the trains are running seven minutes late!" He could not understand why I smiled at his reply: he did not know the chaos our workers created when they went on a wheel-jam strike, and that I would not mind the trains running seven minutes or even half an hour late.

After a long tiring twelve-hour flight from Los Angeles to Tokyo all of us were exhausted and were looking forward to a comfortable night's sleep in a good hotel. A Pakistani official had been asked to receive us, which really was quite unnecessary, as there was a comfortable bus service to and from the airport. He had come a long way to receive us, as Narita airport is over 50 kilometers away from the city, and was justified in insisting that we travel with him in his car. I became so engrossed in talking with him that I left all the loading of our luggage in his car to the porters. When we were seated in his car, again we got absorbed in conversation about good old days, the conditions that now prevailed in Pakistan, and his life in Japan.

An hour later when we were alighting from his car, I noticed that my briefcase containing our passports, about ten thousand dollars in cash and traveler's cheques was missing. It is not difficult for anyone who has had to face such a predicament in a foreign land to imagine the panic that ceased me. All sort of thoughts crossed my mind: How were we going to board our next flight to the Far East without tickets? And how will I be able to find money for buying new tickets if the brief case was not recovered? I was visibly shaken. My friend tried to console me and turned his car back to Narita airport. I was sure we were only wasting time in a wild goose chase. How on earth, I asked myself, was it possible that in such a busy airport, with thousands of commuters crisscrossing its labyrinth of vast halls, I would still find my briefcase where we had left it? After battling with Tokyo traffic for two hours we finally reached the Arrival area of the airport.

Dry mouthed and drained, I could not believe my eyes when I saw my briefcase lying where I had left it hours ago while crowds of passengers walked past it in all directions. It could, I thought with a sigh of relief, only happen in Japan. Nations do not become industrial giants for nothing. The test is very simple. The Japanese cars are being assembled in Pakistan. Which car will you prefer to buy If you had a choice between buying a Japanese car totally manufactured in Japan and one assembled in our motherland by Pakistani workers? Everyone knows the answer. Japanese electronics are now being assembled in Thailand, Hong Kong, Indonesia, Singapore, and South Korea. The brand is the same. The products assembled in which country would you like to buy? The answer again is obvious. The quality of even world-famous foreign brands depends on the quality and business ethics of the people of the country that assembles them. High reputations are not easily acquired: they are earned with hard work and uncompromising morality.

During the Asian games that were held in Korea I accompanied the Pakistani contingent to Seoul. The Koreans do not speak much English. Once when I hired a taxi from downtown, I had communication problem with the taxi driver who was driving me to our quarters in the

Asian game village. Before entering the cab, I clearly told him, "Asian games village." He grunted something, nodded his head vigorously, indicating that he understood me, and drove off at a fast pace. Soon I noticed he was driving me past my destination. I tried to stop him. He again mumbled something I could not understand, nodded his head vigorously and grunted, "OK, OK." That seemed to be the whole of his vocabulary of English.

Soon he entered the Olympic Games village and stopped. Using sign language and bits of English and broken Korean I explained that I wanted to go to Asian village and not Olympic village. He looked around for some time in bewilderment, but soon realized his mistake. He then drove back to Asian games village. I got off at my destination, read the clocked amount on the cab meter and paid him. The taxi driver refused to accept the amount. I thought perhaps the money was not sufficient and offered him some more. He still refused. A Korean-speaking athlete soon joined us and interpreted the situation. I was told that the taxi driver was not accepting the money because he did not want to charge me for the extra mileage we had done because it was due to his fault.

Unlike us, the Koreans have chosen their enemies carefully. 'Can do' in Korea is opposite to what 'Insha Allah' is in Pakistan. Korean's slogan is, "If Japanese can do it we can also do it." Or like Germans, "if someone can make electronics and cars, we can make them more robust." Or like Chinese, "if anyone can make it we can make it cheaper!" Or like Japanese, "If Americans can make it we can make it smarter."

At an in-house party an American ambassador was once asked to describe Islamabad the capital city of Pakistan. "Islamabad is half the size of New York cemetery but twice as dead." He answered.

In Islamabad, architects take sadistic pleasure in constructing houses in two extremes, either like mausoleums and fortresses or like wedding cakes: rather than care for the comfort of its residents and merger with ecology. The life of a city is not brickwork alone; it is linked to the native culture and for that the setting in Islamabad are daunting. Every town has its own distinctive rhythm and pulse that springs from the people and the land. The residents of this city are bland bureaucrats, mysterious diplomats, crooked politicians, and shady businessmen. Culture cannot nourish on hypocrisy; it is very original and genuine. Mores, norms, fine feelings; art and traditions of society are what make culture of a place.

Boota, a simple soul of about thirty, worked in a kiln in a village called Dinga near Gujrat. Like him he had an illiterate wife who used to wash clothes and do the household chores in the Chowdary's (head man of the village) house to supplement their income. They along with their four children lived in a shanty slum close by. It was hard but between the two of them they brought enough home and somehow managed to make both ends meet. In the evening Boota would find some free time to go out and mingle with his friends and with a *hooka* in the middle, narrate stories, discuss politics, and let out his day's pent-up steam. Occasionally he used to take his wife and children to the city for some entertainment and shopping and to a fair where the children and sometime his wife used to enjoy merry go round. Whenever Boota's mother-in-law visited them from her village, he left the children in her custody and took his wife to a cinema to see a Punjabi movie. Life was tough but they were a happy family despite the sporadic dressing-down Boota used to get from his wife for not providing enough to have some homely comforts like his brother who was a bit educated and had a Radio and an old sewing machine in their house.

Somehow lady luck smiled on Boota and as compensation for his small piece of land that got submerged in the lake of Mangla dam, and urgent requirement of labor, Boota along his family found himself immigrating to UK.

New to the culture, not being able to speak a word of English, they found life in UK different and not very hospitable, but they persevered. Being a stoic worker, he found himself a job in a textile factory that entailed little mixing with local population and the requirement was only a pair of hands. He worked diligently and soon was making enough money to afford an old fridge and a used black and white TV. Being a mechanical mind, he managed to repair a broken-down washing machine that their landlady had discarded for a new one. So, life was gradually looking good. Once back from work, the family used to sit around the Tele with children having a piggy ride on their father and enjoyed whatever they could understand. It was the cartoons they loved most. He with his children would enjoy munching his favorite mango flavored ice cream and the other goodies from their fridge while his wife cooked in the adjacent kitchen on a gas cooker. Children started going to school and life was bliss, and they were set to live happily ever after.

Thanks to healthy environment and good food children started growing fast. Boota's wife was very happy but sometime longed to visit home and her village to show off her good fortunes to her friends and family. But they could not yet afford a ticket and saved every penny for such an event. By now her elder daughter reached adolescence and her second daughter was about fourteen. Fearing the free for all local lifestyles shown on TV, Boota's wife watched their blossoming daughters with a hawk's eye; making sure they dress modestly, say their prayers, do not fall in bad company, refrain from mixed gatherings and remain good Muslims. Being illiterate she felt ill at ease not being able to teach the children Koran and other religious sermons at home. She sometime felt uncomfortable at their body language and odd behavior of the children when they mimicked their English friends. She did not want her growing daughters to go astray, and some time felt troubled about their behavior, sharing at night her concern with her husband about her apprehensions and qualms. Boota would just laugh matters away, saying they were only children.

One evening when she returned home after buying some eatables from the market, she was horrified to see a boy in their living room sitting next to her elder daughter. They were obviously very happy playing, watching TV and sipping fizzy drinks. Boota's wife was appalled and furious. She shouted at her daughter and asked her who that boy was?

The girl did not understand the reason of her mother's fury and said, "He is my boyfriend." The word 'boyfriend' struck her like a lightening, and she lost control on herself. With froth fuming from her mouth, she started hurling in Punjabi all the abuses she could muster; threw out the bewildered and astonished boy and gave her daughter a real good hiding. She then locked her in her room, threatening her with dire consequences if she ever brought a boy home. The other children were visibly frightened and could not understand her outburst, and that why their mother was so angry, because in the schoolboys and girls mixed freely. In fact, mothers of the other girls in the class encouraged their daughters to have boyfriends and they would be very concerned if they did not have one.

When Boota arrived home, dead tired after a hard day's work, looking forward to putting his feet up, he saw quite a different house that day. The atmosphere was palpably charged. He asked his wife what was the matter? Hardly had he opened his mouth the dams ripped apart and she let hell loose on him and amongst crying and sobbing shouted at him; accusing him for not taking any interest in raising his children and that they were going promiscuous and were heading for hell and that she had decided to take them back to Dinga.

Boota tried to calm his frenzied, fuming red-hot wife and asked her, "Good woman, what has gotten into you? Isn't it good that she brings the boy home, and they can play before your watchful eye rather than that they spend nights out?" Then after giving her a piece of his own mind, he shouted; that he was quite happy working in Dinga, where unlike here he had plenty of spare time; to socialize with his friends over *hooka* and cups of sweetened tea. It is she who kept complaining about his low income and lack of homely comforts. He asked her; doesn't she now enjoy drinking water from the cold machine, and cook food without smoke? Smoke that used to smolder her face and blacken her clothes while she blew into hearth and that she does not have to wash clothes with her hands, which she used to when in Dinga. Realizing his wife's country background, he thought of a simile she would easily understand. "Woman, can't you comprehend that when you buy a goat it is more than the milk you have bargained for." Then he spoke the words of experience and wisdom that the hard life had taught him. "Coming here in a different culture is a package deal. Take it or leave it, you can't have one and leave the other." Everything comes with a price; not even the roses grow without thorns," he said judiciously. "If you do not want to change, this society also will not change just for you. A drop of ink cannot turn a river blue." He philosophized.

"I was quite happy baking bricks back in Dinga and can even today, pack up and go home if you like. How much is it that I need for myself?" He asked.

John Harvard who established Harvard University at Boston was a liquor merchant. As a mark of respect for the benefactor a bronze statue has been resurrected. This is placed on a pedestal about four feet high in one of the lawns of the University.

There are cultural differences the way the students show their reverence to their peers. In the subcontinent and in Africa the students used to genufract, bow and touch their feet as mark of respect. When I visited Harvard, the great seat of learning; amongst the sites that I was overwhelmed to see was the black statue of John Harvard. And what struck me most was the shining shoe of that benevolent man. I thought the American students must have been following our traditions by showering their veneration on the old man's statue for the services he rendered in the cause of education; by respectfully touching his feet repeatedly, resulting in the shiny shoe. Black stone in Mecca has worn thin due to repeated kissing and caresses of the devotees. What however baffled me was why only one shoe.

Due to a depression in the lawn in front of the statue rainwater had collected after a shower and the students had difficulty reaching the statue. Some Good Samaritan and helpful students had placed bricks in the small puddles a few feet apart in a row to help leapfrog the wet land saving one's shoes from soiling. Perching precariously on one foot on the bricks every student clasped the shoe of the statue which now shone brightly in contrast to its ebony color. I was impressed at the pains the students took to reach the statue.

While students crossed the lawn, each one of them touched the shoe of that great man. Overwhelmed, I enquired from a young student, "you must have great respect for the great man, the way you touch his foot as a mark of your reverence." "Reverence, my foot, she said, "we take this path because this is a short cut to our classes" "After the rain when water wets the lawn, treading on those bricks can be tricky as one may fall flat on the face if we do not hold on to his foot!

10

The Black Continent

One of the interesting assignments being a military doctor was a deputation to some other under doctored countries like Saudi Arabia and Nigeria where I spent four years as a surgeon in uniform.

Landing at Lagos was a pleasant surprise. In the middle of black Africa, where one expected bush and desert, big game, and primitive tribes: a modern and beautiful airport almost like Schiphol of Amsterdam or Changi of Singapore, was the last thing I anticipated.

It was a particularly welcome spectacle, as we had just come exhausted after a visit to Saudi Arabia. Like all good Muslims going past Holy Land, we had stopped over for *Umra*, and the proceedings of entering and leaving that country had drained us. We were required to reach the airport six hours before the departure time and stand in long queues before entering the departure lounge. An indifferent Saudi immigration official browsed sleepily through the pages of different passports. It seemed he enjoyed looking at the long queues. The Saudi authorities would not increase the number of personnel to deal with long queues, as is done in any efficient airport where the number of staff is automatically increased in proportion to the number of passengers to hurry up the proceedings. It is said that all the inconveniences and difficulties that come in the way of a noble deed like *Umra*, add to your blessings. It seems that the Saudi authorities take special pains to ensure as much reward for the pilgrims as possible by creating avoidable and unavoidable hurdles in their way.

At Lagos, the then capital and largest city of Nigeria, the airport not only matched the international standards in design and construction but also functioned to the international standard of efficiency. The arrivals and departures at different levels made the flow of passenger traffic very orderly. The airport had been named after the very popular slain President of the country, Murtala Mohammed, and had been recently commissioned with the help of the Dutch government and KLM, the Dutch Airlines, which was still running the airport. Whatever the reason of the efficiency, it was a soothing experience for my wife and sleepy children after a sleepless night at Jeddah airport. Thanks to my connection with the military, we received a very courteous treatment.

Traveling from the airport on the four-lane highway, I could not believe that I was in a third world country. The capital of the country Lagos was a city in a hurry to develop. Lots of high-rise buildings were in different stages of construction. The seat of government was in a picturesque, postcard-beautiful island known as Victoria Island, the shores of which are washed by the blue waters of Atlantic Ocean. This was the old colonial capital that the British had specially segregated for their use. The beautiful lush green island with its sandy beaches must have enchanted the British who ruled Nigeria for a very long time.

Nigeria is a country in Western Africa on the Gulf of Guinea. The Portuguese, the British and the French were the first to discover it and exploit its resources. Then arrived the Dutch traders in the 17th and 18th centuries. The British created separate protectorates in Northern and Southern parts of the country in the beginning of 20th century, and finally merged them into one colony under the British crown in 1914. The country attained its independence in 1960.

A country with a population of over 100 million, like Pakistan had not been able to find a leader with the strength of character and breadth of vision to come to terms with the problems besetting a newly independent country and win it a respectable place amongst the comity of nations of the world. In 1991, the capital was shifted to a more central place, Abuja, in the hope that this would bring unity to the ethnically divided country. When I worked in Nigeria in the seventies/eighties, the horrors of Biafran war had not yet been forgotten. It was the war, which the eastern wing of the country inhabited, mostly by the better off Ibos fought, to secede from the Republic. The attempt to dismember the country failed after a long struggle, but the scars of the conflict were still visible. Attempts were afoot for the integration of three major ethnic divisions. In the north live the tall dark Hausas, a shade lighter than other Nigerians because of admixture of Arab blood in their veins. Yorubas, mostly traders, inhabit the southwestern region with the port city of Lagos. The Southeastern part of the country is the home of Ibos, who are better educated and dominate the civil service.

The tribal divides in Nigeria were much deeper than any other demarcation and there was intense air of suspicion amongst all tribes, it is said it was the root cause of the Biafran war.

It was a tropical stormy rainy dark night when the head of medical service, a senior General in Nigerian Army was driving home late at night from a party in his heavy-duty Mercedes. The storm was ripping off the tin roofs and the electric poles and the night was dark and blustery. The already erratic electric supply of the hospital under such heavy downpour was affected and for emergencies we had become used to working with torches and lanterns. The General met with a serious road traffic accident and was brought to our hospital. His face was bleeding profusely due to multiple lacerations caused by shattered windscreen. He also had a broken forearm and a leg that was grotesquely deformed. He was in a violent temper and would not let any Nigerian doctor touch him despite being in shock. I was sent for. I lived in the doctor's residence in hospital compound in a high-rise apartment building idyllically located overlooking the Atlantic and reached ER in no time. When I arrived, he was in a violent mood and also in a bad shape; cursing and swearing anyone that came close to him. While in his office he was well known for being a man of few words, stern, severe and almost sadistic. Although to be fair I had found him quite the opposite; a principled, rather quiet and a decent man, won't take no nonsense and who was utterly predictable. This was not his normal behavior and, I wondered if his present state was due to head injury, but I soon realized that he smelled strange and thought it to be due to heavy drinking, as most Nigerians suffered this malady, particularly in the wild parties he was heading home from. Seeing me he pacified. He needed immediate surgery to cobble him up and set the fractures for which I needed to anesthetize him. With non-existent and broken-down logistics, I could not expect any help from any quarters. The only anesthetist I could think of at that unearthly hour was a young raw Pakistani Captain, since he also lived in the hospital compound. He was only an apprentice with some hands-on experience in anesthesia and was yet not qualified. I sent for him, and he also immediately arrived. He had youthful overconfidence on his side and without being too much over-awed from the social stature of his patient; boldly started putting the General to sleep. Before the Captain started, I asked the General if he had any previous surgery or any ailments. He shook his head.

What with no electricity, sleepy assistants, and primitive theatre conditions somehow, we managed to mend him and set his fractures and put his limbs in plaster casts. I then asked my young colleague, the makeshift anesthetist to wake him up. None of us had any clue about his previous medical history because most senior officials had their personal physicians in London where they would fly off for even trifles. All went well and we were satisfied for a job well done. But after completion of the surgery the patient was taking his time and would not wake up. While we waited our concern changed into apprehension and then turned into panic. The thought of a senior general dying on the table was petrifying. He smelled of what I thought alcohol and we presumed that was what was delaying his recovery. The young Captain and I were now increasingly getting vexed, as to why he was not coming around. First mentally and then vocally we ran through the checklist that surgeons and anesthetists learn early in their carriers; as to why an otherwise stable patient does not wake up after surgery: -

1. Still paralyzed, meaning the paralyzing drugs are still not neutralized. Well, he did have a small, short acting dose at the start of the anesthesia; but none since.
2. Narcotics given before or during the operation. He was not given any.
3. Carbon dioxide narcosis due to accumulated carbon dioxide because of shallow breathing. He had been breathing normally on his own throughout and still was.

After that there was a long list in small print.

As the time passed, we got increasingly worried, and panic started to prevail. Since the patient was taking time to come around, I asked my assistant to bring a catheter to drain his bladder. As the urine poured out, my assistant an elderly Nigerian soldier commented on the musty smell. I thought it to be due to the pungent gases of anesthesia. The bladder was full, and the urine was warm and concentrated and smelled strange. My Nigerian assistant, a gray-haired nursing orderly, again commented about the fruity smell and stuck a finger in his mouth after dipping it in the urine. 'It is sweet like syrup, Oga,' he said, and before I could clench my teeth, he tried to stick his other urine-soaked finger in my mouth. Already on my wits ends all I could feel was a bad taste in my mouth, but he was right, it tasted sweet.

Knowing fully well that there would not be any one present in the laboratory at this unearthly hour on a stormy night I still sent the urine sample for the test; the theatre orderly came back with the sample that laboratory was locked. While the anesthetist supported the patient I stumbled into Laboratory. It was pitch dark and I did not have much clue about its geography. In the dark with wind blowing noisily the place looked spooky. Somehow, I managed to find my way towards the shelves with chemical bottles and fumbled onto Benedict solution and a few candles. It is difficult to imagine in this E age such primitive conditions but that was how we used to diagnose glucose in the urine those days. I dropped five drops of urine in the test tube. The test was strongly positive. I rushed back and told my young colleague as to why our patient was not waking up.

Gingerly we administered a small dose of Insulin. It was a long wait but we both agreed he was a bit lighter after that; at any rate he was no worse off. Since there was some response so we repeated the dose, poured in lot of fluids and the General started coming around. Another dose, the patient began opening his eyes, and now started to struggle pulling the tubes out. What a relief, I still can recall and remember it vividly.

Following day after we had established his glucose state and things had settled down, I rebuked the General for not revealing his past history of Diabetes Mellitus. He did not have any recollection of the events. He admitted that he suffered from severe diabetes and had missed a couple of injections of Insulin inadvertently due to his preoccupation. Apart from that he did not show any sense of remorse for a slip that could have cost him his life.

Fortunately setting of fractures was perfect; so more for bragging and a pat on the back than anything else the following day I showed his X rays to a senior Nigerian colleague. The General did not like that one bit and became furious. "How dare you reveal my ailments to a local? Don't you know which tribe he belongs to? He is a Yoruba," he shouted. I had no idea and little did I care.

Nigeria is a vast country inhabited by over 140 million people, has two great rivers, the Niger coming from Niger and flowing southeastwards and the Benue flowing from Cameroon and running southwards, traversing it in the shape of a huge Y. The two rivers meet at Lokoja and proceed to the Gulf of Guinea. The country obviously takes its name from river Niger. It is a very fertile land, rich in mangroves and rain forests so thick that no ray of the blazing summer sun can penetrate its dense growth. The perennial rain and equatorial location ensure that temperate climate makes the country rich in flora and fauna.

All that the farmers had to do to grow a crop was to scatter the seed, wait for some time, and then reap the harvest. Unfortunately, they were not willing to do even that when I was there. Once Nigeria was a prosperous agricultural economy: it was all but self-sufficient in staple food, and a major exporter of peanuts, peanut oil, cocoa, and palm oil, but not anymore.

The oil boom had turned in a doom; mass migration of rural population to the cities causing not only civic problems but also traffic jams certainly the worst in Africa if not the world. During rush hours nobody moves. The ambulances are stuck in the middle of roads. The patients cannot do anything but wait and pray, babies are delivered in vehicles. Since traffic comes to a standstill on major roads for hours on end, vendors have set up almost full-fledged markets along the highways. To rectify the situation the authorities came up with a novel idea. One-day cars with odd numbers on their registration plates would be allowed to ply on the roads and on the next day those with even numbers.

Strangely enough, the ingenious scheme worked well for a month or two. Then those owning even-numbered cars bought second cars bearing odd-numbered plates, and the owners of odd-numbered cars bought cars with even numbered plates, thus compounding the situation further.

We in Pakistan have plenty in common with Nigeria. Ethnic prejudices; frequent Martial laws, rampant corruption and terrible law and order situation. The army in both the countries did not miss any opportunity to intervene and pack up democracy before it had a chance to take roots. Graffiti on the walls of Lahore and Lagos were also the same: -

"We apologize for the temporary democratic interruption Normal martial law will resume shortly."

Military dictators initially are unsure of themselves, and direly need and look around for some sort of legitimacy. Not finding it at home they hunt for friends abroad, while the nation helplessly quivers, that national assets may not be bartered away for petty personal gains and friends do not turn into masters. What precious national interests even sovereignty of the country, they surrender for their chairs is a dark chapter in the history of the Third world.

The impositions of Martial law at regular intervals have made a mess of both the countries, economically and politically. We gained independence much earlier than Nigeria but are still walking in circles even fifty years later. These self-styled crusaders have conquered their own countries many times over like the dictators of banana Republics. Every revolution begins with power of an idea and ends when clinging to power is the only idea left. Dictators are riding on a tiger, and they dare not disembark for the tiger will eat them up.

In our country, it was not the generals alone who were at fault. A people who has voted into power corrupt leaders not once or twice but half a dozen times and have willingly endured Martial Law after Martial Law for an equal number of times, have no one else to blame but themselves. What is stupidity? Stupidity is, "that you make the same mistake over and over and yet expect that the result this time will be different!"

Two men who were neighbors, one a civilian and the other in uniform, go to a nursery to buy some plants. They take fancy for a special identical shrub and buy a sapling each, take it home and plant them in their respective gardens. After a few days the man in uniform noted his plant was not doing well, starting to shrivel, and dried up. He went to nursery and complained to the owner for supplying him a flawed plant. It irked him more because when he looked form his window his neighbor's plant was flourishing. The salesman gave another sapling of the same shrub to the officer, who brought it home and planted it after throwing out the dried-up plant. After a few days the officer noticed again the plant shriveling up. In a few days it was like a dry stick. The officer was very annoyed and stormed into nursery complaining that he was being cheated. Out of awe of the uniform, the salesman provided him with a third sapling and gave him a lecture on how to bring up a plant; emphasizing the importance of regularly watering and hoeing it, like his neighbor did and whose plant was flourishing. The officer and his batman regularly did what the salesman had advised; watering and hoeing but after a few days the plant again dried up. The officer now was furious. He charged into the nursery and demanded an explanation. This time the salesman refused to give him any more plants but out of curiosity asked him, "what do you do to the plants that all your saplings dry up, whereas your neighbor's plant is now a grown-up beautiful shrub and has started to flower, surely you are not looking after the plants." The Major did not like that and retorted, "I look after the plant better than my neighbor does. I have followed all the instructions you gave me like a regimental order; like watering and hoeing every day. I even pull out the sapling every morning to see whether it has taken routes or not, and yet all my plants dry up."

In Nigeria the ethnic ties were stronger than a religious brotherhood. Religion was rather the private affair of the individual and was not as serious a business as the ethnic pride. It was not uncommon to find different religions in the same family. Muslim men married Christian women and Christian men married Muslim women without any hesitation. The children were free to choose their religion. The names were quite confusing. A Mohammed could be a staunch Christian and a Jesus a devout Muslim. Both religions were amusingly mixed, and most people had chosen the best of both the worlds. Muslims drank liquor freely, and Christians married as many times as they liked. This was a land of abundance. Most dwellers had two cars, four wives and innumerable children. The oil boom unfortunately brought with it all kinds of evil, crime, corruption, and wastage of resources, widening gap between the affluent and the poor culminating into one economic disaster after another.

There was a time when local currency Naira used to be equal to a pound sterling. Things, however, began to slip and the Naira became equivalent to an American dollar. In late eighties one Naira used to fetch only a few pennies in the open market. This is even though Nigeria is potentially a very rich country. Rulers had very mercilessly stripped their motherland bare of all its wealth by depositing it into Swiss accounts. When I went to Nigeria in 1979, the corrupt practices of Nigerian hierarchy shocked me. How could, I asked myself, can one be so cruel to one's own country? Alas! Pakistan of the nineties was worse than the Nigeria of eighties.

An American Senator visited the palatial palace of a politician in poverty ridden country of Pakistan, where he was grieved to see so much misery due to poor socio-economic conditions and could not help comparing the difference in the ghettos and luxurious living of his host and asked him how he manages to live like a king in a poor country. The politician took the Senator to a framed photograph hanging on the wall and asked him, "Do you see that river?" The senator replied in the affirmative. The politician asked him again, "Do you see that bridge?" the senator again said, yes. "10 percent." explained the politician.

The politics of the country changed, and it so happened that the senator after a few years went to see the same politician who was now a big shot in the government and again showed his amazement at the filthy collection of wealth. "How do you manage to do that?" The minister again took the senator to the framed picture and asked the same question. "Do you see that river?" "Yes," answered the senator. "Do you see that bridge?" The politician asked the senator. The senator gazed at the picture and could see nothing and answered. "No, I do not see no bridge on the river." "Yes, 100 percent," answered his Excellency.

We in our country have climbed the ladder very fast. In fact, we can teach a trick or two of this trade to even the most corrupt. This is even though we, unlike Nigerians, founded Pakistan as an ideological state in the name of Islam. We have not only pushed ourselves down the drain but also tarnished the name of Islam. The whole world, I believe, respect the principles of Islam but hates Muslims like us.

The stories about corruption, nepotism and other moral evils of our rulers that have been making headlines in the national press for some years bear a striking resemblance to the exploits of the Nigerian ruling coterie narrated in the world press in the seventies. The then finance minister of almost bankrupt Nigeria once went begging to one of the world's financial institution for a loan of a few hundred million dollars. He was told that the amount he had come to borrow could have been borrowed in his own country from anyone of the top politicians or senior bureaucrats who had stashed billions in Swiss banks.

Another scandal that remained on the front pages of Nigerian newspapers for almost a year was about the mysterious disappearance of half a billion dollars. The amount received as the price of exported oil was deposited with the government, but then it vanished into thin air. Every other day one impudent journalist or another would write a story about the missing dollars, but the government kept mum. No responsible government official seemed to notice the hue and cry that grew shriller with every passing day. After about a year, one morning a high official confronted the press, denied all charges of wrongdoing, and declared that the dollars, about which the whole country was crying hoarse, were very much where they should have been, in government treasury, and that anyone was free to check the accounts. There was a sense of relief in the country. Many simple souls sympathized with the poor innocent official who had so patiently born the unjust attacks of the irresponsible press for such a long time. Further investigations revealed the official was telling the truth, when he asserted that the half a billion dollars were in the treasury; they were in the treasury on the day he made the announcement. But for one full year he had kept the amount in his personal account, perhaps to protect it from other predators in the department and had incidentally earned some million dollars as interest.

Then there were stories about the police, the most popular and interesting of which ran as follows: A person whose house was burgled in the night by a band of dacoits went to the police station to report the robbery but turned back hurriedly without saying a word to the officer-in-charge. When people asked him why he had not lodged the complaint, he said that as he entered the inspector's office to speak to him, he recognized him as the person who had led the robbers' gang last night. On my return to Pakistan, I was to hear similar stories about our police. It seems the policemen of our two brotherly countries, despite the differences in their physical appearance, really are brothers in alms under the skin. In fact, the lower, middle, and even top bureaucracies of the two countries, excepting a few honorable exceptions, are mirror images of one another. Bribe culture in fact is like the good old barter system; a manifestation, that the people are still living in Stone Age. The pay they receive is their rightful share of the national cake.

I understand the hypnotic spell that money casts on people, and I also know that some people have more appetite for wealth than their neighbors do. I also accept that there is no limit to depravity of men; but I still wonder why fate has caused all the people with insatiable hunger for illicit money to be born in Muslim countries. These leeches have certainly succeeded in sucking their own peoples white and pawning their countries to the international usurers and piling up heaps of ill-gotten wealth in the dark, hungry vaults of Swiss banks, but there is little chance of their enjoying their loot in peace. They are oblivious of the fact that the corrupt rulers of the third world have never been able to enjoy their ill-gotten money. The recent history is replete with such examples, the Shah of Iran, Marcos of Philippines, Mobutu of Zaire. Not that our rulers are ignorant of recent history; they know what befell their predecessors in this deplorable business, but they hope, fondly and foolishly, that somehow, they will escape the executioner's axe. Even if some of them succeed in escaping retribution and reaching the French Rivera, English country houses and penthouses in London and New York, they will be treated like pariahs. No peace of mind will come to them, and they will spend the rest of their miserable days and sleepless nights, in fleeing, from country to country, from pub to pub, casino to casino till the weight of their crimes drives them crazy. He who sows wind reaps whirlwind. This is the law of the nature, and it will not change for anyone's convenience.

I was posted as surgeon-in-charge at Nigeria's most prestigious Military hospital in the Federal Capital. It catered for the needs of not only the top military brass but also the hierarchy of the Nigerian federal government. The president of the country was our most esteemed visitor. He could trust the Pakistani doctors who naturally were not influenced by any local prejudices, ethnic or political. The officials in the Pakistan Embassy took advantage of this professional relationship, and whenever they had to cut short the long protocol and red tape to have an audience with the President, they would use the good offices of the doctors.

The President once came to hospital for an X-ray of his chest. He took his clothes, the Nigerian ceremonial regalia off and just before the technician was about to shoot, the electricity went. The generator could not pick the heavy X-ray machine. While we felt extremely embarrassed, the President in the darkened room quietly put on his robe, smiled benevolently and left without shaking the earth, not even a tremor!

While in the subcontinent we have abandoned all the good traditions left over by the British, Nigerians still respected and stood in queues. Once I was busy seeing patients in the outdoor clinic of the hospital when I had to suddenly come out on some errand. Outside my office to my utter surprise, I saw sitting on a wooden bench, the wife of the army chief, waiting patiently with her numerous, not so patient children awaiting her turn to see me. This I would not see happen in my country.

In this prestigious position, I had had ample opportunity to work with local Nigerians; and during my over three years' stay in Lagos I came across a cross section of the society. The average Nigerian was a simple and hospitable honest man. In fact, I felt very comfortable with the local population. As a result, I have made life-long friends while working in

Lagos. A couple of them, whenever they have an opportunity of visiting Far East, very graciously break their journey in Pakistan to spend a day or two with me. Needless to say, the great pleasure it gives me to see them again and talk of old times.

One of them Dr. Jibril Oyekan who had earned a doctorate in UK in petroleum technology was a high official in the federal government. A staunch Muslim, he would gather the local and expatriate Muslims in his house every Friday to teach us the Holy Book and what was more important, to put some spine in our rather passive faith. He used to be furious at us for our lukewarm attitude towards Islam. He could not understand why we Pakistanis, coming from the bastion of Islam as we did, were such half-hearted, unenthusiastic, almost apologetic Muslims. He had launched a campaign that the Muslim girls studying in local Christian missionary schools should not be required to wear the short skirts which formed a part of the standard uniform but be allowed to wear the Pakistani dress and the Arab hijab.

My attitude on this issue was rather ambivalent; it would be good if they allow the change of dress, and if they do not; well, it still would be okay. This kind of feeble, casual position on important matters would make him mad. But I remain very confused to this day about the dress of our ladies particularly abroad. Modesty is the main aim of dress. But you do not have to look so different that you stand out like a signpost. If a Muslim lady walks past in a street of Stockholm with Hijab, she will look conspicuous, and people will turn their heads for a second look. If an American or European lady is scantily clad amongst the burqa clad ladies of Kabul, it is not difficult to imagine the reaction. I appreciate the European ladies, the correspondents of Western media dressed as is the norm while working in Iran. I feel within certain parameters one should try to merge with the milieu.

A grateful and well-off Christian patient of mine once sent me a crate full of wines. Being a teetotaler, I knew nothing about wines, but from the French and Scotch packing I could guess that this was expensive stuff.

I did not like to return the gift, for it would be uncivil. So, I sent the crate to my Nigerian Christian Commanding officer who accepted it with great delight. I told this to Jibril. He was livid with rage. "Why don't people know that you are a Muslim? How dare anyone present you alcoholic drinks! Are you ashamed of being known as a Muslim?" When he cooled down a little, I asked him as to what should I have done with this wine? He retorted, "Why don't you know that the Prophet has promised Allah's wrath to those who cultivate grapes for making wine, to those who ferment wine, to those who sell wine, to those who transport wine, to those who serve wine and certainly on those who drink it." Then he pronounced that by sending wine to the commanding officer, I had placed myself in the category of those who transport it. However, he was kind enough to say, "May Allah forgive you for this lapse."

He used to be very cross with the expatriate Muslims working in Nigeria on account of their small families. He said that we were financially well off and, unlike poor Muslims who could not afford bigger families, surely could raise any number of children we liked. "What really is happening", he said, "is that Muslims who can't properly educate and bring up their children are having large families; whereas all of us highly educated, enlightened people who can send their children to UK and America for higher studies are content to have small families. He was convinced that we had fallen a prey to wrong propaganda about family planning.

I am reminded of my friend's remarks about poor Muslims having larger families when I look around, here in Pakistan, and see armies of children swarming the streets, ill-fed, half-naked; uncared-for illiterate urchins left to be brought up in *Madrassahs*. I shudder to think what sort of Pakistan we will have in a few years when this forgotten generation of children grow into uneducated, unskilled, unemployed delinquents.

To my mind this man, Jibril Oyekan of Nigeria who had a total commitment to his religion and would make no compromises on principles and accept no nonsense in the name of enlightenment, came close to picture of an ideal.

I remember the firm reaction of my friend when he was asked to attend an important meeting of a high-powered committee on oil industry scheduled to be held on a Friday at the time of Friday Prayer. It was to be chaired by the Vice President of the Federation. Jibril told the Federal petroleum Secretary, a rather prejudiced Christian that the time did not suit him as it clashed with the time of *Juma* Prayer, and that he would not be able to attend. He suggested that the time should be changed. The Secretary thought that this man was not more important than the Vice President who had agreed to this time and hoped that his absence would give him an opportunity to settle old scores with him. So, the meeting was held right at the time of *Juma* Prayer. My friend did not attend. Now he was the linchpin in the oil industry, and in his absence no useful discussion could be held. No one could answer the Vice-President's questions, who, exasperated with the situation, finally said, "Gentlemen we are getting nowhere. Where is this man who has all the statistics and other necessary information?" The Secretary thought that this was the right moment to strike and blacken the face of the absent expert. So, he told the Vice-President that how rudely the fanatic Muslim had refused to attend the meeting at the time of *Juma* Prayer. The Vice-President, himself a Christian normally a cool man blew up. The Secretary felt very pleased that today he will be able to sort out old score. The vice–President however was annoyed with the Secretary, "Knowing fully well the sensitivity why the hell did you then insist on holding the meeting at the time of *Juma* Prayer?" he asked. "Just to annoy him and injure his religious sentiments?"

Another expatriate who impressed me was an Englishman who decided to convert to Islam after carrying out a comparative study of the religions. An Engineer by profession, he had worked in Muslim countries, and even though we the Muslims by birth were such poor specimen of Islam had joined our faith. His Islam, unlike ours, was quite simple and straightforward. He used to wonder at us why we had no identity to mark us apart from other Western educated people, and whose faith did not give them courage to stand firm on principles and refuse to be influenced by everything foreign. I have observed that those who have studied Islam before converting are better Muslims than us.

The working conditions in Nigeria were impossible. No member of the local staff wanted to work. They were never short of excuses for not doing their duties. Even when a life-threatening emergency was brought to the operation theatre, no one seemed sensitive to the gravity of the situation, and everyone dragged his feet. "We cannot operate today, Sir, there is no linen," the operation theatre sister would declare without any hint of regret in her voice. "In that case, I think, we will have to use operation gowns for linen," I would answer. "But, sir, there is no electricity," someone else would inform me, rather triumphantly. "We can operate with emergency light, can't we?" "The sweeper is off sick," another voice would blurt out as if it was the most compelling reason for postponing the operation. Exasperated with the attitude of my assistants and knowing that people are susceptible to enthusiasm I would pick up the broom and start sweeping the floor of the operation theatre. This gesture would shame them into action, and soon hesitantly and sheepishly someone will join me in the cleaning job, and a little later someone else would take the broom from my hands. Since the responsibility for treating the patient rested on the shoulders of the surgeon, I had to be firm; but my assistants, after failing to dissuade me from going on with the operation, would adopt another line of attack and try to frighten me. Someone would suggest, "What if the wound got septic? You will get a bad name for nothing." Another would add, "You are a foreigner here. People may misunderstand you." "What if the patient died for want of surgery which is his only chance? Who will accept that responsibility?" I would counterattack, and this would shut them up. We would then somehow manage to operate. Although I would succeed in having my way most of the times, this routine fencing match before every other operation drained me more than the surgery.

When I compare working conditions in Europe, the subcontinent and Africa I find a stark difference. While I was in England when an order was passed by the head of the department, it was taken for granted that the job would be done, in the best possible way. Not so in the subcontinent and certainly not in Africa. Back home, after giving an order I expected that the job would be done slowly and in a shoddy way, and half-heartedly, unless I ensured constant monitoring and saw to it that it was being carried out, and to my satisfaction. With some coaxing, pushing, sulking, and gritting of teeth, the job would finally be done, but not of the standard I would have liked it to be. In the African continent, when you give an order, you can be sure nothing will move. There, you would have to get up and do the job yourself. I suppose smart executives would blame it on poor leadership; but that was the only way I could deal with life threatening emergencies.

This explains why nations are what they are. When there is no pride in performance, the work is a drudgery that people tend to avoid, and the nations remain backward. People, nations are made when there are enthusiasm and people take pride in working. Since there is hiring and firing on the spot in the private sector; carrot and stick is used freely and ruthlessly and these produce results. In the public sector people consider jobs as their right, remunerations part of the national cake and are least pushed to work. Job security provided by the state becomes an impediment for progress in the third world.

Traveling during the day in Lagos was risky, traveling at night was asking for trouble. Living in the scanty comforts of a single star hotel, over ten miles from my hospital, courtesy Nigerian bureaucracy, I was once summoned urgently at midnight to see an emergency in the hospital. This was a rather unusual as due to poor transport and other logistic problems the staff in the hospital normally slept on even worst of emergencies. The telephone system mostly was out of order and due to law-and-order conditions only a few doctors would venture driving on their own at night any way.

The Nigerian driver, driving a vintage 3-ton ambulance of MASH looks arrived to fetch me. He had no clue what the emergency was all about. I climbed into the front seat of rickety old ambulance. Inside, the heat and humidity were unbearable. Even worse, the stench of beer bellowing in wafts from a half-drunk driver was nauseating. I lowered the windowpane to let in some fresh air of wet Lagos. The jalopy made noises of all descriptions and slowly lumbered its way towards the hospital.

A concerned middle-aged theatre sister greeted me when I alighted from this Sherman-tank like vehicle. She took me straight to the operation theatre where on the operating table laid her adolescent daughter, moaning and writhing with pain. For a change all the instruments were ready for surgery and even a couple of operation theatre assistants were standing scrubbed up. The anxious sister told me the history that the young girl had been having pain all over the abdomen for a few days and now it was worse on the right side.

I examined the girl who was burning with high fever and experiencing lot of pain in the lower abdomen. Burst appendix perhaps I thought. But the expression on her face did not look as if she was suffering from peritonitis. I took some time examining the girl to the annoyance of the theatre sister who thought I should get on with surgery.

After thorough examination I came to conclusion that this was a case of pelvic inflammation and not acute appendicitis and that there was no need for surgery. I started heavy doses of antibiotics and sent the patient to the ward. Walking back to our changing room the sister, the mother of the girl who by now was quite confused whispered in my ear, "Doctor you do not think this pain could have something to do with Jane going out with dirty boys?" Surgeons are tough nuts and are used to such embarrassing occasions, but I felt my ears burning and could only blurt, "I am afraid so." The nurse heaved a sigh of relief, "Thank God," she said. "I thought it was appendicitis!"

Driving back in the old ambulance, I thought about the incidence and the cultural difference that spanned here and from where I came and why was I always summoned to hospital when least required. But then I thought of the theatre sister who worked so closely with me, and I felt relieved that my visit had done her some good.

We had traveled only a couple of miles when the ambulance stopped and would not start again despite repeated turns of the ignition key. The Nigerian driver got out of the vehicle on a deserted highway in the early hours of the morning and lifted the bonnet to find the cause of malfunction while I shivered in fear. All I could hear at that unearthly hour were barks of a few stray dogs. Fears of gangs of robbers who would soon pounce upon us in the darkness were uppermost in my mind. Such happenings were not unusual after the breakdown of vehicles on deserted roads after sunset when people had been deprived of their belongings, maimed, and even murdered. And the advice by the experienced expatriates was that always keep a few hundred Naira in the pocket for presenting to the highwaymen. I put my hand in the pocket and could only count a few notes of God knows what denomination. I wondered if this much money would be enough for a machete-flying robber.

The loud noise made by the driver banging the bonnet in disgust who swore audibly shook me up. He came over to me on the passenger side of the ambulance and announced, "Oga, there is no petrol in the vehicle." "What no fuel in the ——," I exploded, my fuse being short already and I was at the end of my tether. The military officer in me tried to take over. But soon sense prevailed. Losing temper at that late hour at the now fuel and beer smelling driver would not have solved any problem, so I kept my cool. "What do we do now?" I asked. The driver thought for what appeared a very long time, took a deep puff at his cigarette and then came up with a solution. "I will walk back and will try to find a gas station if one is open at this hour. Have you some money on you sir? Without thinking I gave him the few notes I had in my pocket, and he marched off into the darkness leaving me all alone in the dark eerie night. It was hot and humid, and I could not roll up the glass as I sat in the hot ambulance sweating, wondering at my plight. I thought to myself, there must be easier ways of earning your livelihood than risking your life in far off lands. I sat there waiting for the driver and looked desperately towards his trail. It had started to rain in the meantime, and it had become even more humid, till I could no longer see through the hazy windscreen.

After what appeared an eternity, I saw a distant figure walking towards me and braced myself for the worst. Fortunately, it was only the driver. I heaved a sigh of relief as he was carrying something in his hands, which I could not discern in the darkness. These were cans of beer instead of petrol. "There is no gas station open at this hour Oga. I woke up this shop keeper and brought a few drinks for us." I looked at him in amazement as he carried on, "he also runs a small hotel on top of the shop. We will walk up to him after a drink." He opened a beer can and took a deep pull and then offered me, a strict teetotaler the other can!"

There were all sorts of foreigners working in Nigeria, Europeans, Indians, Pakistanis, and people from the Far East. The Nigerians would group them all together as the 'pale ones.' The color of skin as a criterion for differentiation between people has always baffled me. An Asian settled in South Africa recently described his plight to me. While comparing his position in present South Africa to former Apartheid State, he lamented, "I am very confused where I really stand. During the apartheid regime I was not white enough to deserve respect. Now when there is black majority rule, I am not black enough!"

The color of skin does not make a man what he is, nor does it invest him with what he is not. Under the skin people are not much different from one another. Even visible differences in culture of peoples do not decisively divide them into separate species. The chopstick culture of the Far-Easterners, the tuxedo culture of the Europeans, the curry culture of the Indians and Pakistanis, and the yam culture of the Nigerians are all cultures of humans and none of them has its origin in Mars. Local customs, climatic conditions, geographical location, and natural produce of a region, more than anything else, determine customs, the way of living and the patterns of behavior of people; and there is no justification for belittling or ridiculing a particular culture. An experienced traveler has very rightly said: The locals know best which dress and which foods are appropriate in their conditions. So, respect the local culture and follow them wherever you are. You can never be smarter than the people who have lived there for centuries. 'While in Rome do, as the Romans do' is a very sound advice.

I remember a colleague of mine who went with me to Nigeria. He thought that he had been sent to Africa to replace Albert Schweitzer, to reform the country and he mounted a one-man crusade to 'civilize' the people. He was soon sent home with a one-way ticket. Those who have traveled widely know very well how to respect the local customs and culture because these are time-honored traditions handed down from generation to generation through centuries. A newcomer cannot hope to understand the people and their customs within a month or a year. Of course, I do not mean that cultures remain static: these adopt other cultures and people change slowly, one may say, painfully slowly and that too with education. Any reform, any improvement must evolve within the context of local conditions. Evolution is the best form of revolution. Love His creatures as they are, do not wait till they become as you would like them to be, this may not happen—not in your lifetime.

A Nigerian Major, whose father was admitted to the military hospital in a serious condition, looked very apprehensive about his father's welfare. He would sob and break down seeing the deteriorating condition of his father. I was really touched by his concern. The way he danced in attendance and looked after him, at times put me to shame, since I had left my old mother back in Pakistan. He would plead repeatedly to do more to save his father. I was doing my utmost anyway and had involved all the other relevant specialists in the treatment for better management of the patient, but the prognosis looked bleak. It must be the tribal culture, the way this Major was looking after the old man, I thought. I appreciated his concern and left no stone unturned. The Major, one day while talking to me broke down and with tears rolling down his cheeks pleaded, "Sir please, do not let my father die." He told me that after the death of an elderly person it is customary in his tribe that there are long festivities and the whole clan collects to celebrate the occasion and please the spirits. This can last for several days, and he will have to bear all the expense. "I am only a Major and am broke. Please doctor, do not let my father die," he pleaded.

Parents of a young girl hardly ten brought her to me with a painless swelling in the lower abdomen. No other history was forthcoming; she had not yet started menstruation. I examined the girl with a couple of medical students breathing down my neck and we started discussing differential diagnosis. By an amazing flare we reached a diagnosis that I had only read in the gynae. books—-congenital obstruction of the female genital tract causing obstacle to the outflow of menstrual blood. Having made rather an unusual diagnosis in a branch of medicine I knew nothing about, I felt very pleased with my theory and clinical prowess. There was no gynecologist posted to that Military Hospital for a second opinion. In fact, that must be the reason why this girl came to me in the first place. This being a surgical condition, the pant up menstrual blood that had collected in the uterus would be drained and swelling would subside.

While we were planning surgery, in walked my anesthetist, a sari--clad Indian lady who had two young boys of her own. She had come to inform me about the emergency case that was awaiting surgery. I grasped this opportunity to request her to examine the girl whom I thought we could also operate in the same sitting. When she emerged from behind the curtains she pronounced the diagnosis confidently, "she is pregnant," she said. "Pregnant!" I nearly jumped, "the poor child has not menstruated yet." I protested. "She is pregnant," she repeated. Period. There was finality in her tone. Subject closed. She turned around and left, leaving us all bewildered and feeling very stupid.

11

Persona Before A Person

White coat of doctors used to be considered a symbol of mercy, of healing, of compassion and empathy. Not anymore. White coats are now routinely worn by salespersons on the shop floors and when even the butchers started donning the same white coat; in disgust or may be in protest, the healers decided to doff off this time-honored dress and slip into the most menial dress used by the cleaners. The medical authorities in Britain put a final nail who thought that the white coat was too 'authoritarian.' Now the doctors in America wear cleaner's outfit, called the scrubs.

In this age when the world is said to have reduced to a global village, the Western dress is fast replacing the local dresses of Eastern countries. Sometimes Pakistan's regional and national dresses arouse interesting reactions in Western countries where our dresses are not a familiar sight. Our Sherwani, for instance, seems to confuse the Westerners who take it for some form of an overcoat or overall.

No military dictator howsoever benevolent he may claim to be at home has any credibility outside the country and is looked down upon as a pariah. Howsoever arrogant they may feel in uniform, before leaving home they sheepishly shed it off and slip into something less galling. It takes a brave man like Fidel Castro to travel abroad in his military fatigues. While on a visit to France, the President of Pakistan was received by his French counterpart at the airport. As it was an official visit, there were a lot of ceremonies. President Zia always wore the national dress; white Shalwar and black Sherwani. While the two Presidents were going for guard of honor, the French President said something to his staff officer who went to President Zia and whispered in his ear. President Zia ignored the young ADC who went back to his place in the parade. The French President motioned to his ADC again. The ADC again whispered in General's ear, but he still did not pay any heed. Thereupon the French President, thinking that there was a language problem, himself asked President Zia if he would like to take off his long tunic before inspecting the parade and hand it to the ADC. President Zia flashed his famous toothy smile and protested, "But Mr. President, I am not wearing anything underneath this tunic!"

The president of the World Bank was caught off guard when he visited a mosque in Turkey and had to remove his shoes. The holes in his socks were displayed all over the world press. Destitute women weavers of Bangladesh who sustained on a few takas from Younus's Germeen Bank offered to send him a new pair of socks!

May be General Zia did not wear his vest underneath his 'tunic' because of its holes.

On another occasion, the President was on an official visit to an African country. Early in the morning, while everyone in the state guesthouse was either asleep or getting ready for the day's engagements, the physician to the President, an early bird, a fair-complexioned man dressed in his black Sherwani, buttoned tightly at the neck and white Shalwar, decided to go for a stroll in the lush green lawns of the state house. The morning was so calm and serene that he decided to take a walk outside the compound.

Outside he came across some African families who lived in hamlets near the guesthouse and seemed in a festive mood. Seeing the fair physician clad in black and white one of the Africans went up to him and requested most humbly, "Father, God has blessed me with a son. Now, while you are here, it will be indeed gracious of you if you will kindly baptize him." The physician kept his composure. He was a kind, noble man, and did not want to disappoint the African. He accompanied the man to his hamlet, followed him to the interior, picked up the infant boy in his arms and recited loudly the 'Azan' in the baby's ears, one after the other, while a crowd gathered around them and witnessed the baptizing ceremony with great reverence. Having finished his duty, the physician blessed the flock. The grateful father, while escorting him out thanked him most profusely, but could not help commenting, "But father, this is not quite the way I have seen baptism performed before." The physician affectionately patted the African on the shoulder and explained, "Son, strange are the ways of the Lord."

The dress is like the cover of a book. In some unknown way it makes you form your first impression about the man inside; and first impressions usually endure, but sometimes they are misleading. In early seventies, I was working as a surgeon in the Air Force hospital. One day the duty doctor awakened me in the middle of the night to see an emergency case. When I reached the hospital, I saw a middle-aged man wrapped in a coarse, homemade cotton quilt lying on a crude cot. Four villagers wearing turbans and wrapped in thick, coarse clothes to ward off the December cold stood round the cot. The poor man, they told me, while chopping off wood had fallen off a tree and was paralyzed waist down. This was bad news. I got the patient X-rayed. There was a fracture-dislocation of the spine. I was searching for words to tell the peasants that unfortunately the paralysis was permanent and there was nothing I could do. Helplessness and hopelessness writ large on my face, when one of the villagers from within his wrappings spoke out, "You should at least try steroids."

I was taken aback by this advice coming from a seemingly illiterate villager, but I realized that it was the only thing to be tried. I admitted the patient and put him on steroids. I found out later that the 'simple peasant' was Dr. Malik, a neurosurgeon. We became friends, and our friendship has blossomed since that chance meeting. He is a leading neurosurgeon, an authority on arteriovenous malformations in America. His rustic clothes did not give any clue to the real man inside, a highly qualified surgeon. The jacket of a book does not always tell about the book.

In Tokyo, I sent my *shalwar* and shirt for washing to the laundry. The clothes, nicely washed and pressed, arrived on three hangers, one for the shirt, another for the *shalwar* and the third for the '*nala*' or 'azaarband' in Urdu, —the string used as a belt to hold the baggy pants in place. I was rather intrigued by this special treatment shown to the little string, but as soon as I looked at the bill, I realized the reason for it: the money they had charged for washing this oneand-a half yard long string was more than the total cost of the suit.

The impression a uniform makes on people is also interesting. People respect your uniform if you can do something to or for a person. An officer in a uniform was driving from his place of duty to another station on a temporary assignment. On the way his car slowed, coughed a couple of times, and stalled. All efforts to start it again failed. The officer was stranded on a road along a canal in the wilderness. There seemed to be no help in sight. So, he locked the car, took his brief case in his hand, and started walking along the canal. After some time he came across a villager who seeing a man in an impressive uniform offered to carry his brief case. The officer thankfully handed him the case. The Martial law had just been lifted. As they walked along the canal, the villager wanted to know who the officer was. The officer introduced himself.

The villager asked him, "Can you set free a man who is in jail?" The officer replied in the negative. Baffled the villager asked again, "Can you help catch a man and put him in the lock up?" "I am only a surgeon," said the officer apologetically, "and cannot do anything of the sort." Thereupon, the villager threw his briefcase in the running canal saying, "You cannot arrest a person, and you cannot set free a prisoner from the jail. What sort of an officer are you?" Then muttering to him, he went his way towards the village.

Your dress grades you arbitrarily, but it is the first thing that other people notice. When I was a house officer in British hospitals, the advice given to doctors appearing in a court of law, or before a gathering like a clinical meeting, or an interview board was "Dress up, stand up, speak up and shut up."

Once I was an advisor on a selection committee that interviewed candidates for the posts of Associate Professors etc., when an unkempt, unshaven candidate dressed in a stained and crumpled *Shalwar-Qameez* suit entered the room, I could not help commenting, "This is an important day in your career. Shouldn't you have given some thought to your dress?" He looked at my well pressed Western clothes and decided that the best way to defend him was to put me on the defensive. He said, "I am wearing my national dress." I could not keep my cool and I retorted, "How about a vest and a loincloth that would be even more representative of our rural culture?" It was not his national dress that incensed me, I believe. What really troubled me at that time was the thought: How would this man who did not take the trouble of dressing properly on the day that was to make or mar his career; look after his patients? He must be casual and careless in all matters like standards of sterilization, surgical techniques, and other matters concerning the welfare, even the lives, of his patients. I think that the way you dress, often, reveals your state of mind.

"We shape our dwellings and afterwards our dwellings shape us."

Winston Churchill

The white overall of the doctors is symbolic of the mercy and compassion that should be the hallmark of medical profession. The man inside this gown of mercy must rise to the highest professional and humanitarian standards articulated in the Hippocratic oath. If a doctor behaves like a playboy or a bureaucrat, he insults his profession. The doctors in the armed forces wear blue, khaki and white uniforms; but the uniform does not change what they really are, or should be—'healers,' first and last.

The school and college uniforms give a sense of pride to students and inspire them to uphold the traditions of their alma maters and encourage them to behave in a proper, dignified way. I still remember the feelings of pride and euphoria when I wore the red blazer of Government College, Lahore with the flaming torch embroidered on the upper pocket. I experienced a similar feeling of superiority on wearing the blazer of the King Edward Medical College. The *Ravians* and *Kemcolians* really felt on the top of the world in those good old days. They were, perhaps, justified in feeling rather superior, for admission to these premier institutions placed them on a higher pedestal and admitted them into an elite, of talent and excellence, and required of them to live up to the brilliant traditions of the previous generations of students.

I have friend, a Brigadier in the Education department who oversees all the schools of the cantonment. He was telling me the effect of change of uniform in the boy's schools. Boys through a federal law wore *shalwar qameez* of a drab color. Fed up with complaints of infighting and bad discipline, he thought of trying the attire of his academy days. He changed their uniform to trouser, shirt and a necktie. The result was astounding; there was over 50 % drop in the truancy, indiscipline, and delinquency!

Uniforms are not just distinctive clothes; they not only set apart one group from other groups, but they do something more: they make the person in uniform an heir to certain traditions, certain attitudes, certain norms of behavior, some which may not be officially discerned. Thus, each uniform has come to acquire a 'reputation' in the public mind.

The police uniform is a very visible emblem of authority and almost unlimited powers. It makes the man inside feel ten feet tall. If this uniform strike terror in the hearts of criminals and gives the common law-abiding citizens a sense of security, nobody would grudge the policeman their powers; but unfortunately in our country it has come to acquire an unenviable reputation. Many of our minor police officials are neither civil nor helpful, and it is these officials with whom the majority of citizens come into contact. The result is that the police uniform does not arouse positive reactions. An immigration officer has only to stamp your passport, but he performs this simple chore in a highly arrogant way that very plainly suggests that he is doing an immense favor to you and your descendants, and that you should acknowledge this magnanimous act with some kind of tribute in cash or kind. The custom officer's uniform, too, has come to be associated with bribery: one would suspect him of negotiating a 'deal' even when he is seeing off his own mother at the airport.

In the army the rank determines everything even the professional competence of a physician or a surgeon. It seems logical that a surgeon wearing the insignia of a senior rank should be more experienced than a raw, young Lieutenant. When I joined army as a surgeon, I was temporarily given the rank of a Lieutenant, stop gap arrangement till I get my permanent rank of a Major pending the paperwork. One day I admitted a soldier with a stone in the kidney and advised him surgery. The patient readily agreed. But when he found out that I, a petty Lieutenant, would be performing the operation, his face dropped, and he changed his mind with the usual excuse that his mother or someone else was ill and that he would undergo the operation some other time. We struck his name off the operation list. The very next day I was promoted. When I went round the ward in a Major's uniform, the reluctant patient immediately changed his mind again and told me that his mother had recovered. He had his kidney stone removed by me the next day.

White is the color of purity and sincerity, and the nurses' white uniform symbolizes selfless service to the sick. Army nurses once enjoyed an excellent reputation, and they really deserved it. I still remember how they used to look after patients and would even scrub clean the patient's room after scrubbing the patient. I also can never forget the inquiry the first day of my uniform in the military hospital ward by an elderly Anglo-Indian in charge nurse who took nursing like her religion. Quietly comparing my starched stiff uniform of a Lieutenant with her scrubs she asked me in her broken Urdu,

"Afsar banye ga ya doctor bunaye ga

Do you want to become a doctor or an officer?

One Chief of Staff was so impressed by their dedication to their profession and the quality of their work that he decided to award them ranks like other officers of the army. They now join the army after a passing out parade, introduced by General Zia and presided over by a four-star General, and wear insignia of ranks. Unfortunately, this measure, which was intended to give them, added incentive for a deeper commitment to their vocation proved counterproductive, and they began to behave more like rest of the officers. Gone is the compassion and hard work the army nurses were famous for. In our bureaucratic culture, officers do not work with their hands, they only dictate and shout orders.

The uniforms of the armed forces give them a distinct identity and set them apart not only from civilian services but also from one another. The sailors, soldiers and airmen wear different uniforms and work with different machines. It is an interesting subject to speculate about the mental attitudes fostered by the environment in which they work. The man in white tends to be slow and unhurried, doing things patiently and ponderously, like his ship, which used to take 24 hours for priming. The man in blue is inclined to think and act swiftly, for he lives in the world of Mirages and F-16's where a split second decides his fate. The man in the khaki uniform works with heavy guns, tanks, and trucks. He does not need to react at the speed of lightening like the fighter pilot, nor as leisurely as his brother in white. He has enough time to think and plan his action.

The soldiers, sailors and airmen are fighters, they know what they are, and their uniforms proclaim what they are. A doctor wearing a military uniform, however, faces a dilemma: What is he—-a doctor or an officer! He is a doctor by profession and the discipline of this profession is quite different from the discipline of the forces. I think the very hierarchical organization of the armed forces with its protocol and formalities, the salutes, and acknowledgments, are not conducive to the development of the professional competence of a doctor. Dressed in khaki uniform, with brass and tags on shoulders he will always consider himself on parade.

Many years later when I had resigned to my fate, one of the surgeons, now a senior consultant at Hammersmith hospital who was my colleague while I worked in London was invited by Pakistan Army to render some advice on a surgical project. Being an old friend, I went to airport to receive him with my crisp ceremonial uniform complete with Sam Browne belt. He was very pleased to see me but could not help commenting, "What have they done with you Munir?" He asked. "With all these ropes and leather around you, you look more like a horse!"

12

The Children

In the early sixties, when I was in England for higher studies, I worked as a resident medical officer at a hospital in a town in the North, famous not for its scholarship—but for its pottery! I used to look after the emergency and accident department of the hospital. One morning an immaculately dressed urbane English couple brought a smart young boy of eight or ten to me. Their appearance and manners clearly indicated that they belonged to an elite class.

The young lad had hurt himself in the school and had a cut on his arm and the first aid bandage was soaked in blood. The parents and the boy waited very patiently for their turn, without creating any fuss and commotion as is the routine in our casualty departments where the patient who shouts loudest wants to be seen first, especially if he or she, or his or her parents, happen to be well off or influential.

The boy was still in his school uniform. He seemed to be very well brought up. The cut on his arm was four or five inches long and it needed stitching. I took the young boy to the emergency operation theatre, helped him to lie on the table, and prepared to proceed with the job. The regular sister who used to assist me in the theatre was not available, so a young nurse was standing in for her. I scrubbed while the nurse prepared the trolley we needed during stitching. I washed and cleaned the wound and asked the nurse to hand me the local anesthetic syringe. In order to prepare the boy for what he had to undergo I told him, "I am going to give you a little prick around the wound. It will sting a bit but then the wound will not be sensitive to any pain as I stitch the cut. You will not feel any pain; but if you do, let me know. Do you understand?" "Yes sir" was the simple answer.

When I injected, the child controlled his emotions not a word, outcry or commotion. While waiting for the anesthetic to take effect I chatted with the child. He was a very intelligent kid and was studying in a very prestigious school. He told me that he planned to study law when he grew up. "Why not become a doctor?" I asked. "Oh! It is a very demanding profession and then you have to be very clever to become a doctor," he said. I do not suppose the boy wanted to flatter me, but his remark delighted me.

Thinking that the local anesthetic should have produced its effect, I prepared for stitching the wound. The nurse gave me the silk threaded on a needle and I proceeded. While I stuck the needle in his arm, the boy winced, but said nothing. I thought that perhaps the anesthetic needed some more time to act. So I stopped. After a pause I started again, but every time I stuck the needle, the boy would flinch and go ghastly pale. Each time I asked him if it hurts, he would answer "Just a little, doctor." I thought it was the touch sensation that made the boy uncomfortable. The local anesthetic numbs the area but the sensations around remain intact. So, I proceeded with the job. Still with each jab the boy would go ashen pale but won't say anything. I kept asking. "Does it hurt, son?" "Just a little," was all he would answer. I completed the procedure while the nurse kept talking to the child, cutting, and counting ten stitches. I dressed the wound and looked at the boy. Beads of cold sweat like big drops of dew covered his forehead. His color was deadly pale. I felt his pulse. It was very slow.

I feared he might have an anaphylactic shock from the local anesthetic; some people do although it is very rare. I pulled a stool and sat down next to the boy and started talking to him about his family and school. He was not on top of the world, but still he answered me very politely. I was thinking of setting up an intravenous line when color started returning to his cheeks. He gradually picked up and soon was his normal, bouncy self again. In a few more minutes he felt well enough to jump off the table, saying, "Thank you kindly, Sir."

When the child had gone, I asked the nurse casually. "Did the child really feel the stitches?" "Shouldn't have," she said confidently. I was a bit uncomfortable though. We both went back to the trolley and while she was clearing her things for the next patient, she suddenly stopped and called me. She had inadvertently filled up distilled water from the ampoule, while the local anesthetic vial was still lying on the trolley untouched. We both looked at each other in embarrassment thinking the same thing: What pain we had inflicted on the sweet little kid! The courage with which he endured the pain of ten stitches in his arm without any anesthetic and without any protest amazed us. I remember that sweet kid to this day; and whenever I see a grown-up soldier letting out a scream of non-existent pain on getting an intra-muscular injection, his words 'Just a little, doctor' come to my mind.

The best thing I love in children is innocence and spontaneity and the way they express their original and genuine expressions.

I was the only foreign resident in an English hospital and would occasionally visit children ward that housed patients from all disciplines of medicine. Whenever I had patients there, I would go on a round to see them. A permanent resident of the ward in the corner bed was a pale, sick looking little girl. Her gaze would follow me wherever I went in the ward. Perhaps she regarded a doctor with a brown face in a white coat as an object of interesting curiosity, an amusing oddity. Due to nature of her illness, she would be repeatedly admitted in hospital. Although not my patient we used to smile and wave at each other during my rounds. When I found out that she was suffering from a fatal condition; Leukemia, my affection for her deepened and I would sit down with her for some time, and we would talk small talk. She was a lovely, sweet girl and would giggle at the stories I would tell her and the caricature of Mickey Mouse that I would draw for her. As our friendship blossomed, once during a tete-aetat, she gave me a friendly innocent suggestion, "Doctor why don't you wash your face with soap and water like I do?" Sadly, soon after, the little girl died and the corner bed she used to be in remained vacant for a long time, which brought back moving memories on my rounds. And for a long time, each time I would scrub my face I would see her angelic face in every soap bubble.

While working in Lagos I used to visit children ward, where I would have a couple of patients with fractures on traction. Being long stay patients, they used to become quite friendly with me. The children who were mobile would sit next to each other, socialize, and make friends. Whenever I used to visit the ward, small children would wave at me, and some would come running and dared to shake my hands. When in a group, they would greet me with respect, the African style. They would *en mass* bow, put their left arms over their backs and courtesy with their right hands and genuflex gracefully. Shiny, copper faced, giggling, scantily dressed because of intense heat; almost all had umbilical hernia, which to my surprise would disappear on their own without surgery as they grew up. I found them very cute. After the round once I would turn my back, the children used to hide behind the doors and would sing in a course, a long song starting with, "*Oh Ebo pepe. Ife ife pepe. You go yellow momo*...." I asked the Nigerian sister in charge what were they saying. Embarrassingly she translated the song. In sham rage I would rush back and run after them shouting.... "Who said that?" The little rascals would scramble and run for cover to the far end of the ward to escape my wrath. But when I would turn my back and walk towards the corridor, they would again regroup and impishly giggling, start chanting the same song, this time even louder!

Every child is born with a genuine mind as he knows his destiny clearly and he is all set to change this world. He or she is a dreamer and there is no moratorium on dreaming. Every achievement in this life begins with a dream and a child when born is programmed to think independently and if encouraged can change the world. A child on the average thinks of 60 alternatives to a given situation in contrast to an adult whose thought process over the years continue to shrink; to a single digit! If one answer to a problem does not fit, an alive mind thinks of another, still another and yet another, does not give up and does not take no for an answer. As the curiosity of the child is curbed, the alternatives keep on shrinking. This seems a very good way of judging your creativity age; in contrast to the chronological, as to how much of you are still alive!

There are three situations where the curiosity and enthusiasm of a child is curbed: -

1. 'Disciplinarian' parents who continuously keep checking the child so that he or she behaves like a 'good' boy or a girl. From the very early days, it is like series of shocks to freeze his motor, to undercut his process of thinking. "Do not ask so many questions. Parents know best. It is right because I say so! Do as I say. Do not struggle, compromise." Meaning let me think on your behalf.

2. Regimental teachers, who want 'order' in the class and school and spread terror. The students are afraid and do not venture to question them and live in a culture of silence. Young students generally have curious, imaginative, idealistic minds, but it takes a real good teacher to develop their eager minds and guide them into using their talents for worthwhile purposes. It is very easy for a cynical, insensitive teacher to destroy their idealism at this very critical and formative period of their tender lives. Fear is fatal for creativity of a child.

3. Finally, our examination systems, which do not evaluate enquiry.

How should one bring up children? By developing a very strong bonding and then giving them freedom of thought and action but discreetly keep a hawk's eye to watch as they grow. The babies and toddlers need to be soaked in an elixir rich in love, girls requiring double the dose. But as their bodies start growing, the intellect does not keep pace and there is a need for a constant watch like a shepherd of a flock, so that they do not go astray. Overprotection certainly stunts the growth and should gradually recede, and children be let on their own. Children brought up in insecurity and poverty mature much earlier. Warren Buffet when he donated his billions to charity was asked, "What have you left for your children?" Replied, "I have left them enough to do anything with it but not enough to do nothing."

Raising children require a soft but firm hand, like a lion's paw. Children respect authority. It is important to say 'No' when the situation so warrants. It takes time for children to make correct decisions on their own. Left alone they may get lost in the un-chartered terrain. Watch them from the corner of the eye rather turn a blind eye. It is prudent to raise the family as a single authoritarian unit where everyone knows the limits and the guidelines are loud and clear.

In the West, young children are thrown in the cruel churn of economic juggernaut long before their maturity. They are exposed to alien culture at a tender age when hormones are more powerful than the neurons. The parents shirk and withhold their advice and for wrong reasons like; 'we do not want to interfere in their autonomy and stand in the way in the development of their personality!' The need for guidance is from womb to tomb. Democracy is not such a good thing in raising children; when all that glitters seems gold and the poor child is left to fend for him or herself in this unkind world without any guidance. When young, the children consider their father as a role model and think him hell of a guy but as they grow a bit older, the eggs soon start teaching the hen. Once they have matured, only then they realize that their father after all was not such a bad guy!

I also wonder, as to what is best for the education of children—-staying put at one school throughout as I did, or changing schools every couple of years, as my children had to do not only in different towns or countries, but also in different continents. One thing about which I am sure is that as far as the development of personality is concerned there is no better way than by traveling. One discovers things along the way that one would otherwise never have experienced or had the courage to try. The formal, academic side of education probably suffers, if you are a rolling stone but other gains are worth the repeated dislocations. I was made aware of this fact when my children were admitted in a Nigerian school where I had gone on deputation. After a month of their admission in that school a prize distribution ceremony was held to which I was also invited. My children were new to the school and to the country, so I did not expect that they would be winning any prizes. To my surprise, however, the name of my daughter was called out, and she was given a prize for 'Quick Adaptation' to the new surroundings. This not only attested to her ability to adjust to the new environment, but also demonstrated the high quality of the system.

After my return from Nigeria, I was posted to Rawalpindi. It was an ordeal for me to find a good school that would accept my children in the middle of the academic year. Every week I would visit a local convent school and return after getting the routine answer from the Principal "There is no seat." Finally, I do not remember after how many trips, she relented and told me to bring my daughter for a test, but the nun from Dublin did not forget to warn me, "If she does well, only then she will be considered for admission."

My children had not formally studied Urdu in the schools they had attended abroad, though my wife had made some effort to teach them their national language at home. I was, therefore, afraid that my daughter would not be able to do well in Urdu.

After the test I was waiting outside the principal's office, when with lot of airs about, in walked a Brigadier in battledress with medals dangling on his chest and marched into her office. Sitting outside the office I could not help overhearing what went on inside. He started with a resume of the important duties he performed and had he not been there, how the edifice of the GHQ would crumble. The Brigadier said that he had a letter for her from the Chief. She asked him what it was about. "It is about the admission of my daughters in your school," he said. "I have no vacancy," she answered coldly. "But this letter..." the Brigadier protested. The principal, slip of a woman, cut him short, "I have no time to read such letters," she said returning to him the unopened envelope. The petit nun then unceremoniously ushered the big Brigadier out. Sitting outside I shrank in my seat. I had difficulty understanding her but looked like, that like her Lord she also hated arrogance. The way through this nun's heart must be through humility, I thought.

She, a woman of few words reminded me of a past American President who was well known for his quiet disposition and a poker face. He and his wife were religious, God-fearing couple. Every Sunday they faithfully went to church and listened most intently to the sermon of the preacher, however boring that might be. The President was a no-nonsense man and did not believe in wasting a syllable whenever and if at all he spoke. One Sunday it so happened that his wife being indisposed could not accompany him to church, so she instructed him to go alone but record every word of the sermon and recite it to her when he returned; the President agreed. When he came home his wife seated him on a comfortable sofa, prepared a hot cup of tea and sat down to listen to what the preacher said in his sermon. The man would not open his mouth, so she had to ask him, "What did the father say today?" The President shuffled in his chair and with great stipulation said, "Oh, he spoke about sin." He then started sipping his tea in silence. The woman wanted to know more, so she asked him again.

"What did he have to say about sin, dear?" The President answered, "He was against it!"

When this President died a correspondent rang his home to check up the news, "Yes, the President is dead, someone confirmed on the other end of the line.

After a hesitation, she thought aloud, "how can they tell?"

After marking the papers of the test, the sister brought the answer sheets and showed them to me with a glum face as if Farah had failed. She had scored more than sixty percent marks in English and Math's: but forty percent in Urdu, which I thought was pretty good for admission. But the nun's expression remained dour. I was reaching the end of my tether and commented that for a new arrival in the country what more can you expect. And with an equal firm expression that matched hers I said, that had she come from abroad and appeared in the test in a new school, she probably would fail. Her demeanor looked a bit softened; and I guess there seemed a semblance of flicker of a smile and I quickly added, "Look sister if after the first semester she does not top in her class I will withdraw her from your school."

She admitted my daughter, but her manner made it abundantly clear that it gave her no joy. She warned me that my daughter might not fit in the school. But about that, I was sure that she would fit in all right. I had testimonials to that effect! And fit in she did very well indeed.

After her Secondary School Examination, in which my daughter had secured cent per cent marks in mathematics and ninety-eight percent in English; and had also, to my surprise, done very well even in Urdu. I went to thank the Principal and congratulated her on the quality of education in her institution. I reminded her of how curtly she had treated me and had almost refused admission to my daughter. She remembered the occasion very clearly. But did not in the least show any regret for her then blunt attitude, even though since then she had brought to me a number of her elderly colleagues with broken bones, whom I had treated with extra-ordinary protocol!

I had so much difficulty in getting my children admitted to a school in my home country, but while in England, where I had taken up the job of a resident surgeon in the mid-seventies, the education authorities seemed keener on educating my children than I was. After joining the hospital, we were just settling down in the new environment when an official letter arrived. It said that I had been in that area for a week, but my two children had not joined any school yet. The letter asked me to get them admitted as soon as possible. There were addresses of the schools in the area. I took my children to a school the very next day. To my surprise I did not have to introduce myself. The school authorities were waiting for me.

My daughter was eager to join school. She did not know any English but settled down very quickly and made lots of friends who keep writing to her to this day. One day I was asked to see her teacher. She told me that every time Farah was offered some food during a break, she refuses it saying, "No Miss. Muslim, Sargodha." Obviously, her mother had worked hard on her as to what to eat and what not to.

My wife and I would find my son sleeping between our sheets when we woke in the early hours most mornings. From his room next door where we encouraged him to sleep, we would hear thumping of his footsteps on the wooden floor running to our room to sleep between us. Scared of his martinet mother, he with his tiny hands would locate a rough unshaven face in the dark and wrap his arms around me. He was still very young and did not like the idea of going to school. He would protest, "What is the hurry, why don't you let me grow up first?" I drove him to school while he bawled his head off. The teacher was very friendly. She told my wife to leave him under her care and go. She assured my wife that he would be all right. My wife, however, stationed herself outside the classroom and kept peeping through a window to see how Omar was doing. He soon settled down and started conversing with a kid whose language he did not understand. When he came home, I asked him, "What did you do in school today?" He said, "There was a little boy 'Licher', who sat on a skate and said to me, 'Puss me', and I pushed him. Then I sat on the skate and Richard pushed me and soon we were friends." After this, since he had such fun in school, he would wake me up even on weekends and holidays and ask me to take him to school. It was really amazing how quickly my children learnt English and spoke fluently and that too without native accent, unlike their parents.

I had read in a book of' psychology that if you ingrain in the minds of your kids at an early age what they were to become in future, they would start developing a liking for that profession. With that in mind I began to plant, directly and indirectly, in my son's mind, barely seven at the time that he would become a doctor—-a physician if not a surgeon like me. We lived virtually in the Hospital compound, and he had accompanied me on my visits to hospital so many times. Thinking that he had accepted the idea of becoming a doctor, I asked him one day to accompany me to the operation theatre where I was going to perform an emergency appendectomy. He was thrilled at the opportunity of seeing an operation. So, I took him along. He was given sterilized clothes to wear before entering the operation theatre, and he seemed to be enjoying the special attention and treatment given to him.

The patient was anaesthetized, and I started cleaning his abdomen, taking special care not to expose what I did not want my son to see. He stood all wrapped up in front of me. I explained to him what I was going to do and gave an incision for the appendectomy. He watched closely as I operated. I proceeded step by step, so that he could understand. Soon he started moving to one side and leaned against the wall of the operation theatre. Then he sat down, stood up again and, opening the door of the theatre, hurried out. I could not figure out why? I sent a nurse after him to find out what was the problem. She took some time coming back. When she arrived, she told me that Omar had been feeling sick and had thrown up his entire breakfast on the table in my office next door.

After finishing the operation, I went to my office. The boy was still pale and uncomfortable. I took him home without saying a word about the incident. Later his mother told me that Omar had found the atmosphere in the theatre stifling and sickening. He had also told his mother that I was cutting the patient like a cake!

I have a friend, now a Cardiac surgeon in America, who while studying medicine with us in Lahore, had fainted and fallen, when blood was drawn from the arm of his mother for investigation. Now the sight of blood in his operation theatre does not worry him. I, therefore, thought that the reaction my son showed on first seeing blood coming out of a man was a natural reaction, and that he would soon get over this incident, and that I would be able to persuade him to become a doctor as he passed his Secondary School examination. But I was mistaken. He had firmly made up his mind not to become a surgeon or even a physician. I was dismayed when after passing the secondary school examination he insisted on taking up pre-engineering subjects in college. I allowed him, of course with a heavy heart, to choose his own way. Genetic pull, I lamented was not strong enough.

With my daughter it was quite the opposite. I thought that my hectic and demanding professional life which left me little time for my family would deter her from ever thinking of taking up this profession. Not that 'intellect in a woman is unbecoming,' Medicine, I believe, is not an ideal profession for women who wish to marry and raise a family. Raising children and managing the household affairs is a full-time job. It is due to the presence of a woman; mother, wife, or a daughter that house becomes a home. If a woman chooses to enter an exacting profession like medicine, she must leave her children to the care of hired help, which is not good for them. If she tries to do justice to her responsibilities in the house and her duties in the hospital, she will find it extremely difficult, for both demand undivided attention. It is cruel to ask a woman to do two full time jobs simultaneously. My wife voluntarily gave up her handsome job soon after our marriage. My friends keep telling me that the times have changed, and that now circumstances demand both husband and wife to work to make both ends meet. Maybe they are right, but I am not convinced. I still feel that the first duty of a woman is to look after her home and children. Call it male chauvinism or whatever else you like, but that is what I think. I therefore did my best to dissuade my daughter from becoming a doctor, but she stood firm. She has become a doctor entirely by her own sweet will.

So much for child psychology, career counseling and influencing people!

Now I know what Peter Ustinov meant when he said, "My children often disagreed with me. Thank God! I had no objection at all to their being disobedient. Parents should remember that besides being parents they are also the bones on which the puppy can shape its teeth."

Not only their teeth my own persona has been influenced the way they have grown.

Although learnt the hard way both my children turned out to be rebels; yet I would still concede that letting children make their own minds is the best course of action. This helps them develop a determination and doggedness that is of use to them in later lives. Another rather cunning, cynical advantage when children select their own career is that later when the goings get tough in their chosen line and life is not so rosy and they have to struggle, they cannot turn around and blame the parents, 'you told me so!'

When Farah went to America to study, she started her career as a Research scholar in an honorary position at Massachusetts General Hospital. She worked with extreme devotion and dedication and soon completed material for a couple of research papers. Wherever there was any academic activity going on in the hospital, she was sure to be there. Her omnipresence baffled the chief who asked her one day, whether she was a resident or a fellow. He was amazed to see her commitment when he found out that she was only a researcher and not even on the staff and yet spent all her time in the hospital. He on his own volunteered a reference for her residency. That testimonial would make any proud father fly without wings.

After the residency, for her fellowship she had to move to Bible belt in a new and a very different place and was thrown in the deep end the very first day; 'sink or swim' was entirely up to her. From a quiet hospital she had arrived in a big teaching hospital on the other side of America amongst the red necks and hillbillies. Farah found the place bewildering, and the change required some time for acclimatization; the time she did not have. The first day she arrived she was assigned duties in the Intensive care unit where over two dozen, patients were struggling to keep alive, most on life support machinery. With blinking lights and whirling discs, the place looked like a workshop with equipment and wires all over the place. Like Alice in wonderland, she was confused and dazed and did not know where to start. She had difficulty even finding her way around, what with, arranging investigations, run to laboratories, X ray, MRI, the pharmacy, and the lot.

She was flabbergasted, dazzled, and lost with little help coming from any quarters. But she never gave up and struggled, thanks to her stoicism and soon got to know the routine of investigating, treating, and presenting cases on ward rounds, the teaching programs, and the conferences. Every day she gained more and more confidence yet the change from a quiet place to a crazy one was traumatic and at time she would be close to crying. While all this was going on and her hands were full, her chief called her one day to give her yet another rather taxing assignment: preparations for an international moot. She started her work earnestly for this conference. Seeing her breakneck schedule, the chief must have felt bit guilty and had second thoughts; he called her the following week and asked her, 'since you have so much on your hands already I can give this task to someone else'. Up to her eyebrows

Farah considered the offer for a moment; a thought did cross her mind that just by accepting the offer so much extra burden would be taken off her shoulders. But then quickly she was her own self; 'that would be accepting defeat,' she thought and that she would not do come what may and she declined the offer saying, 'no thanks I will do it', and did she very well indeed.

Later, at her passing out ceremony her chief spoke about her, "When you arrived here Farah, you were a walking disaster. You were like a deer in front of headlights! But over the period you grew and grew and now you are our best fellow and we cannot do without you."

"In these difficult days of international conflict, when one reads mostly in the newspaper about the harm that Western and Muslim nations seem so capable of inflicting upon each other, it is refreshing to read of a life that illustrates the opposite. Dr. Munir Cheema took the best of a Western medical education and skillfully applied it with great benefit in his home country of Pakistan during his career there as a military surgeon. Now he offers the many insights he has gained over the course of that career, spiced with by his own personal vignettes and passages from the Koran, to further our education in what it takes to become a doctor and a worthwhile human being. Dr. Cheema's book well illustrates one of its own sentences: 'The horse that you have taken to water will only drink if the water is palatable.' Statesmen take note."

Roger K. Pittman, M.D.

Professor of Psychiatry

Harvard Medical School

Massachusetts General Hospital

13

Learning Skills

After my furlough in England, I spent three years with Air Force. While in uniform I now had only one objective—-to establish Orthopedics and Trauma as a separate, full-fledged specialty in the Armed forces. I earnestly believed that in the Forces, Trauma management and Reconstructive surgery should be given top priority. The establishment of a Medical College was the most important event in the Army Medical Corps. This was a breath of fresh air in the rather stifling military atmosphere. Academic freedom in its wake brings broadening of professional horizon. This college was to play a vital role in raising the standards of military hospitals. Military hospitals were cleaner and more regimented, but professionally no better than other hospitals. Within a few years of the inception of the College the hospitals changed into teaching hospitals and the standard of the patient care catapulted. This transformation to teaching hospitals entailed adapting to a different culture. The culture of a military hospital differs from that of a university hospital in its orientation, practices, and training of its medical staff. The culture of the hospital influences the behavior and attitude of the physicians and the staff working there. The academic culture of university hospital fosters inquiry, learning, teaching, and questioning. It emphasizes the scientific identity of surgeons and because of the types of patients treated leads to proliferation of new subspecialties and training programs. The safest thing for a patient is to be in the hands of a doctor engaged in teaching medicine. Good hospitals do two things, first they look after their patients well and secondly, they train good doctors and the staff. I was fortunate to find a place in the faculty of the Medical College in my chosen field. Now academics were the priority, the pressures of military routine and discipline eased, and life became bearable and more congenial.

Ranks will always have their import in the army, but in the college academic prefixes did blunt some of the arrogance of ranks.

Teaching is a profoundly rewarding experience. My work in England as a surgeon for many years had made me feel that teaching students would be a child's play. But as soon as I entered the classroom I was cured of this illusion. It took time to find out that an experienced surgeon did not necessarily make a good teacher. Unfortunately, I was never trained to be a teacher and had no idea what teaching was all about. I had to learn teaching while trying to teach; and whatever I learnt, I learnt the hard way. In fact, I used to kid our colleagues who went for teaching; "Those who can, do. Those who cannot, teach!" The first few years in medical college, I wasted, trying to impress indifferent students with the misguided display of my knowledge in rather a superior, arrogant manner. Then I learnt that a good teacher had to be down-to-earth, less interested in showing off his knowledge and more concerned about the students' capacity to learn. A good teacher does not have to be a genius. He should begin with the assumption that the crowd sitting before him knows nothing, nor is over-anxious to learn. It is the teacher's job to bring himself to the level of the students and employ every trick he knows to attract their attention. If he works hard patiently, he may see the day when students reach up to his level.

It is a common observation that good teachers stay young at heart perhaps due to their company and an enthusiasm that can be catchy.

The best way to stay young is to have childlike inquisitive nature and infectious enthusiasm. People are susceptible to enthusiasm.

Oratorical skills and charismatic personality help for a while but not for long, rather to my utter surprise I found out that the teachers whom the students liked best were just plain and unimaginative persons. To me they looked rather plain folks; grown up children perhaps, who had lot of curiosity like children and with whom they could identify themselves. I remembered the story, Rudyard Kipling wrote for his daughter to stimulate curiosity, where the characters were named——What, When, How, Why and Who. The best gift of God given to us particularly to the young is child-like curiosity and the joy of discovery. We cannot, in fact do not have to teach our children everything; the best we can do is to exploit their curiosity, make their minds inquiring, instill the wonder of 'Why'; and that will make them lifelong learners. Medicine is a lifelong learning, the learning does not stop after exit from classroom, it lasts the whole life. To remain a teacher of medicine a doctor should always be a student.

I can never forget two teachers that I knew of as a student. One of them would tear off pages from the book of surgery, the famous Love and Bailey and then read that to us till everyone would yawn and fall asleep. I have not come across a more soporific teacher.

The other teacher came prepared with notes and then would dictate them to the class and the students would write down the 'lecture' as in a press conference. He then expected that the students would regurgitate everything verbatim; coma, full stops included. Their 'teaching' reminded me of spoon feeding to infants and forced feeding to the inebriate patients.

They had developed an impenetrable aura around them and thought very highly of themselves and insisted that everyone else should also think highly of them. They were like sacred cows whom no one could touch, who gobbled up all the printed pages from the books written ages ago, but they never digested or pondered over them. They never wondered for themselves; they read and repeated, read, and repeated and the students who listened to them read and parroted, year after year.

Some teachers have twenty years of experience; others have only one year's experience multiplied by twenty.

Garbage in—garbage out; class after class. Today, I realize that they knew little about what they pretended to teach.

Many are called, but only a few are chosen. The two teachers who I believe were chosen were from the Royal College of Surgeons: Professor R J Last and Professor Slome. They taught us Anatomy and Physiology respectively. Their best skills probably were the art of communication and the sound basics, and they never distanced them from students. They had charm, flair, infectious enthusiasm, showmanship, taste, and distinction. They gauged their audience well and the lectures used to be more of a conversation rather a one-way stampede. They would inspire and encourage students to think ahead of them while they spoke, and we came to our own conclusions after they had laid down the facts before us in a most pleasing and interesting way. Professor Last while teaching upper limb compared it with the lower limb all the time; the bones, the muscles, the vessels and how the requirements were different in upper limb as contrast to the lower. The lower limb just had to carry us and do a donkey's job, while the function of versatile upper limb was to plant a hand at its end. The hand he described as the 'only mobile part of the brain,' the most beautiful creation of nature. 27 bones with meticulous muscles and sensitive ligaments work as in a concert.

The hand is refined and nimble enough to thread a needle, work on a violin and at the same time powerful enough to deliver a right hook or a left punch. Precision with which a surgeon holds a knife to the brute force of a laborer. Can work jack hammer or a crane and yet can caress a lover or write melodious poetry. The sensory part of hand is even more fascinating and is represented as a homunculus in the sensory cerebral hemisphere. With eyes closed you can differentiate air from water and solids. You can tell whether the object is wood, plastic or a metal. Without even seeing the face of a woman, just by looking at her hands one can gauge her beauty.

So by the time he finished upper limb, we already had fair knowledge of anatomy of lower limb; how according to the role required, the foot molded itself from hand and we just needed filling in the blanks. He stressed the principle that it is the function that determines the structure. While Professor Slome emphasized that function is at its best with the anatomy given to us by the Lord. I remember his examples: why dogs have longer snouts than Homosapiens. The extra space was required to lodge more organs of sense of smell, which in dogs is hundred times better. Why people living in the tropics have dark skin and why their nostrils are wider and shorter as compared to people living in snow who have longer noses. We did not have to think hard because pigment protected from the abundant and harmful rays of Sun in tropics and the cold air needs to be churned warm in the nostrils before reaching the lungs in the cold. Lungs would freeze solid if people on the Poles did not have circuitous air passages in their long noses.

You did not have to parrot these examples; it seemed so obvious. In fact, how could it be otherwise?

Learning lesson from such teachers, I wondered what a good lecturer should be like. Daily lectures by teachers are much more challenging than the moving speeches delivered by orators like Churchill and Martin Luther King who not only spoke with passion but also knew how to seize the moment. They fired imagination, stimulated the audience, and could set them ablaze.

First and foremost, it is most important for a teacher to know his audience, their mental aptitude, likes and dislikes and then speak in the language they understood. In our country cricket has achieved crazy proportions. If one were teaching students, Stress Fractures of the long bones; to illustrate one's point, two names or preferably photographs, of Dennis Lillie and Imran Khan, who had suffered from this malady would wake up, even the dead from their graves. The horse that you have taken to water will only drink if the water is palatable. A good teacher should have the ability to make his subject fascinating.

How important it is to speak the language people understand; even a little boy knew that.

When he returned from school one day his mother thought of checking how his child was getting along in his class. "What did you read in school today, Johnny?" She asked.

"Oh, it was about the tribe of Israel," the child replied. "What about Israelites?" The mother wanted to know more. "Oh, the teacher narrated the story from the Bible, how the wicked Pharaoh with his army was chasing Moses and his people, who were fleeing from Egypt, fed up of the atrocities inflicted upon them, and had decided to emigrate. While on the run they were trapped, as there fell a big river before them blocking their onward journey. Pharaoh's armies were chasing them in hot pursuit. "What did Moses do then?" The mother thought of checking her child's grasp on history. "Well, Moses ordered his Engineers to quickly fabricate a bridge over the river. The engineers complied and immediately floated a Pantaloon bridge over the angry waters and Moses along with his entire tribe crossed over the river. Once the last man was home and dry Moses looked back and saw that Pharaoh's army was following them towards the bridge and was very close. He immediately ordered his Engineer's to destroy the bridge. The Engineers quickly laid ammo: along the bridge and blew it up. Pharaoh's men some drowned and killed were stopped and could not follow the Israelis; and were left on the other side of the sea swearing and cursing the cunning Moses."

"But, son," protested his mother, "that is not quite the way this story is told in the Bible or Koran." "Mom," said Johnny, "the way this story is told in the Bible, you would not believe a word of it!"

Any communication, a speech or a lecture consists of three parts; a beginning, middle and an end—the 'Three Tell triad'.

1. Tell the students what you are going to tell them.
2. Tell it to them.
3. Tell them what you have just told them.

The lecturer should state the goal of his lecture quickly, soon after the preamble. He must then bring out the salient points not numbering more than half a dozen. His use of slides and Power point must be very judicious, and he must not start reading the slides which should only have a few lines written on them. Be very particular about the punctuation marks. Punctuations marks are like traffic signals. These are akin to good manners and are like a thread stitching the words of language. Explain each point by giving examples, quick but preferably narrative. No canned jokes. One picture is better than a thousand words is a famous axiom. This will stop the students' mind wandering off too far and also would give them respite.

During the lecture a good teacher should always size up the audience repeatedly. It is difficult for anyone to remain captive for too long. Instead of going on in a monotonous note, the teacher should move zigzag. This little mental gymnast to follow the tracks would keep the students on their toes. To hold the interest of students it is necessary for the teacher to recognize the first symptom of student's lack of attention and do something about it. The students become bored and jaded if a lecturer deals with the subject robotically and lifelessly. If the lecturer has done his job well, students should be able to reach the conclusion of the lecture before the teacher announces it in the end.

While the teacher is assessing the students, the students are also sizing him up, trying to read as to what stuff is he made up of. It is most important that a teacher exhibits the highest standards of both, a noble human being and a compassionate doctor. What is called bedside manners, the students emulate their peers. Medical ethics learnt by the students come from what the teacher betrays rather than what he says, it is the silent influence of character over characters. All the time we are sending moral signals to our students; we let them know the kind of people we are and what kind of a person we expect out of them. When I look back, it is not the oratory of a brilliant teacher teaching me high tech science in the lecture hall that has left a lasting impression on me but the person behind the persona; the body language, how he dealt with patients, ordinary people and especially the very important ones; and how he did not make any distinction amongst them. A good teacher through self-example should be an ideal in high morals. The students are like little monkeys who will do what they see and not what they are told. Sermons alone do not cut much ice.

"A teacher is best with whom the students feel at ease.
Not so good when students praise him.
Less good when students stand in fear.
Worst when students are contemptuous."

One of the best starters in a lecture that I have had the pleasure to listen to was by Professor Hadfield: an authority on treatment of breast cancer, which to date remains a controversial issue. In the lecture hall there were experienced surgeons and post-graduate students. He must be close to seventy then. He began thus:

"If any one of you sitting in the audience can tell me the right treatment of cancer of Breast, I will write a citation for him for a Nobel Prize right away."

When he started speaking everyone thought the old man had forgotten who the audience was, as he was addressing undergraduate students. But soon he took off and swayed his audience like a conductor in a symphony. When he finished his lecture there was pin drop silence in the hall, but every one's mind was buzzing with curiosity. I think that is the quality of a good teacher.

All the knowledge that teacher wants to impart is printed in the textbooks and the students can read it on their own. What might take a student a whole day to acquire; a good teacher should be able to teach that in an hour and in a way that the student should find enjoyable, and it would remain indelible in his mind. The difference is, between browsing through still frames and actively participating in a live show. On its own the student may get lost, like a sheep in a wood and wander off astray, while meandering from pasture to the barn, if there were no shepherd to guide his flock.

One can divide the neophytes sitting before him in the lecture hall into three categories. Those sitting in the first couple of rows are innocent souls, and would gobble up anything, even garbage dished out to them; they listen most intently to the teacher however dull or pretentious he might be. Skinny, stoop shouldered, cadaveric, wearing thick bulletproof glasses, fill page after page with frantic scribbling. Those adorning the back benches are 'strong characters', athletic, six footers most with handlebar mustaches and long flowing hair; exhibiting real rascal looks; with their minds firmly made up that taking any part in the proceedings of the class is a waste of time. They would not even try to listen to a teacher, however sparkling he might be. Those occupying the middle rows have open minds; they will lend an ear to the teacher if he has the talent to attract and hold their attention; but if he were a pompous bore, they would soon find other things to occupy their time. It is however the backbenchers whom the teacher should accept as a challenge. Experience over the years has shown that if the students in this group are somehow persuaded to become doctors, these are the ones who excel afterward and make their mark; whereas the Rote group probably will manage to qualify but in due course will peter out into oblivion and will never be heard of. All plants look alike when small. It is later when the flowers bloom on them that you know the difference. Till the age of fifteen there is little difference to tell them apart.

Our examination system unfortunately only encourages the regurgitation of parroted facts, where the examiners take sadistic pleasure to know what the students do not know rather than what they do.

At a viva voce practical examination in a medical school, a candidate was presented a pickled specimen of uterus in a jar and was asked to recognize it. The big student with handlebar moustache looked curiously by rotating the jar around but since he had never attended the Anatomy museums seriously, he was at a loss to diagnose the specimen. Seeing the blank face, the internal examiner thought of helping him and told him, "It is because of this that you and I are here." The candidate peered at the strange object and could make neither head nor tail of it and was sure to fail. The examiner felt sorry for the student as he had failed many times before. This could be his last chance and he really wanted to help. He tried again, "All right, I will give you another lead. Neither you nor I have this in our bodies." The candidate suddenly perked up and with a big smile he confidently answered. "Yes, yes, it is the brain!"

Real purpose of education is to stimulate the mind to think. A good teacher should have the ability to stimulate his or her students to learn. In fact his function is to over-see the students learn and how to learn. He should inculcate a process of thought and develop a reasoning mind. The students should be able to arrive at an answer to a question on their own and should be able to complete the learning process themselves. The students should learn and know facts, think, and revolve them over in their minds and then learn its usage. Students should appreciate the joy of importance of learning. A good teacher should be able to listen to the mental cogwheels whirring in the brains of his students. Mind is an attribute of an individual. No teacher can give his students the capacity to think. When students start asking questions the teacher has succeeded.

A good teacher should be more of a facilitator, like a mid-wife: the efforts and the ecstasy at the end are that of the mother.

Once I went to see a friend, he was in the bath and his four-year-old son did well in keeping me company before his dad arrived. He told me what his name was, how many friends he had. This and other small talk from that little boy kept me engrossed. Then he volunteered his knowledge about the facilities in his house. Pointing to different sockets of electric plugs in the living room he said, "Uncle, this plug does not bite while the other two bite when I stick my fingers in them!" His father arrived in the meanwhile and told me how curious the child was and how he kept sticking his fingers in the electric sockets. He was seriously thinking of disconnecting all of them lest the little boy got electrocuted.

Now this child had the curiosity and was learning the hard way. He knew about one characteristic of electricity and kept wondering in his little head about it and used this knowledge by not sticking his fingers in the live plugs; only in the one that did not bite! This is reverse of learning that we practice in schools; that is knowledge—thought process and then attitude.

On the other extreme are we the good Muslims of the sub-continent, who read a book whose language we do not know, like the rote group. Whatever instructions it gives, some of us even memorize them by heart; but never think of putting that in practice. Our daily lives do not show its application, which the little boy now practiced. Unless our actions exhibit the instructions of the Koran in our daily life, we are wasting our time. Koran must be the only book in the world that is read without understanding, pondering over it and certainly without any will in its application.

The instructions of the holy book that we have parroted without pondering are being practiced in Scandinavia.

The goal of medical institutions is to prepare students and trainees to learn medicine and create an environment where it is possible to do so. The students should be able to devise their own ways of learning and the postgraduate trainees should display that they use in their clinical practice what they know.

During my school days once while on a picnic early one-morning curiosity led me to climb a lofty tree. There was a creeper that climbed up the tree well over fifty feet tall and I was intrigued how far this creeper had gotten to. Young and enthusiastic I climbed almost to the top of the tree. Just short of the top, the creeper changed its course towards a branch of the tree. I followed it on that branch well over forty feet from the ground. The view from the top was exquisite and I was beckoning my friends to come up and join me. The branch of the tree could not take my weight and it suddenly snapped and I came crashing down. This sky jump took only fraction of a minute and I do not have any recollections of that tumble. When I landed on the ground my left arm was in a grotesque shape. Surprisingly this was the only injury I sustained thanks to the branches of the tree enroute that must have slowed down my descent. Although stunned, while I was being transported to hospital, I remember that I thought that it was a miracle that falling from such a height I got away with only a broken arm, but little did I know what was coming next. As an American adage goes, "you haven't seen nothin yet." I hadn't.

I was in considerable pain and my sisters rushed me to the nearest medical facility, a rural hospital. There a young lady doctor was in charge, there being no other medical facilities available. She pulled my arm straight and without any padding of cotton or a bandage slapped plaster bandages on my bare arm. My arm was now encased in a heavy plaster from knuckles to my axilla. With some medication she sent me home. After the initial pain subdued, I was becoming comfortable and by the afternoon was well enough to take my dinner. But as the evening passed my whole arm started throbbing till, I could bear it no more. The young lady doctor was contacted who prescribed some painkillers, which did not make the slightest difference. As the night descended my pain became unbearable and I was in agony. The lady doctor was again disturbed, and she sent an injection of pethidine. I was doped for an hour or so but when I woke up I thought this pain in my arm would kill me, as it was now intolerable. My fingers and thumb by now had swollen to enormous size and looked dusky in color. In the early hours of the morning, I could stand the pain no more and the lady doctor was again disturbed at that unearthly hour; she sent another injection of pethidine. This time even pethidine could not work, and I kept yelling in agony.

Early at daybreak the lady doctor was summoned, and she came to see me; a tormented nervous wreck. By now my fingers were like a bunch of bananas and were blue and cold and multiple blisters were leaking lot of fluid from disfigured fingers soiling the bed sheets.

Looking at my plight the lady doctor was horrified and immediate asked for a kitchen knife and a saw. She set to work to cut the cast. Plaster was heavy and she was having little effect on it. It was an agonizing experience, as the slightest movement of my plastered arm would send me into terrible spasms. She being a slight person and not used to manual work could not free my entombed arm from the vice. The men in the family came to her help and after doping me with yet another injection of pethidine they struggled hard to cut the plaster off. Despite the severe pain due to their pulling and tugging, the relief that I felt at the removal of plaster was immense. My hand and fingers were now a mangled mess and poured out blood-stained fluid. Exhausted and drained I dozed off.

In our villages people equate plaster of Paris application with gangrene and not without reason. No wonder they instead of turning to literate doctors seek help from unqualified wise men, who simply hold fractures with wooden splints and a majority do well. Being literate is one thing, to be educated quite another. Education is what remains in the head when one has forgotten everything learned in school.

I later found out that this lady doctor, fresh from medical school had all the medical knowledge, secured a position in her finals; her knowledge was solely gathered in the classroom and had no hands-on experience of application of plaster and I was her first patient she had put the plaster on. I think it is just luck that she thought of cutting the plaster off, rather giving me another shot of pethidine that my hand although scarred for a long time is still with me, otherwise I would be writing this story with only one hand.

If we as teachers produce doctors like this, fault lies with us. For a teacher it is not enough to just regurgitate a lecture, it is his bounden duty to ensure how the knowledge imparted is of help to his students; in treating his patients. In medicine, rationale and application of the medical knowledge is more important than the rhetoric.

The three essential steps for learning—-intellectual exercise are: -

1. Memorization of facts,
2. Use of facts in a thought process—-synthesis of information, and then
3. Practice them in daily life: which should be visible from the behavioral pattern of the students.

Medical teachers should ensure that an average doctor before leaving the medical college has his basics right and is reasonably conversant with initial treatment and first aid of the ill and resuscitation of the injured. It is very unlikely that he or she will be called upon to do a heart or a kidney transplant, the sort of stuff we keep stuffing the students with.

The way to learn is by on job training.

1. Demonstration by a teacher. What and how to do it.
2. Replication. Become a copycat of your peer. He has traveled on these roads many times.Correction. Polish up your repertoire by knocking off the extras as the sculpture does.

3. Repetition. Only practice can make a man perfect.

Failing to prepare is preparing to fail. The great benefit of having peers is that they can dilute the stigma of failure.

Whatever else medical education may be achieving, it does not seem to be educating students in growth of pattern of thoughts—in abstract reasoning, in syllogistic thinking, in the principles of reduction and absurdity. This high education so much needed is not given in medical schools, is not to be bought in the marketplace, but is to be wrought out in each of us for himself. Everyone has to travel that road on his own footsteps. But it is the same road.

The responsibility for producing bad doctors squarely lies on the shoulders of the teachers who had been teaching them abstract art. The difference between a popular teacher and a good teacher is the difference between a politician and a statesman, who will always practice the truth and would not stoop to appeasement. A teacher must not seek cheap popularity by ungraciously holding back the stick where required. The evil must be nipped in the bud and no wrong should either be tolerated or allowed. All wrongs permitted will become habits and would remain so for the entire life.

A little neglect may breed mischief and may end up in a catastrophe by snowballing effect. Nip the evil in the bud; a stitch in time saves nine. So goes a time-honored military dictum:

> ***"For want of a nail, the shoe was lost, for want of shoe the horse was lost, and for want of a horse the message was lost; for want of a message, the battle was lost; for want of a battle, the war was lost, and all for the want of a nail."***

Benjamin Franklin

The best teachers from whom I have learnt the most were those ruthless arrogant surgeons who never tolerated any slackness in the management of a patient. If a patient needs surgery now, in the dead of the night, it must be performed now; notwithstanding, your personal conveniences or any other excuse. Patient comes first. Medicine is not a 9-5 career. Diseases do not take a holiday outside working hours and weekends. If a post-operative wound ever got infected, my teachers would grill me and raise hell: chance and Providence was not in their lexicon. No lapses were ever accepted. Human life is far more important than interpersonal pleasantries and the compromises. Surgeons must be a different breed anyway, where profession is the primary passion.

You give an inch; soon a foot will be taken. Also, all the wrongs will be accepted as norms and will become lifelong habits. This practice will then last the entire life of a doctor.

"A teacher affects eternity; he can never tell where his influence stops."

Henry Brooks Adams

The fate of individuals and the destinies of the nations are made by teachers. A shining example is that of an extraordinary, dedicated teacher Mr. Catchpole, an Australian national, whom the Gods sent to come to work in Pakistan; and how he dedicated his entire life in educating his students. Several of them went to forces and changed the fate of our nation. Due to his commitment, he shaped the destiny of the Air Force, which is what saved Pakistan in 1965. Once this lot of officers he trained superannuate from Pakistan Air Force; the difference will be too painful to take.

While in school Salim Nawaz, was a very good student and one of the favorite pupils of Mr. Catchpole. A bright student, who would always take position in the class, once fumbled, and could not stand first in an examination when the result was announced. Mr. Catchpole used to return all the papers after correcting mistakes. On receiving his paper Salim Nawaz felt dismayed for not winning the top position. While walking back to his hostel he was very cross with himself and in utter disgust, he tore his paper into smithereens. He then threw the bits in between a hedge to forget all about it. During the night a storm blew the bits of the papers all over the compound of the college. Next morning Mr. Catchpole while walking to his class saw a few of the bits in the lawn and picked up a small piece of the paper with hardly a few letters on it. His dedication and commitment to his students was so intense that he immediately recognized the handwriting of the student. Despite having hundreds in his school, he knew each one of them personally. He sent for this student and after giving him a lecture on tidiness broached the subject, about which he had a fair idea. Young lad broke down in desperation for not winning the first in the class. After a heart-to-heart session he then narrated to him the story of John Bruce the king of Scotland and read to him the poem, "try, try again," which the officer really took to heart and rose to be a two-star Air Marshal. It is tragic that he crashed before he could attain dizzying heights.

If we the medical teachers produce doctors like the lady doctor who treated me and had I lost my arm because of her lack of knowledge or even died due to negligence, how much blame should fall on the shoulders of the teachers? Whose duty it was to train the students to be skilled doctors rather than stuff their heads about abstract and ethereal effects. Should not the nonchalant attitude of teachers be questioned? It was because of their poor coaching that a human life or limb was put at stake. Did the teachers ever refuse their perks because they had not delivered? It seems teachers are accomplices, certainly in part, in such crimes and cannot abrogate their responsibility; teachers who do not teach well, teachers who pass such students to become doctors, let them loose on the hapless patients and the professors who select such teachers to the faculty of medical schools. We swell up with pride if our students do well in academics. We should also look inwards and ponder over when one of them is charged with negligence.

"One who kills a human life has killed the entire humanity."

Al-Quran

Patients are the best teachers. I am so grateful to them that they come to me from far off places taking me to be a wise guy and keep saying 'doctor you know best' which at times even I find embarrassing to accept. They hold me in high esteem, give me the respect I know I do not deserve and at the end of the session pay me as well! Scars on their bodies make me feel guilty for the shoddy job I had done on them. I have become a surgeon at their expense by experimenting on them. If they are still grateful, I can only hang my head in shame. I have climbed the ladder of success by stepping on their maimed and dead bodies.

If we want to excel, we should also know our history.

"The physician must know what his predecessors have known, if he does not wish to deceive both himself and others."

Hippocrates.

"The longer you can look back the farther you can look forward."

Churchill

As the best way to learn, is to teach, the best way to learn to teach is to write. Why treatment and teaching are of high standard in scholastic institutions is because teachers are always busy writing. By writing a teacher is forced to think, arrange and re-arrange his or her thoughts in an orderly language and if he or she is an artist, into a mellifluous prose—-may be poetry, where thoughts and words form neat and orderly lines and columns, as military men do at a parade so unlike a jumbled crowd. This not only helps to discipline the thought process but also opens new vistas and will broaden the horizon of a teacher.

The real challenge in Medicine is Research; by searching for unknown cures one is contributing to will of God. Medical research has been invested with reverence of a religious duty. Researcher walks in the path of God. The ink of a scholar is holier and more venerated than the blood of a martyr. Striving for knowledge has been ordained.

"God created no disease without creating a cure for it."

Al-Quran

What is the challenge? Our knowledge of ills that beset humanity is woefully inadequate. Today we can boast of empirical cure of just over two dozen diseases, while ninety eight percent of the diseases are treated by guesswork and only symptomatically; and are still crying out for help. Man will continue to find cure to diseases. With each discovery a curtain causing darkness between man and God is torn and he comes closer to his creator. The process of scientific discovery in reality is continuous flight from wonder. Every second of research is an encounter with creator. But do whatever we might Nature will always keep enough secrets to make humility the watchword of any scientist. Research means trying to know what we do not; thus, furthering the frontiers of knowledge. It is the cutting edge of Medicine. From bedside, through laboratory and to the bench and vice versa; in fact, it can work either way. Some of the greatest scientific discoveries were not made but stumbled upon. Fertilization of ideas and scientific intuitions flashed in high-powered laboratories but also at mundane places; like discovery of X-rays and Penicillin: Even in a bath and a shower; remember Eureka! But in the field of scientific observation, chance favors only the mind that is prepared. More one prepares luckier he gets. Intuitions are sudden dip of soul into universal current of life.

I find the discovery of Insulin very inspiring, not only because it has helped so many diabetics but that it was discovered not by a celebrity but a plain mortal; a medical student (Charles Best), and a failed orthopedic surgeon (Frederick Banting). I therefore cling to hope; I still may have a chance! And the journey goes on.

"What is possible has already been done
What is not possible shall be done."

By publishing research papers, one can extend frontiers of knowledge and spread it to every nook and corner of the world, which no other means of communication can do so effectively. By writing one also exposes oneself to criticism, comments and sometimes appreciation. The standard of education and hence the treatment is thus enhanced.

Nothing has been invented, only discovered.

Reading great lives is inspirational as it inculcates the spirit of being a gentleman and reading great writers is part of medical education. People, who think well, also write well. Reading makes a person better; better persons make better physicians.

19

Priorities And Sense Of Proportion

Life is more than work; it is a gift and a man at peace with himself must have not only his priorities right but also possess a sense of proportion. For professionals, surgeons included, to keep a balance amongst different values can be tricky but without it one would suffer lot of tribulations. To drain the most from every moment of life this balance is essential.

There are five prerequisites for a poised personality and full life. Each one of them is important. If under pressure one component for a period relegate the other four, which is commonplace in professionals trying to find a place in the sun, attempts should be made to come back to equilibrium as soon as possible before a personality becomes scruffy and permanent damage is done. Man does not live on bread alone. What does he live for?

1. Talent to be explored.
2. For the love of children and family.
3. Nostalgic memories.

4. Sound health is essential to enjoy life.
5. Faith: that there is a better tomorrow.

Now if you draw these five values as equal lines, a pentagonal star, like a starfish is formed. Each of the value when equally represented makes a balanced person. To excel in one field at the cost of others will deform the shape of this starfish. It is easy but it will fragment your personality.

To be successful in one's profession takes top priority, usually at the expense of other components, certainly in career men, like surgeons who to excel, leave no stone unturned to reach the top. The professionals work so hard in their chosen field that soon they distort the balanced look of this starfish like equation, into an obtuse shape and a lopsided figure will result. And this can only happen at the expense of other sides of the star, which shrink. This obtuse shape has resilience for some time, to come back to its original shape, but not for long. Soon you will be like an eccentric professor who knows nothing else except his profession.

There was an elderly professor of science, bit absent minded lost in his scientific work all the time to the great annoyance of his wife and children. His forgetfulness was proverbial, like kissing the porter and tipping the wife when he went to see off his wife at the railway station. The family bought a new house and the day they were to move to that house, his wife repeatedly reminded him, "We are moving to the new house today, so do not lose your way." He assured her that he wouldn't. At night he returned from the university and went straight to the old house. He could not figure out why the house was dark and deserted and why there was no body there. Then it suddenly dawned on him that he had to go to the new house tonight. He was rather confused, as he was not sure where to go since he could not remember where this new house was. Suddenly he saw a little girl in the twilight and asked her, "Little girl, do you know where the Smiths have moved to?" "Yes dad," said the little girl, "mother sent me to fetch you."

There is usually a woman behind every successful man and so can she be behind a failure. She can make all the difference between success and failure; domestic peace and rancor. After the first heart transplant in history, the surgeon was on top of the world but the response he got out of his spouse quickly doused his enthusiasm. He was ecstatic and after finishing the operation in early hours of the morning excitingly rang up his wife to share the good news with her. She was fast asleep and quickly dumped his spirits by asking. "Did you have to wake me up at this unearthly hour just for this?" Surgeon's wives are nicknamed House surgeons, except that their cut is deeper. We in the East are lucky that despite so many pressures, our marriages do not break up. Being mostly arranged marriages these are based on broad and sound values and joint families can withstand lot of insults. Our spouses expect very little from us, in contrast to in the West where the marriages reel under pressure. The result is we can work in peace and due to their sacrifices, can take up lot more pressures than in the West; where families tear apart on petty matters resulting in broken homes. These effects are also reflected at our place of work. It is difficult not to carry your domestic problems to work. You just cannot close the front door in the morning and leave the luggage behind.

Couple of my friends got married to foreign wives later unfortunately got divorced, when they had grown up children, with a very strange plea that I have not been able to figure out. Both these ladies said they wanted to 'discover' themselves. Once you have grown up children of marriageable age I, for the life of it do not know what more there is left to discover. But there must be a sound reason; thank God my wife does not know it! No professional success, however sublime can compensate for a failed marriage. Concomitantly, there is no greater stress or distress than that arises from rancor or problems at home. Home is one place where I would like to be myself; no veneer, polish, mannerism or affectation and that can only happen if my wife is akin to me. We in the East are lucky where the strength of extended family buffer and compensates for lot of our weaknesses.

How important the support of our friends in keeping our balance is, I found out when I stayed abroad for some time. I have worked in countries, where law and order situation used to be atrocious. In Lagos, Nigeria for instance, getting out at night was asking for trouble. You could be robbed, nabbed or worse still, could be lynched. The traffic jams even at night used to be so thick, that one could not get away, as no vehicle moved. Yet most expatriates took the risk and got together some place every weekend for food, or a drink, just to converse and socialize. One senior officer used to be so adventurous that he had voluntarily taken upon himself to pick and drop the latest Pakistani movie videotapes at odd hours, even at night from house to house, providing ladies an occasion to lighten themselves by shedding tears watching these soap operas. I wondered why we took so many risks; just to be together which we never did while at home, till I carefully read the contract that the foreigners working in Nigeria were required to sign. At the end of the contract in small print, were given detailed instructions and procedure of repatriation in the event, the officer went insane!

While working in London, the weekends used to be very lonely despite living in a jungle of people. I had a very dear friend since my college days who is now a professor of ophthalmology. He used to work in Wales. At one lonely weekend I thought of giving him a surprise and traveled all the way to Cardiff to see him. He thought likewise and wanted to give me a surprise and without informing me he traveled to London. Wasif spent his weekend stranded in a strange hotel in London and I languished in Welsh speaking environs, but we both remember this incident and have a few laughs every time we remember the occasion.

Harry Truman a past American President when he moved to Washington said, "If you want a friend in this town buy yourself a dog." I am not so sure. It must be a very unfortunate man who has no friends. Friends are relatives you pick and choose yourself. Family can be more than biological. To lose a friend, whom time and sweat has nurtured over the years is a catastrophe. Like a sapling in a nursery, friendship is delicately brought up, pruned, watered, and saved from the elements till it becomes a massive tree. To lose a friend on a petty matter in fraction of second, in the heat of a moment is possible and easy but is disastrous. Friendships are not developed overnight. Friends are worth their weight in gold and must not be lost at any cost. Remember the prayer, "God give me friends the best but never to need them." If a friend in his folly thinks he is using you, let him. Do not let him know that you know that you are being used, pretend naiveté, look the other way. Let him use you but do not lose him. One day he will regret. In fact, one should bow one's head before the Almighty in gratitude for granting this superior pedestal where other people need something from you, rather placing you in that inferior position where you may have to beg. It is a small mind that worries about being used. Surely there is plenty of you to share with friends. Riding a fast train, they are riding on the foot pedals, but we have enough empathy to carry them along. Our profession basically teaches us to shoulder the burden of others. Friends are like roses, thorns, and all. No one is perfect. Love men as they are, ideals do not exist in this world.

On the other hand, some friends will humble you with their affection. I was constructing a house I now live in. Building a house needs a big investment and one is always short of funds. I was happily cruising along and was trying to pool in all my savings and resources without giving anyone the impression that I needed money. One day one of my very dear friends came to see me. He pulled out a gunny bag bursting at seems from the boot of his car. Once I opened it, it was filled with bank notes of all denominations; looked like he had just robbed a bank. He said, 'I know how much it costs to build a house. I have built one recently. One can always do with additional funds. I have brought some amount that I thought would come handy at this hour. Please do not put your mind to any stress that you must return it. I feel I have just transferred this amount from my right hand to left. One day once the house is built you may return it if you like but please I repeat, do not be under any pressure about this amount." This speech, which I found more valuable than the accompanying bag full of bank notes, touched my heart. I had never given him any impression that I needed this money he just thought about it.

Friends in your life are like the pillars of your porch. Sometimes they hold you up, sometimes they lean on you; sometimes it is just enough to know that they are there; real friends are there when you need them most.

I operated on the father of a very dear friend once. All went very well, till time arrived to send the elderly gentleman home. I was perhaps not graceful enough to suggest it more diplomatically, that the patient could now go home. My friend, a very decent man, for whom I have greatest of regards, perhaps thought that his father was being pushed out prematurely, for whatever reason, though experience has taught me that the earlier these old folks get back to their own familiar surroundings, earlier they recover. Otherwise quite a few of them get disorientated in hospital settings. My friend did not like it. He, in front of some other people in my office gave me real hell. Short of hitting me on the head, he spared no insults; making it abundantly clear what he thought of me and in no uncertain terms and tone. I could not believe myself, the extents he went to.

Not used to such high handedness I could have retaliated but I knew his attachment with his father. Tears rolled down his eyes when the old gentleman met with this accident. I, to this day am thankful to Allah that I could keep my cool. I knew that the wounds caused by the bluntest knife of a surgeon heal, but those caused by a sharp tongue do not even in a lifetime. May God bless him and his father, I still consider him a good friend.

Professional jealousies are commonplace in all vocations; we are no exception. Some surgeons are gifted more than others are. Not many like a cleverer number two and in our profession, as elsewhere plans are hatched to see him fail. If you step slightly out of line, the superiors do not like it. To side with the victim, even when he may be right, can land you in trouble, as you will be labeled as friend of the accused. But to win favors with the superiors, at the cost of your personal relations and leave a friend in the lurch, who is being unnecessarily hounded would be mean. Looking back, it has been a satisfying experience even at the cost of burnt fingers.

Maybe it is because I am a doctor that I wonder that if I were granted just one wish to make, I would ask for—Health, anytime; my mind is very clear about it. I was replying to the greetings of a friend, "How do you do?" "Thank God I am usefully employed." She said, in fact reminded me, "This you are doing because you are keeping good health." I reflected on what she just said. How true. If it was not for my good health I would not be working as a surgeon almost full time at seventy. Helen Keller wrote, "Use your eyes, as if tomorrow you would be stricken blind; hear the music of voices, the songs of a bird, as if you would be stricken deaf tomorrow. Touch each object as if tomorrow your tactile sense would fail. Smell the perfume of flowers, taste with relish each morsel, as if tomorrow you could never smell and taste again." And pray as if it were your last prayer. "If I should die before I wake."

Health is not just absence of disease it is physical, psychological, and spiritual harmony. In health one should not only feel on top of the world, but also be at peace with oneself, at least most of the times; mood variations and diurnal ups and down, notwithstanding. Physical fitness and exercise make tremendous sense, not just because we enjoy outdoor and sports but also because exercise stimulates brain to generate stem cells and release chemicals such as Endorphins and Enkephalins, which reduce anxiety and create a sense of well-being naturally, without drugs. Pain threshold is increased, and immune system is strengthened preventing disease. The blood in all the vessels particularly coronaries and cerebral arteries gushes vigorously, the muscles pump forcefully, hormones some known, and quite a few still unknown are released into circulation and the feeling is that it is good to be alive. The reverse is also true; one's mental flabbiness can be gauged by palpating the tone or the lack of it in the muscles of calf and abdomen.

The importance of regular exercise cannot be over emphasized. Remaining physically fit is the only recipe for long healthy life. Sports, preferably outdoor activities are not only enjoyable but now are considered part of medical treatment, like pills, injections, and surgery. Research and science have proven the virtues of regular exercise. By burning calories, it keeps weight in check. Obesity is mother of most ills and is aggravated due to injudicious use of cars, computers, and endless hours of watching the tube. Just simple regular walking can do wonders to the body and to the tranquility of mind.

One may not live longer with regular exercise but certainly will live better as exercise will improve the quality of life. The time that might have to be spent on wheelchairs and in hospital beds may be spared. Someone who cannot find time for exercise will have to find time for illness in hospitals and disease can take away one's self-esteem.

Then there are diseases that make life a burden for the patient and relatives alike. There is dignity in dying that the doctors dare not deny their patients. There is no better way to die than with boots on, rather in intensive care wards of hospitals with tubes everywhere. Under such circumstances death indeed is a blessing that rids a person of pain, misery, indignity, dependence, and vegetative existence.

While I was working as a resident in Bristol Royal Infirmary, an injured young motorcyclist, hardly a twenty-year-old boy was brought to our ward. He was involved in a road traffic accident and sustained fracture dislocation of his cervical spine leaving him quadriplegic; all his four limbs were paralyzed. Immediately we put him on traction and resuscitated him. He soon started breathing on his own and we were wondering what would happen to him. Chances were the damage was permanent and he would not recover the use of his limbs again. It was sad to imagine what sort of life he would lead, being so young. Doctors are not allowed any euthanasia but if this person were an old man no one would have felt so sorry for him. Most doctors leave alone patients with terminal cancers and those suffering from incurable diseases and let nature takes its course, instead of resuscitating them energetically unlike for diseases where there is even a faint chance of full recovery. Quadriplegia is a different story. The patient was reasonably comfortable with cervical traction and was beginning to realize extent of his injuries. We had a young bright Registrar who had recently joined us and he at rather a young age had passed his fellowship and all the time lived in high spirits as he could see a bright career ahead.

Following morning the professor with his entourage that included a horde of medical students of all description went around the ward on a teaching round to see the patients. I had been off the night before and was surprised to see the quadriplegic patient on a respirator with lots of nurses running around. When the professor reached this patient, the young Registrar very proudly announced that last night at about two in the morning this patient suffered a cardiac arrest and he rushed and resuscitated this patient, who was now stable on a ventilator. Being surrounded by the medical students the consultant was tongue-tied and kept nodding his head as the Registrar went on and on describing his heroic efforts last night. After the end of the ward round when the students had left and we entered the office the consultant, an Irish man with an ill endowed temper let lose the tirade on this Registrar telling him in no uncertain terms what a stupid thing he had done in reviving this patient, thus prolonging the process of dying and denying him the dignity of death.

"Now in this vegetative state he would be on a respirator and only God knows for how long and at the end of it all it was highly unlikely that he would walk away from hospital." The Registrar new to the place was taken aback and could not understand why the consultant, instead of appreciating his heroic effort was so angry with him. Mercifully the patient died in a week's time but that week the entire nursing and medical staff was in a spin looking after a comatose patient not to mention the agony and pain the parents suffered.

Modern lifestyle of rich food and no physical activity is turning people into couch potatoes. There has emerged a class of novae riche who think good health means eating a lot of meat and sweet meats, having a double chin and a potbelly. The amount of beef, mutton and chickens consumed run in hundreds of tons. The number of sweet meat shops selling tons of sweets is a recipe for disaster. No wonders due to obesity complications of diabetes are on the increase. While eating rather a tasteless bland dish in a Japanese restaurant in Tokyo I asked the waitress to bring me some salt. She looked askance, bit confused and asked in her Japanese accent, 'rat poison?' Looked like we had difficulty understanding each other due to different accents and I repeated my request 'table salt please.' She repeated, 'white' poison. Fearing she may not bring me some harmful stuff, I approached the headwaiter who spoke better English. He brought me the salt with apologies for the confusion. He said we Japanese sparingly use salt and sugar and call them 'white poison'! Sweetmeat shops in any city show how much poison is being consumed daily.

We not only eat too much, but we also eat incorrectly; we eat food that is too hot or too cold, cooked badly with wrong ingredients. Researchers have doubled the life span of mice just by decreasing the food by half. The calculation is very simple; for a sixty-year span of life destined for you on this planet you are allotted say a ton of edibles. It is up to you whether you consume this food in a decade or stretch it beyond a century. A glutton by overeating is literally digging his grave with his own teeth.

Excessive consumption of rich food, sugar and salt has raised the incidence of heart diseases in men. We do little exercise and damage our health by smoking and drinking. Nicotine, saturated fats, and grilled meat are excellent sources to produce free radicals which gradually but surely are gnawing us on the quiet. We use less of raw vegetables and fruits that are the best antioxidants. Younger women, who think to look like a toothpick is a sign of beauty have increased incidence of osteoporosis. The irony of modern lifestyle is that the grandfather who is in his eighties is alive and well, the father has had a moderate heart attack but the grandson hardly thirty has had a bypass or has died because of a massive myocardial infarction. The tragedy of stressful man today is that he earns wealth on the expense of his health and then must spend the same money to regain health. Contentment, simple living; not preserved but fresh food straight from mother earth and regular exercise is time tested and time-honored principles for good health.

As a medical man I find working of human body fascinating. How are we built and how we function is bewildering. Our body is even more astounding than the world around us. It is a universe. Trillion of cells, each with its own code of conduct and constitution, working harmoniously in a mysterious way; from the same raw materials, some produce lubricants, other juices for digestion, yet others, hormones, and some neurotransmitters. It is no less wonder how these are manufactured, what controls them; and how they control us. Soon after an injury a complex healing process starts, proceeds inexplicably, and continues till the damage is undone, who tells the cells when to stop, whereas the cancer cells do not know when to. Conception and birth of a baby is the biggest wonder of all; how from a couple of cells such a beautiful being is born. What goes on in the womb is indeed a miracle. A sperm or an ovum each carries information equivalent to 750 megabytes of a computer!

Men risk their lives to climb high mountains and leap in the deep sea for ecstasy. We wonder at the motion of stars and yet pass each other without wondering; even without a second look—-man who himself is the biggest wonder of all.

The anatomy of the human body is perfect and so is its physiology; the third dimension, body-mind-spirit axis; as how we put our body to use and what we make out of it, is under our command. One path leads to heaven and the other straight to hell, depending upon how we use this wonderful machine, the choice is ours and ours alone All the parts of this body will obey us faithfully; they are at our command absolutely;

whichever way we want to take them.

Faith is the backbone of our personality, like steel meshwork in a building, it holds us together. Belief in a supreme force; God, is needed for all those phases which are beyond the range of human perception and cannot therefore be proved or disproved by scientific observations: Ultimate meaning of time and Eternity, Resurrection of the dead, the day of judgment, paradise and hell, nature of beings, the angels; is all beyond us. Even if there were no God it would have been necessary to invent one, was a statement made in utter bewilderment. Man being a spiritual animal, belief in a superpower is his necessity. "Thank God I am an atheist," was not a reflex exclamation but proves that deep inside everyone is a believer. This craving is in the genes. For unforeseen eventualities, tragedies, the tribulations man has no control on; one needs to fall back upon something, or someone. When chips are down, and the mind is troubled you need a shoulder to cry upon. The real peace can transcend only through a faith. Agnostics have nowhere to turn to. Believing in nothing results in an inability to believe in oneself.

I envy people who can adhere to a faith with complete conviction. They are placed on a certain set course, like on railway tracks from which they cannot derail or go astray. By traveling on it they will reach a destination—whatever: unlike people trying to reinvent the wheel on their own and wander on uncharted routes in empty spaces where there are no signboards or directions to guide them and soon, they are lost as in a maze. In search of truth, one undergoes the torture of 'why'. Anguish and pain that seems quite unnecessary; when there are branded routes which are already tried and tested. And after all that, hitting the head against the wall there is no guarantee of finding nirvana by limping on one's own, in deserts and jungles where the tormented retreated. And the land is littered with the appendages of philosophers and thinkers who went on solo flights and those who perished. Bones of the skeletons of those loners are strewn all over the place that wandered on their own and failed. But the quest for finding God is a human thirst and a spiritual need. Like a passport showing nationality everyone must have an identity—a faith; call it a religion. Beyond logic and science there is a twilight zone, where man has no say. There is nothing but good in every religion. Prayers are the way to find God. Prayers that are not divorced from their daily lives and do not help forget life but to understand it better by remembering Him. God then seems so close to them. Skeptics who keep wandering aimlessly in blind alleys are organically unhappy. You can do only so much and can go no further before you will be humbled. Scientific notions evolve from one point and progress in a linear fashion to find concepts; thoughts on religion do not.

Most of us, the believers however live our lives sitting on a fence and are always in two minds. A man slipped from a mountain cliff and hurled down but somehow stopped before falling in a dark crevice deep down below and die, his fingers clawed on to ledge of a rock and he started dangling in midair holding on only with his bare fingertips. In distress and utter desperation, he looked around and yelled; "Help, help, is somebody up there?" A voice came from the heavens above; "Yes, faithful I hear you, do not panic, and trust me. Now do as I say; Let go the ledge."

The man looked down the dark bottomless abyss and nearly passed out, he could hold on to the cliff no longer. After thinking for a moment, he cried again, "Help, help, somebody up there." Again, the instruction was loud and clear, "Let go the ledge." The man was exhausted and drained. Hanging in midair he looked around and after a little pause and in extreme trepidation yelled again, "Help, help. Is somebody else up there?"

But a faith that keeps a people backwards is not a true faith. Religious cults which defy science and technology, and progress are not worth following. Any religion when followed in its true holistic spirit, results in peace. The principles of Islam are same as enshrined in Judaism and Christianity, and flow from the same source. These three great monotheist religions have not only a common root, but also a common trunk; we are all followers of Abraham's traditions and teachings. Religions demand from us to be as close to perfection as possible treading on a tight rope, differentiating between right and wrong and hold oneself accountable at every moment of life, be careful about other's rights, particularly of the weak and those who follow different faith.

While in London Hammersmith I had several Jewish colleagues with whom I got on splendidly well as I found their culture, their living, strong family values, eating habits, and the kosher; in fact, almost everything very similar to mine. I found them very decent people, highly intelligent, hardworking, and very principled; would never tell a lie, always kept their word come what may. In fact, living with them at times I felt so small that I was developing inferiority complex. The maximum number of Nobel Prize winners, the eminent professors, scientists, scholars in fact teachers of the world are mostly Jews. Due to excelling in science and technology, they control economics and the Media and virtually rule the world. But I could not help wondering that a race with so much creative intelligence could be so myopic. Downtrodden as they were after the Second World War, there is plenty to learn from them. How they rose— from the ashes of holocaust when half of their race was wiped out. But unfortunately blindfolded by heightened sense of self-righteousness and selfishness they have never stopped to ponder why Europeans hated so intensely such a decent people? Even today Zionist's rabid parochialism, arrogance against other nations has not changed and I am fearful of their future; that history may not repeat itself. It is only love that vanquishes all in the end. It is much better to win the hearts and souls of people rather than occupy their lands. Not very many people know that as Muslims it is essential part of our prayers that we pray for Jews and Christians over dozen time each day.

The practice of religion should not make us opium eaters. God has given us intelligence; all the tools and energy and one should use them to the maximum and only when no options are left God comes in. With every advance in science and medicine God's role in our everyday life diminishes. To leave everything to God as we do without striving is forbidden; first do your best. Do not expect Allah to toil for us in this world while we wait for rewards in the hereafter.

The famous adage of Caliph Omar we all have heard of when he said, "That even if a dog dies of starvation on the banks of Tigress River, he as the head of the state would be held responsible." The one most of us do not seem to recall is, when he said to his people on assuming power. "Oh faithful's, I have come to highjack (filter) your prayers. It is my duty as a ruler that I solve as many of your problems that I can and only those prayers should reach heaven which I cannot resolve."

During earlier part of inception of our country there were severe food shortages and millions of tons of wheat used to be imported. It was feared that there would soon be famines. The head of the state worked very hard and got river water problems sorted out. He asked the farmers to change their man with the hoe, farming ways and follow the latest techniques in agriculture. By following science and modern methods of farming the country, through green revolution soon became self-sufficient in food. He sent several delegations of farmers and agriculturists to different countries to learn new techniques of modern farming to increase per acre yield. One such delegation went to atheist Russia where they were taken to a desert and the members were amazed to see for themselves as to how the desert was being reclaimed bit by bit, through hard work and by artificial rain. The delegates had never heard of artificial rain. It was pleasing to see an oasis in the middle of a desert. Lush green paddy fields spread over miles next to and at the edge of a barren desert.

Spellbound by the miracle an astounded faithful could not help asking, "What did you use to do when you had not developed the artificial rain system?" "Then, we were at the mercy of the vagaries of nature," answered the Russian guide gravely, "and like you, we also used to pray hard for the rain."

Man is influenced by his surroundings. Almost all of us like a herd blindly follow the set routes and adapt to the environs where we are born, bred, and brought up and become a creature of habit and not many of us find it necessary to question the traditions, value of rituals and the customs of our peers. Slowly and surely the impressions imprinted on the mind are so deeply etched that it is difficult even to think otherwise. Our names for instance have imprisoned us and put a label that no one can change; unless an outright rebel. Those who try are considered pariahs in their own society; so, most of us find it convenient to lamely limp along on the beaten tracks. A time however does come in every one's life when second thoughts begin to trouble, and one starts to question and become skeptical of the values and significance of the routine. Those who do not doubt or do not want to, become lukewarm, lose interest, become indifferent and look the other way. Most people around the world are like that, retreating from religion. Paying only lip service to their faith; being so much involved in their daily chores and the rat race. The die-hard group: the wailing gyrating skull capped Jews, the hardened crusaders, the hirsute suicide lunatics, and those who adhere to the rituals verbatim become self-centered and feel so self-righteous that they not only become intolerant of other's viewpoint, but also intolerable to live with. By closing their minds, they feel self-righteous and are prone to dogmatism. Rituals alone seem to make people spiritually blind. Such practice of religion per se breeds selfishness and overemphasizes the importance of the individual spirit. Religion preaches nothing but a single concern—the salvation of one's own soul and those who practice it blindly start to claim themselves self-styled champions of all the virtues. The tyranny of certainty is that one becomes intolerant of other's viewpoint. It closes minds to other possibilities, makes people dogmatic and intolerable.

Real test of one's faith however is whether it is strong enough to tolerate other faiths; and the test of strength of a man is that he should be able to accept his weaknesses without hesitance.

The religion we are given however is like an arranged marriage where love does not precede but is expected to follow the marriage. Similarly in religion conviction is left to follow—after having inherited a certain faith, which is decided for us long before we know and when have no choice. As we grow, unknowingly and unwittingly we feel our environs and see our parents, practice certain rituals; by going either to a church, mosque, temple, or a synagogue. This leaves indelible imprints on our young minds, and we inherit the religion of our parents, monkeying even before they start to preach us. Each one of us continues to follow the faith of his parents and dare not question its sanctity. Once we reach mature age and quest the significance of rituals which now look hollow, it is too late as now we had already started teaching our children the same parochial thoughts as our parents did, perhaps with not same ferocity.

The real spirit behind all faiths however is the same; how to live graciously in a crowd; shielding the weak. The real aim is to prepare decent human beings.

I do not feel it fair that anyone ought to be culpable due to mere accident of birth; for following a certain faith that was given to him in inheritance long before he was even conscious of it. What I am accountable for, are my deeds and what sort of a human being I become. The English description for it is 'Gentleman.' By gentleman one implies qualities enshrined in any faith: virtues like honesty, integrity, sense of honor, directness, and fear of God. A man who is generous and compassionate, proud towards brutal force and humble before goodness and above all realizes man's ephemeral insignificance before the Infinite and the Eternal. Confucius defined a gentleman, 'a superior man who has intelligence, dignity, grace, kindness, resolution and forcefulness.' It is said that it takes at least three generations of rigorous schooling, apprenticeship and on job training to produce a gentleman. By gentleman I do not mean old Estonians and all that.

"Arsh tak ho nein sakti jo risai na sehi, yehi insan ki mairaj ha kai insan ban ja ai."

Iqbal

Cosmos, may be beyond my reach; so be it,

Zenith of man is that he should become a (gentle) man.

Some consider these values above everything. An English Chief justice was interviewing candidates for the post of judges. He was asked what qualities he was looking for in a candidate. His reply applies to all the professions where trust and ethics are important pre-requisites. He said, "first and foremost a judge should be a gentleman, and if he knows bit of law that helps."

We try to infuse this spirit in newly selected cadets in military institutions, calling them Gentleman Cadets. Due to the intense training and with a sense of pride in being called gentlemen, the under-officers are groomed into excellent human beings. The army picks up raw young urchins from the street and then with grilling, intense training, and coaching works to rebuild them into gentlemen who with further guidance can become leaders, develop confidence to take up any task, write, speak well, behave and command. The real endeavor is to come close to Iqbal's vision of *marde-momin*. No other organization can claim to have such a program of rigorous structured training. Most successful leaders of the world at some stage of their lives had the benefit and privilege of military grooming.

How are gentlemen made? The first academy is the mother's lap, where the foundations are laid. Then the school and there is no better instructional manual than the letter Abraham Lincoln wrote to his son's teacher: -

"He will have to learn. I know that all men are not just, all men are not true.

But teach him also that for every scoundrel there is a hero;
For every enemy there is a friend. It will take time, I know
But teach him, if you can, that a dollar earned is of far more value than five found...
Teach him the secret of quiet laughter.
Let him learn early that bullies are easiest to lick...
Teach him, if you can, the wonder of book...

But also give him quiet time to ponder over the eternal mystery of birds in the sky, bees in the sun, and flowers on the green hillside. In school teach him it is far more honorable to fail than to cheat...
Teach him to have faith in his own ideas,
Even if everyone tells him they are wrong...
Teach him to be gentle with gentle people and tough with the tough.
Try to give my son the strength not to follow the crowd when everyone is getting on the band wagon.
Teach him, if you can, how to laugh when he is sad... Teach him there is no shame in tears.
Teach him to scoff at cynics and to be aware of too much sweetness...
Teach him to sell his brawn and brain to the highest bidder; but never to put a price tag on heart and soul. Teach him to close his ears to howling mob...
And to stand and fight if he thinks he is right.
Teach him gently; but do not cuddle him because only the test of fire makes fine steel.
Let him have the courage to be impatient... let him have the patience to be brave.
Teach him always to have sublime faith in himself
Because then he will always have sublime faith in mankind.
This a big order; but see what you can do...
He is such a fine little fellow, my son."

On this pedestal and psyche the child now can build up a towering edifice.

At Asian games in Seoul our team had done poorly in every department and the only gold we had won was in Yachting the hosts Koreans were runners up. The performance of our hockey team, we had pinned high hopes on proved dismal. After the yachting gold was announced at the port city of Pusan, the yachtsman unfortunately tested positive for a drug Ephedrine, which is a banned drug. The sailor, a junior naval officer was suffering from cough and cold and one of the Korean doctors had inadvertently prescribed a cough syrup that contained this drug. The award was cancelled pending an inquiry.

The thought of returning home empty handed and facing a hostile nation gave Chef de mission cold feet. Being the team doctor, I was to represent the sportsman in the court. A high-level meeting was held in his office where I, being a worldly-wise physician, was asked to represent him and keep the sailor under my wings. After all he did not take any drug on his own. The syrup the Korean doctor had prescribed was the responsibility of the doctor. The sailor was instructed to 'cooperate' and say only what he was told. The reply of the sailor stunned us all. "Gold or no gold," said the yachtsman bluntly, "I am not going to tell a lie or conceal the truth." Not content with that he shamed us further with a sermon, "The desire to win is inborn in all of us. To win is a matter of training but the manner of winning is matter of honor." It became difficult to look him in the eye. This was the only gold for a contingent of over a hundred athletes and we were desperate to keep it, but the sailor was adamant and refused to 'cooperate' and lend me a hand. He spoke the truth and nothing but the truth. With the medal his physical strength was apparent to all, but only a few of us knew his inner strength; strength that anchors on truth and honesty. Because of this incident I kept track of him in the Navy and it gives me immense pleasure that he has not lost any fervor despite being a senior officer now. I have not seen a man more at peace with himself; a grace and harmony that is an expression of the magic consonance between a human being's conscious and the world that surround him.

Honesty remains the best investment.

In our school days we used to be asked to recite an axiom, the significance of which I can only now appreciate. In fact, during those days, it was easy to memorize but difficult to understand and now it is difficult to memorize but easy to understand.

"If wealth is lost nothing is lost.
if health is lost something is lost.
But if character is lost everything is lost."

15

The Bitter* Half

*The 'e' in BETTER was reluctantly changed to 'i' at the insistence of an anesthetist friend.

There is lot in common in the working of an anesthetist and an airline pilot. For a pilot the critical times are while taking off and at landing of an aircraft and for an anesthetist, while putting the patient to sleep and while waking him up. In between both relax and usually put their machines on auto function and can get involved in crossword puzzles or some more interesting past time. The pilot can stare at the horizon from his cockpit or rub shoulders with his passengers down in the cabin, (to the chagrin of the passengers!) while the anesthetists find the surgeon an amusing object and sometimes a punching bag. Both the pilot and anesthetist suffer hours of boredom and fortunately and rarely, moments of terror. The mettle of both is proven in an emergency.

The anesthetist is an uncrowned king of the Operation Theater. He along with the theater sister reigns the arena, while the poor surgeon does the donkey's work. Tense and taut with tension, he looks up to anesthetist for succor and support, who can make his life hell or heaven. Their compatibility is essential for the smooth running of an Operation

Theater. It is teamwork and if the working runs smoothly, the ultimate beneficiary is the patient. On the temperament of the anesthetist depend the atmosphere of the Operation Theater, as the temperament of a housewife determines the peace and tranquility of a home. It is amazing how much they can put up with and tolerate idiosyncrasies and inadequacies of different and difficult surgeons they work with. We the surgeons love to play God, suffer a complex and think ourselves a different breed and perceive the rest of the doctors to be bit dim! We carry this conceited notion in our heads that only the live ones become surgeons, the left over become internists, pathologists, or anesthetists—and in that order, depending upon the amount of fervor left in them!

Operation theaters are tense and bleak places. There is an ongoing battle between life and death all the time. In these somber settings, the need for some light moments is intense. It is a good anesthetist, who can provide some comic relief and entertainment to lift off tensions. Most anesthetists since they have plenty of time and spare energy manage to create some humor, usually at the expense of the surgeon and cut him to size.

I was trying to repair the skin loss of a badly injured patient who had lost lot of skin in a road traffic accident. The patient was a paying private patient. My anesthetist as always on a look out for an occasion to have a dig at me and for a change was watching the proceedings with unusual interest. He saw me take a big slice of the skin from the donor site of the patient, ready to be planted onto the defect. Being a paying patient the anesthetist with tongue in cheek commented, "I am very impressed from your surgery. You are at your best in operations like the present one; how to skin a patient alive!"

A trauma surgeon was hard at work operating through a ghoulish incision and had made an untidy mess due to profuse bleeding; there was blood everywhere and the scene looked macabre. During one of the maneuvers a splash of blood spluttered onto the glasses of the surgeon, and he could not see anything through the opaque glasses. He asked his anesthetist friend to help him; remove his glasses and clean them. The anesthetist obliged and after wiping the blood off, put the glasses back on the surgeon's nose. Surgeon was not getting anywhere and when stuck we usually look for scapegoats. The surgeon requested the anesthetist again to please wipe his glasses clean. The anesthetist was already fed up due to the length of surgery and the bloody mess that had drained his patient. He looked at the shiny glasses and then the gruesome scene on the table and commented, "If I were you, I would leave the glasses as these are; I am sure you do not want to see too much!" Some trauma surgeon are traumatic surgeons!

A tardy surgeon was struggling on and on, taking unduly long time for a simple procedure. The patient had been under anesthesia for a considerable length of time to the chagrin of the anesthetist who was getting worried about the prolonged anesthesia in a poor risk patient. He had had enough. As is the practice with such surgeons when stuck, they blame the difficulties encountered and the delays on everyone except themselves, usually the anesthetist and grumble, like 'the light is not properly focused' or 'the patient is not relaxed.' This surgeon complained to the anesthetist that, 'the patient was moving'. Fed up the anesthetist retorted, "The patient is not moving; he is growing!"

No one can realize the importance of a good anesthetist more than a surgeon can. In fact, we surgeons are what we are because of the cooperation of anesthetists. It pays to have good relations with him or her. The competence or otherwise of a surgeon is also best known to an anesthetist, who knows the inside story. The ideal combination is an experienced surgeon and an equally experienced anesthetist. The worst is when both the surgeon and anesthetists are raw. Lot of morbidity and mortality, sometimes catastrophes can be prevented if at least one of the two is experienced.

Once, as I entered an operation theatre to fix a broken hip of an octogenarian and I noticed the young anesthetist peering closely on an X ray of the chest placed on a view box instead of putting the patient to sleep. In a lighter vein and to hurry up the proceedings I said to him, "Son, it is the hip that is broken, you are looking at the wrong X ray!" The nettled young anesthetist who took his job very gravely recoiled and started off enumerating a list of abnormalities he saw in the x-ray, like enlarged heart, unfolding of aorta and fibrosis of lungs etc. Before he could go on further in entered the senior anesthetist to whom this young man recounted the ailments of the unfit patient. The senior anesthetist a cool man went up to the X-ray of chest and said, "Yes, I agree with you it is an 80-year-old chest. So let us take all the precautions and do something about them while we put her to sleep."

The question of fitness or unfitness of patients for surgery often poses problems. Surgeons are usually impatient and would be eager to get on with surgery, rather to worry too much about unfolding of the aorta or an inverted T wave, with which patient has lived so far. The criteria of fitness also vary from person to person. A junior or inexperienced anesthetist would dig out a list of ailments to declare a patient unfit. A confident anesthetist would be sure of himself that he would not let the critically ill patient suffer not even a moment of hypoxia during surgery rather than depend on expensive investigations and other specialists for second opinions, because ultimately, he is the man on the spot.

For surgeons the criteria are quite different than for the anesthetists. Not as enlightened as their anesthetist colleagues they have rather crude but practical yardsticks of determining fitness rather than go after sophisticated investigations, which the patients in the third world can ill afford. A urologist operating as emergency on a case with retention of urine used to say that 'if a patient can get out of bed, walk around it and then get into it from the other side, he is fit for surgery!' In our country, if an old man before a fracture of neck of femur could walk up to a mosque to offer his prayers; is fit for surgery and does not need a thallium scan or a MRI. I know of an anesthetist friend, who very confidently used to say that "If an unfit patient were alive breathing air he would not die breathing oxygen in my hands!"

We in the third world have to compromise for lack of, a lot of facilities the rich countries can provide to the physicians and surgeons. What we lack in gadgetry and in technology must be compensated by being over and ever vigilant. Prevention is indeed better than cure in our set up. Pre-empt any complication before it develops and start with the presumption that if a complication can happen it will.

The requirements of a surgeon and an anesthetist on the operation table are diagonally opposite, in fact poles apart. The surgeon would like the patient under anesthesia to be limp, relaxed, bloodless, senseless absolutely still, in deep sleep; in fact—'lifeless! The anesthetist would like to see blood gushing, the patient pink and warm, lungs bellowing vigorously and heart pumping powerfully.

An incisive anesthetist can cut surgeon to size who tend to play God. A tardy surgeon worked very hard at an operation, which he thought was difficult and took rather a long time. By the time he finished all his clothes got soaked with blood. Sweating profusely, he triumphantly came out of theater after performing what he presumed was heroic surgery. Feeling very pleased with himself, he was walking to the changing room. The anesthetists, who usually are not easily impressed from surgeons and even if they are, rarely express such sentiments; when he saw the surgeon in this 'bloody' state could not help commenting, "I hope you have left some blood in my patient also!"

The sense of humor of anesthetist varies from amusing to weird. It must be due to the inhalation of gases they breathe while at work!

As a part of preoperative checkup, and to develop personal rapport with a young soldier, who was to be operated next morning, I was asking this patient some personal questions, just to put him at ease, although the resident doctor had jotted down a complete history of the patient. It was only a small procedure. The anesthetist was incidentally sitting next to me during this examination. "How many brothers are you?" I asked. "Four." He replied. The anesthetist without any rhyme or reason interjected, "Say, three, count yourself out. You are having an operation tomorrow, remember." I am not quite sure, how much confidence such remarks infuse in a frightened patient.

A diffident surgeon was trying to remove an adherent appendix. He was very scared of any bleed or a complication and was proceeding with utmost caution and was taking his time, a very long time. The anesthetist was getting worked up at the length of surgery and was trying to hurry up the proceedings but to no avail. The surgeon would go near the organ and then would change his mind. The anesthetist finally got so fed up that he blurted out, "Look here mate, only you are going to remove this appendix. It is highly unlikely that it will jump out of the abdomen on its own!"

Good anesthetists in hospital are always looking for occasions to oblige anyone that comes their way. A psychiatrist in a hospital was having trouble with one of his elderly patients who was convinced that he had a cat in his belly! The psychiatrist did his utmost to explain to the patient that it was not possible to have a cat sprinting in a human belly. The patient would have none of that and kept on shouting, "I have a cat in my tummy." The distraught psychiatrist was at his wit's end. Luckily for him it so happened that one day this patient suffered acute appendicitis and needed urgent surgery. The poor crest-fallen psychiatrist went to the operation theatre and sought help of his colleagues. He requested the anesthetist earnestly that once the patient came around from anesthetic after the surgery, "Would you be so kind to show the patient a cat, telling him that on operation we found a cat in your belly and the psychiatrist was wrong all the time."

The anesthetist decided to oblige and as the patient was gaining consciousness after surgery, he sent one of his residents to catch a stray cat wondering in the hospital corridors. The poor resident after a long chase and with scratches on his face, inflicted by the infuriated uncooperative cat managed to grab her and brought it to the patient who was recovering from the anesthesia. The anesthetist seated the cat close to the waking up patient and patting her head said to the patient, "On opening your abdomen we found this cat in your belly and took her out and she would not bother you anymore." The patient was relieved and heaved a sigh of relief. Everybody around including the psychiatrist was delighted at the 'successful operation.' The patient was still staring hard at the cat and then suddenly sat bolt upright in his bed and started shouting at the top of his voice, "This was not the cat in my belly. This is a white cat. The cat in my belly was jet black!"

The way the anesthetists treat the surgeons, at times is far from civil. We were planning to operate on a very ill fragile old man for a fracture around the hip, which for us is an emergency as the patient, if not quickly mobilized after fixing of hip surely would die. While the patient was being wheeled into the theater, the anesthetist looked aghast at the sight of this frail mannequin and advised us sarcastically, "Why don't you fellows leave him alone and at least let the poor man celebrate Christmas, before you get at him," the Christmas festival was falling within next few days.

I was working in an English hospital where we had a husband-and-wife anesthetist team, manning the department of our theater. We all were very fond of our jovial and very cooperative anesthetist, but his irate wife scared us. While the operations were in progress, one afternoon, the husband and wife alternated in putting patients to sleep. The sister in charge peeped into the Operation Theater and called out the anesthetist. There was an urgent call for him. As he went out of the theater everyone thought it must be about a seriously ill patient. The surgery continued while he was away. His wife in the meanwhile was looking after the anesthetized patient. When he returned, he was walking as if in a trance. The color had drained from his face, and he walked back very slowly like a Zombie. In almost a croaked voice and looking very glum, he announced that he had just received a call that his father had died in an old people's home. We all felt very sorry and condoled with him on the sad demise of his father. His wife, who we thought would have similar sentiments, spoke her mind quite differently, "George," she said addressing her husband with a frown on her face, "Your father has not done one thing right in his life. Not even in death. Look what has he done now? He decides to die on a Friday, spoiling our weekend!"

How much reverence we have for our elders was in stark contrast to her statement. My father-in-law suddenly developed Retinal detachment. The treatment was race against time. Facilities in Pakistan those days were very elementary. Being a doctor and very concerned about his health, I insisted on accompanying my father-in-law, for urgent Retinal surgery to England. After the operation, there was need for follow up for some time. The Ophthalmologist in London wanted to see him again in a month's time. We were wondering what to do in the meanwhile. I decided to take up a locum post. A sea resort would be ideal for his convalescence. So, I picked up a job on the eastern coast, a holiday resort in Lincolnshire. When we reached the hospital, I requested the hospital secretary for accommodation, "I will require two apartments." I spoke. I being alone he wondered why. "If your girlfriend is with you, why should you need two rooms?" He asked. "My father-in-law is accompanying me," I explained. He looked very perplexed. "Father-in-law!" He exclaimed. "We do not know much about our fathers in this country, you are concerned about your father-in-law!"

It was a pleasant occasion however, when my old English consultant invited my father-in-law over for a dinner. Knowing our Muslim culture, he had ensured there were only fish and vegetable dishes. He was a decent man, and my father-in-law enjoyed the time spent in his house. The best thing that we liked in his blessed house was that he had both, his centurion mother-in-law, and his own equally old mother, living with him gracefully surrounded by their grandchildren.

Old folks suffer a lot of fractures around the hip that we keep operating upon and to follow them up, I have visited several old people's home. Polished handle rails, Mica white floors, the physical comforts the welfare state provide are like five-star hotels but what the state cannot dole out, is the love and affection. The glint in old ladies' eyes at the sight of their grandchildren still glows fresh in my mind.

While in the West, regional blocks have completely taken over, particularly in the elderly patients and are being used extensively; our anesthetist colleagues in the third world are still trailing behind with general anesthesia. The disadvantage of general anesthesia is that while the patient is asleep, the machines have taken over the functions of the body and there is no better machine than the God made machines. Lesser the patient has to be dependent on them, the better. By not interfering with vital functions of the body, like respiration and the brain, we can help the elderly recover from surgery quicker. In a country like ours, where there is not so much sophistication in medicine and people are not so well off this form of anesthesia should be employed more often, as it can prevent lot of hazards. The only catch is that since the patient is not asleep during surgery, you must keep shut or at least mind your language.

A soldier was having his foot operated under local anesthesia. To ward off infection all operative precautions and proper protocol were observed. The patient was well draped and even his face was covered with a green operating sheet. I was so deeply involved in the procedure that I did not notice the arrival of one of the unemployed anesthetists. As is their habit, when they are not usefully engaged, they would wander around, give unsolicited advice, and pass rude comments about the surgeons, to create some life in the dull proceeding of the Operation Theater. Standing behind me he started watching the proceedings. The operative field was remarkably bloodless due to a vaso-constrictive injection, and we were doing pretty well. The anesthetist watched us for some time with bored interest. Seeing no blood in the operative field, he yawned and walking away wryly commenting, "Is he dead?" The soldier heard that. Pulling apart the sterilized sheets off his face, he lifted his head and said, "not yet, sir."

16

In Rome Do As The Romans Do

One of my anesthetist friends, who deals with patients when they are asleep and does not have to be much of a 'salesman' as we clinicians must be, once visited my clinic while I was dealing with routine patients. He started watching the proceedings with amusement.

A new patient a middle aged illiterate heavy-duty woman from a village was brought in moaning and supported by a hoard of worried relatives. Once she settled down, I asked her, "What is the problem?" "you tell me what the problem with me is. That is why I have come to see you." I swallowed the rebuff and asked again, "Do you have any pain anywhere?" "I have pains everywhere." She answered. "How long have you had these pains?" I asked again. "I have had them all my life, for as long as I can remember." I tried again, "Do you have pain in the legs?" "I have pains in the legs that radiate to my head." She said, "It is all because of eating okra," chimed in a fat woman who had accompanied the patient. "I have been advising her not to." She said sagely.

Keeping my emotions within and trying to look wise I helplessly looked at her relatives who volunteered, "she says she has wind in her belly that travels to her head and then hands, and then she has these terrible pains. These pains then travel in all her body, and she keeps crying with them." I thought I would try another symptom, as there was mention of belly. "How is the appetite?" I asked, "Have not eaten a morsel in days," she answered. She looked well fed, in fact over-weight without any signs of dehydration. "Since when have you noticed loss of appetite?" I asked. "Ever since I have had these pains," she said. Baffled, I tried another symptom. "Have you lost any weight?" "I have lost lot of weight and feel very weak, and I can hardly stand," she said. I thought for a moment of backache. Oh no, I suddenly realized, I am not going to ask her about backache; there is hardly an obese woman in town I know who has not got backache. I will be caught in a quagmire. I skipped that. "Do you have any cough?" I wavered. "I am coughing all the time and cannot sleep at night or during the day," she said. "It is all because she ate okra," again came, the unsolicited wise advice from the fat old woman. Oh, what a tangled web some patients can weave, I gritted my teeth.

Reminded me of a notice I read in a doctor's office. 'To avoid delays please have all your symptoms ready!'

The English medical books and teachers had hammered in our minds, the importance of the clinical methods in this sequence, history first then examination and last of all investigations. I also knew an old axiom that a doctor who cannot take a good history and a patient who cannot give one are in danger of giving and receiving bad treatment. Tongue-tied, I felt helpless in history taking but I remembered a saying that doctors learn much more about the illness from the way the patient tells the story than from the story itself. We had been taught the sequence of examination as in the books. Inspection first, then palpation, then percussion and auscultation last of all. The loud noise still echoes in my ears when I remember the answer we used to shout in a chorus when the teacher asked us, "which is the least important tool in your kit?" and we used to chant, "Stethoscope, Sir." He used to say if you have listened; looked, felt, and percussed you should expect what to hear. Despite dazzling array of technologies, language and physical remains the bedrock of clinical practice.

Another holler that used to bring smile on his face was when he would ask, "Which is the best instrument God has blessed us with?" In unison we would shout, "The hand, Sir." Hearing the cacophony even the very sick patients lying in the ward would turn their necks to find out what had gotten into these healers huddled around their teacher.

My friend the anesthetist was enjoying my plight as I battled to get a foothold for diagnosing this woman. After I somehow got over the ordeal, he said that he wanted to narrate one incidence about a history he took in his examination. He appeared in his final FFA in London that he passed with flying colors. It was a middle-aged man who was given to him as a long case to diagnose. Apart from his cockney accent, the man was cooperative. He said, "I asked him what the matter with him was?"

The patient started like this. "I have been smoking for as long as I can remember. In fact, I am a chain smoker. My doctor had warned me many times, but I paid no heed. I started having this nagging cough that I attributed to smoker's cough, but it persisted. I finally went and saw my doctor who examined me and after listening to my chest, sent me for an x-ray of the chest. Seeing the x-ray the doctor said, "Mr. Smith your x-ray shows a suspicious shadow, and I will like you to consult a chest surgeon." Giving me a letter, he sent me to a chest surgeon in the teaching hospital. Next morning, I went to the hospital. The surgeon looking at the x-ray said. "I don't like the look of this shadow in your lung Mr. Smith. I want to take out a small piece of this thing and would like to see it under a microscope." "He took me to Operation Theater and passed a thin tube down my throat and took out a piece." When the report arrived, he said, "I am afraid this report is not good; looks like we will have to operate on you Mr. Smith." Showing a long thoracotomy scar on his chest he said he had this operation about two months ago. Thumping his chest he said, "I feel fine now. Fit as a fiddle." Our training makes us envy such patients who would go straight for the point and to diagnosis.

All our surgery training is from the books that are written by either British or American authors and English is a language we adore. The patients we deal with however are not the same as described in English textbooks. There are cultural and socio-economic differences and their way of description of symptoms is poles apart from the way the European and American patients would describe their symptoms. 'Hakeems' (native doctors) are perhaps more at home with the language of our patients; we should perhaps take a leaf from their practice. People in different cultures are taught to think differently. How we gather information, process, rationalize, justify, and communicate our ideas is culturally determined.

Not all patients are alike. From some it is very difficult to extract the real problem. A very senior officer along with his wife and a young son brought his sweet eleven-year-old daughter for a problem with her right hand. She was born with a supernumerary finger that the parents now wanted removed as the girl felt embarrassed at the comments of her friends and would keep holding the two hands together to hide the offending digit. The officer seemed an important person as he had arrived with a lot of protocol and several telephone calls from senior officers preceded his arrival.

The problem was minor. I sent her for an x-ray of the hand. The staff officer brought back the x-ray that showed what everyone knew already, the extra digit. A date was set for the operation under general anesthesia. The officer being an intelligent person I took some time explaining the details. The parents were quite satisfied when they were leaving. The father of the child had stepped outside my clinic, and I called the next patient in when his wife again peeped in and asked me. "Doctor, while she is here would you have a look at her knee as well. She has a bump; I fear she may have fallen over." I looked at the knee of the girl and asked her about any fall. She had not fallen over. After having decided about the removal of the extra digit this consultation was more of a formality; and I was supposed to say, 'not to worry and that it will get better in due course.' I looked at the painless rather odd solid swelling close to the knee and was quite perplexed. Nevertheless, I sent her for another x-ray, now of the leg, feeling bit annoyed that this second trip to x-ray department could have been saved had the parents or the girl mentioned about the swelling earlier on. When the x-ray film arrived, I was stunned. The parents must have noticed drained blood from my face and came close to me. The girl had a deadly bone tumor that required an amputation of the leg.

The happy family almost in picnic spirits that had arrived for a cosmetic operation on the hand could not have in their wildest dream imagined what was going through my mind. How would they take this traumatic announcement? I ran short of words. How should I break the terrible news? To soften the impact and gain some time for the news to sink in I said I needed more tests to confirm the diagnosis. Unfortunately, my worst suspicions were proven right on biopsy and the girl had an amputation of the leg and also of the extra digit. Amputation for malignant tumors was safe treatment in our hands those days. With un-calibrated radiotherapy and chemotherapy, the poor patients used to be so miserable that they found the treatment worse than the disease.

The ambassador or some high up in the Pakistani embassy in Washington was a close relative of the father of the girl. He asked the officer to send all the papers of the girl for a second opinion from an orthopedic surgeon in Washington D.C. I wrote the detailed report and the patient's father brought back the opinion of the American surgeon. He blasted me for doing an amputation, instead of a local resection of the tumor. In the end he suggested to the parents to sue me!

Every time this girl catches even a minor cold, the distraught parents rush her back to me; fearing that the metastases from the tumor have spread. I keep wondering what would have been their mental state, had I not performed radical surgery.

The working conditions vary at different places and so do the surgical practices. What type of surgery should be carried out, on what sort of a patient and where, depends on: -

Who is the patient?

Who is the surgeon?

Where do they live?

Pragmatic management of the patient is based on practical considerations. The operations should be tailored to suit the needs, the pocket, the requirements, and the working conditions of the patient and the surgeon. The surgeon may be the best in the world, but he may have his hands tied because of local unhealthy conditions. By operating one may aggravate a condition the patient has been living with so far. Remember the first principle, primum non Nocera. First, do no harm to the patient. It is better to accept a workable mal union of a bone than, by unskilled operation give the patient a pleasing x-ray but a septic non-union. Our working conditions in the third world are quite different from those in the West. It is derisive that after an excursion trip to the clean Alpine airs of Davos— Switzerland, we start opening every fracture and fix with implants in the filth of our over-crowded filthy peripheral hospitals. The working facilities are a very important factor in decision making, particularly in orthopedic surgery. A fracture of femur would be treated differently in different places according to local considerations. If the patient were in a European hospital, one would deal with him quite differently than if he was in a field hospital. It is so alluring to open and fix all fractures with nuts and bolts. This temptation must be resisted in public hospitals where the hygienic conditions are atrocious. A surgeon must hold his hands and find an alternative method of treatment even at the expense of reducing himself from orthopedic surgeon to an orthopedic physician. A surgeon who cannot guarantee the sterile conditions of the surgical procedure must not open the fractures. An operation is culmination of decisions; of which three fourth is reaching the right conclusion and only one fourth is dexterity of the hands.

Several of our North American friends visit us annually and would like to impress us by their surgical prowess. But our local conditions of work are daunting. In fact, I keep taunting them that they are cowards, escapees from hard facts of life. They could not stand up to face the local challenges. Working in a set system is easy; we hardly have any.

I am everything for my patient, from a janitor to a consultant. I must make decisions according to local conditions. Decisions not only mine but quite often on behalf of the patient as well, like a father does for a child. This is why that until these highly experienced specialists understand the local mores; long forgotten, cannot succeed here and will always run back to their glass houses.

A highly experienced immigrant orthopedic surgeon visited home on talent exchange program from an Ivy League university. He was demonstrating how to replace a destroyed hip in an operation theater of a local teaching hospital, with a crowd of local surgeons gathered around him. Once he had fixed the hip component, he asked his local assistant for the other part of the joint. This would not fit the hip component. Unlike his armamentarium in North America where there is so much variety from which to pick and choose, here he had no choice. With the wound open people rushed to the market. He could not have waited whole day.

He cut a very sorry figure for no fault of his. The patient never walked again. The day he boarded the plane back home foul-smelling pus started leaking from the wound. No wonder they run back to their greener pastures. Our local conditions are far from the glass houses they are used to. The natives know their local conditions best. One would not have operated in that teaching hospital in a crowd, polluting and infecting the Operation Theater. Then since we know our limitations, we ensure that the two components fit before opening the patient. If a surgeon does an excellent job by replacing the hip joint and same night the patient dislocates it, due to poor postoperative care the blame will be on the surgeon. This, the foreign trained surgeons will not see it happen in USA.

In orthopedics in addition to anatomy and physiology; the principles of Engineering—architecture also play a very important role. The axis and alignment of a bone is vital. If it does not fall in the line of gravity, it can play havoc with adjacent joints. Without the knowledge of Anatomy or—-geography of the body, a surgeon is blindfolded and will only grope in the dark. Without this road map he won't know which way to travel and would get lost in a strange world. The entire physiology is based on just two elements, water, and oxygen. Both are distributed through blood and its channels, the numerous blood vessels, most abundant in live muscles. Pink contractile live muscle is a reservoir of oxygen. Whereas a live muscle is life, a dead muscle is dark death, which becomes a prolific plant for the growth of deadly bacteria that can be lethal.

A laborer with a diseased painful hip should be treated differently than an executive doing a desk job. A poor man, who can ill afford two square meals a day; it is cruel to even suggest an expensive arthroplasty, the cost of which he cannot afford especially when a simpler operation would serve his purpose. One can live with a malady but not with starvation. In orthopedic surgery implants are made for fractures: not the other way round. We are not here to promote any specific brand of implant of a specific company. Simpler and cheaper the implant, the better it is for the patient. If one screw will do two should not be used. If a joint can be repaired, never replace it with prosthesis.

Respect the native culture. It takes time to understand local conditions of the place you work in. No one knows Rome better than the Romans. Surgery is more than tailor's job and orthopedics, more than carpentry. Our working fabric has sensitivities. Each human being has different social and psychological make up. The hopes, the aspirations, the psychic built up of each patient are different. The scientific basics however are universal. Despite problems as surgeons our life is gratifying.

You do not have to be a great thinker in deciding which operation for whom. It just requires understanding of local socio-economic and psychosomatic conditions. For an Asian, the requirements are different for allowing him to kneel, bow and squat or what sort of toilets the patients use and so on. Treating physical ailments seems easy. I pity the poor psychiatrists, how on earth can they read a human mind when its depth is so unfathomable.

So, before surgery think hard; plan the treatment that caters for the patient's pocket, his living conditions, and your working conditions: -

What to do?

When to do it?

How to do it?

And most importantly,

What not, when not, and how not to do it.

Treatment in orthopedics is triaged. Patients with mild aches and pains require simple reassurance, pat on the back, pep talk; may be some analgesics. The sprains, strains and fractures after immobilization need physical therapy. The category needing surgery is small.

This is even more important in natural disasters and accidents. At the site of accident and at the site of a calamity like earthquake all you need to do is splint the fractures and dress the wounds, no heroic surgery. In the field hospitals and A & Es, resuscitate and assess with the help of investigations. It is in a proper hospital with well-equipped operation theatres that you should treat patients requiring open reductions. Closed methods remain the hallmark of a good orthopedic surgeon. I remember when a young hyperkinetic surgeon would be posted to a field hospital, the experienced commanding officers used to confiscate implants from the inventory of the theatre to stop his temptations of opening closed fractures. Infection in a bone is a lifelong misery. The golden principles are: -

Leave close fractures, closed. Open, all open fractures.

Opening all open fractures implies: -

Surgical toilet, flush off the muck and Debridement— remove all the dead tissues.

There are four tissues that need debridement: -

1. Skin.
2. Facia.
3. Muscles.
4. Bone.

A nursery rhyme we used to chant as students describes the procedure best:-

At the edge of the skin take a piece very thin
Of muscles much more till you see a fresh gore
And muscles contract at the least impact
Tenser the facia more you slash her
Only bits of the bone, pieces left quite alone.

And bury no implants in a compound fracture unless you are prepared to bury the limb.

In the English National Health Service where I was trained, we the residents were forced to change our jobs and the consultants every six months or so. These repeated dislocations inconvenient as these were, nevertheless, gave us the opportunity to work with many consultants. Each one has taught me something. One always learns from one's peers, their shortcomings, in fact much more from their failings than successes. From some I have learnt what to do and watching others what not and how not to do it. I feel that perhaps has been more instructive. When not to operate is more difficult a decision, when to hold your horses? For a surgeon the easiest thing is to operate because he has been trained to. For him it is more difficult—-to hold his hands and not to operate. To put his own mind at rest or just out of curiosity a surgeon might find it safe to cut open and confirm a malady that may get better on its own. The increased number of Caesarian sections is one case under review. The problem may lie in the obstetrician's mind than in the patient's belly. In medicine to do nothing at times is a good remedy; also known as masterly inactivity. Let nature take its course.

Parents of a young girl noticed something odd the way she walked but never took it serious enough to seek an orthopedic opinion till she was ten. The girl was regular in her school, took part in sports and was for all practical purposes leading a normal life. X-rays of her pelvis revealed she had congenital dislocation of both of her hips. The parents of the girl were alarmed.

They took her from one surgeon to another till they found their way to the most experienced surgeon in town who, as expected confirmed the need of urgent surgery. She was taken out of her school and was operated upon. The surgeon with lot of effort and a prolonged operation managed to put the hips back into sockets. He then encased her in a plaster cast chest to the toes. The girl spent next couple of months glued to bed encouraged by a pleasing X-ray picture that revealed both her hips now were normal. The parents heaved a sigh of relief. When the plaster cast was removed, she was stiff as a board. Extensive physiotherapy did not make the slightest difference. The parents consulted a number of other specialists, and the girl had a number of further surgeries but no movement returned in her earlier on mobile hips. When I saw her, she was stiff as a board. A sweet young girl in her early teens she could hardly walk and moved like a mermaid. There were no movements in either hip or she had difficulty even to clean herself. It was a pitiable sight and

I thought I was the right person to cure her—a Messiah.

I was young, upbeat, and enthusiastic and lots of thoughts crossed my mind about the previous surgeons. If you want to know something about a man— person behind the persona, there is no better time than when doctors are pronouncing judgments on their colleagues and previous surgeries. You can form an opinion about them from not only what they say about other doctors but also what they betray. In the hope of conciliating clients and competition of 'business,' the little character that is left in them is squeezed out. Some crude doctors even in front of the patients and their relatives would not mind letting loose a tirade criticizing the previous physicians harshly. Others would not say as much but will say it all with their body language. It is an unethical doctor who speaks ill about his colleagues. If the patient's next of kin join in the course, it is certain that the same relatives of the patient would be equally vocal, perhaps even more when another doctor will be consulted after the present consultation. It is naïve to believe that the window-shopping will stop at your window. Patients and their relatives are lay public, and it is our job to educate them; they need guidance, even in ethics.

It is strange that we praise our preceptors of the past, way out of proportion, yet will speak ill of our colleagues whom we know so well; it seems one has to be dead to earn favors.

Honesty remains the best policy; do not play to the gallery, you are not a conjurer but an honorable professional, watch your every word. It is an evil person who speaks ill of his colleague behind his back. Backbiting has been likened to eating rancid flesh being torn from the bones of your dead brother.

If you do not learn this lesson, your own blunders and failures will teach that to you in more humiliating ways in the not too distant a future. It is usually an inexperienced and insecure doctor who has not achieved much in life, who is most critical of his brethren. It is good practice that if you do not know the previous doctors say nothing about them. Try to be magnanimous. People ultimately find out the truth. But when giving an expert opinion one must be entirely professional—without any fear or favor.

I operated, the entire time remembering an old saying, 'fools rush in where angels fear to tread.' There was no hip joint; the pelvis and the femur had become one block of bone. I cut out the bone where the hip joint was supposed to be and created a space for a metallic hip joint and fixed the prosthesis. Post-operative X-rays were very pleasing, and the girl was delighted to regain movements in her hip. Sailing on a crest I was planning to operate on the other hip when the girl after a couple of months noticed her operated hip feeling bit stiff. When one cannot think of any bright idea one usually takes refuge by passing on the buck. I sent her for physiotherapy again. No help, rather her hip was progressively losing further movements. A look at her latest X-ray sank my heart. The metallic implant was gradually becoming entombed in new bone. Soon she lost all the movements in her hip and was back to square one.

The other day very worried parents brought their young bouncy daughter who had only a few symptoms, took active part in sports, with a pile of investigations and orthopedic opinions to the most experienced orthopedic surgeon in town; that was I, fully prepared for surgery. This congenital dislocation of both her hips was diagnosed ten years too late. Parents were aghast when I advised them to keep her as far away from orthopedic surgeons as possible, I have no right to convert this sweet girl into a mermaid, I thought.

17

The Surgeons

Like good, bad, and ugly, there are also three types of surgeons. It is a poor surgeon who while operating gets into trouble and then does not know how to come out of it. An average surgeon after creating a mess finds his way out. Good surgeon is the one who stays well away from trouble in the first place.

Good judgment comes from experience, but experience unfortunately is gained through poor judgments. This, one learns over the years the hard way: by your failures, bloody noses and hitting your head against the wall, time and time again. It takes a short time to learn as to how to operate, it takes much longer to learn when to operate and a lifetime to learn when not to. Wisdom does come after exhausting all the wrong routes. It is a smart surgeon who can learn from mistakes made by other surgeons.

The most important person in a hospital is the patient. His or her interests are supreme, and the aim of a surgeon is to cure the patient, without surgery if possible. Most patients get well without and some despite the surgery.

We should help nature repair the damage done rather than stand in its way and obstruct the healing process. If one does not know the difference between surgical intervention and surgical interference, surgery can be harmful. Our tissues can repair themselves, if left alone or may need only a little help. The human body is a wonderful machine. It is a symphony of sounds that if harmonious play a lovely melody and if out of tune only need a bit of tweaking of a string or two. Like natural re-forestation of charred mother earth, when after an ecological disaster left alone for a while, our body also is auto bio-remedial able and has a self-repairing mechanism. And bone and blood are the two tissues unlike the rest that replace themselves with exactly their own kind.

Surgery which basically is cutting and stitching consists of three steps: -

1. Approach. Getting there; reaching the trouble spot through a safe route.
2. Trouble shooting. Removing the miscreant or repairing the damage done.
3. Retreat. Closing.

I hate to recall the morbidity we have been inflicting due to collateral damage. For removal of a pea sized stone in the kidney we used to cut the patient into half by dividing and denervating all those dynamic and powerful abdominal muscles, which despite best of repairs were never the same again. Now with better instrumentations, cameras, and operative imagery the same operations can be performed through key holes in much lesser time and with minimal morbidity. Minimal invasive surgery minimizes the unnecessary collateral damage to the surrounding tissues.

Surgery and an operation should not be taken lightly. So many things can go wrong, and some complications can be lasting, some even fatal. The key principles are: -

1. Do not fix what is not broken.
2. If broken and it can be fixed without surgery, do not operate.
3. If operation is unavoidable, operate with minimal trauma and time.
4. If it can be repaired do not replace with an implant.

The decision to operate will become easy if the doctor remembers the aphorism, "to do unto others what he would like to be done to him," when to, and when not to operate and how much to do. Before elective surgery I must ask myself a question, "Will this patient do vastly better after surgery?" If the answer is yes, I must use all my faculties to ensure that he does. But if the answer is vague, think again. Rather than to invent new operations it is much better if you can prevent one.

Nature has provided us with covering materials, the mucous membrane, the epithelial linings, those that cover the brain, the lungs and heart, the gut, the bones, and the skin. These are major players in the healing process, gifts of nature to the surgeon. All surgical processes will come to a naught if there is a problem with healing of the tissues like when there is paucity of building material as happens in malnutrition or in immuno-compromised patients. The best the surgeons can do is approximate the tissues by stitching or in case of bones with plates and nails, but they cannot make tissues heal. The sutures, the screws after some time become redundant—once the tissues have healed or have failed to. If there is no healing, holding materials cannot stand the forces that prevent the tissues from break down. There will be incisional hernias and in case of bones, non-union and metal implants can break down under stress. This shows how much nature helps the surgeons. Surgeons can play havoc with human tissues and these coverings cover our sins.

It is best to perfect your craft at the beginning of the career rather than at the fag end. There should be style and grace even with the basics; even holding a knife that should not be held like a dagger or a pen. It should be held like a violin bow with the tips of the fingers. Even tying of the knots should show more finesse than your camping days while being a boy scout practicing reef knot. All the wrongs that you learn become part of your practice and last whole life. Economy of operative time, drugs and material is hallmark of a good surgeon. The speed while operating should be the achievement and not the aim of a surgeon. The surgical techniques one has practiced over the years should not be abandoned nor changed just because a patient is socially important or politically powerful; otherwise not only the surgeon, but the patient may also come to grief. Regardless of the clamor about ethics, surgeons can snitch, as much as anybody else when a celebrity is concerned.

Over the years one learns by one's mistakes and finally perfects operative techniques best suited for that place of work. This should not then be suddenly abandoned or even changed whosoever the patient. To be a VIP patient can be hazardous!

Once the chief justice had a medical condition for which he wanted to consult one of my teachers while I was his house surgeon. The surgeon had to interrupt his operating list to listen to the call and was irked when the secretary of the judge made him wait before the judge came on the line. "Can I see you ten o'clock tomorrow morning? The judge asked.

"Sir, are you seeking an appointment or giving me one?" The judge being good at reading people visualized the ruffled feathers and rephrased his statement. "I have this nagging pain in my belly and have been indisposed for a while. My superior, one of your old patients has strongly recommended me to seek your advice. When will it be convenient for you to see me?" After rather an uncomfortable pause the surgeon spoke, "I will see you ten o'clock tomorrow morning in my office." How much can you be pushed around or taken for granted is entirely up to you. You must draw a line, because no one can be insulted more than one is willing to take. Empathy cannot be ordered and, in our profession, it is most important that the doctor-patient relations are not flawed by a bureaucratic tinge.

By watching a surgeon operate you can predict the outcome of surgery. A surgeon, who loses planes or unnecessarily opens new ones, tears, and damages the tissues, is not a good surgeon. There should be no crushing, no pulling and tugging. A trauma surgeon need not be a traumatic or a neurosurgeon a nervous surgeon! The kindest instrument in the theater is the sharp knife. The best surgeons that I idolize are the ones who had respect for the human tissues and treated them gently and delicately, as if these were fragile. It is a treat to watch such surgeons operate like artists at work. Despite the tensions, the kick such surgeons get out of their work become their joy. No wonder they become workaholics. For them it is a pleasure and pride to operate.

I have found out another fact the hard way: a surgeon must know his anatomy like the back of his hand, otherwise he would get lost in a strange unknown territory. A good surgeon must also be a very good physiologist. What are known as healing hands must have done their homework in these subjects very scientifically. Even a genius' inspiration will not be of much use to him unless he has perspired long and hard to acquire the ability to recognize and interpret the problem correctly. Edison who said that 'genius is one percent inspiration and ninety-nine percent perspiration' was not making a philosophical statement but expressing a truth his experience had taught him. There is no short cut to success and no substitute for hard work. Once someone listening to an excellent, informal speech by the legendary British Prime Minister Sir Winston Churchill turned to the man sitting next to him and lauded Churchill's ability to extemporize. That man happened to be Churchill's son. He said he knew how extempore the speech was; his dad had worked for hours on that 'off the cuff' speech.

A model surgeon I hold in high esteem used to brag that, with clean instruments, washed with tap water alone—not sterilized, he could open and close a knee joint and guarantee absence of sepsis and that too without any antibiotics. Soil is perhaps as, if not more important than the seed. It is a poor-quality surgeon who after surgery has to resort to high quality drugs. The best surgeons are those who can cure complicated problems with simplest of procedures.

The surgeons scrub ritually before the operation and then raise their hands for the water to rinse from the elbows. Surgeons should grasp this occasion to spread their hands in a silent prayer before the operation, asking for prudence and wisdom to do what is best and save this patient from our inadequacies. Overconfidence, not humility kills. I can only care; it is He who cures. Being a human, I am fallible; my knowledge is limited.

In ablation surgery the principles of treatment are standard. A gall bladder if diseased will need to be removed. An appendix if gangrenous will be amputated. If tonsils or uterus has become a source of trouble instead of being a useful organ will be removed by cutting out. The technique and the steps are the same the world over. There may only be minor differences from place to place and from surgeon to surgeon. Not so in reconstructive surgery, where there is more than one method of dealing with the same malady depending on the expectations and requirements of the patient; and the realities on the ground.

Anatomy of internal organs is the same, so whether you remove a diseased gall bladder by an open operation or through a laparoscope, depends on where you practice. We are alike inside whatever the exterior, thank God. Having traveled widely and wildly and having worked with pitch blacks to absolute albinos; I can vouch for the fact that all people are the same. God has not discriminated, man has. So, whether you remove an appendix of a pauper or the president, the internal relations, in fact everything is alike. A surgeon's life would be very difficult had it been otherwise. In medicine, Anatomy alone would not fascinate you unless you corroborate it with physiology and the pathology. A famous pathologist who had performed numerous postmortems said. "I do not wonder as to why people die, what fascinates me, is how with organs so diseased and damaged they still go on living."

Reminds me of a conversation I had with my car mechanic. Every time I would go to pick up the car there would be further delays, as he needed further instructions. I got really irritated by his repeated queries and had to tell him off, "Look here young man, I repair human bodies every day, and I do not make so much fuss about the job as you are doing." "But sir," he said very respectfully, "you work on only two models." Used to classier conversation than I was having with my car mechanic, I found his cheeky remark irksome and retorted; "Ever tried replacing a spare part in a running engine?"

But we owe a lot to these technicians and engineers, who have contributed in many ways in improving our repertoire and implants by their clear thinking of problems that we face. Bioengineering now is a highly developed science. The job of a mechanic must be perfect, because once he is finished that is the end all. Look at the NASA Engineers how many times they have to delay their spacecrafts, because they cannot leave anything to chance. When I approximate tissues, the job is half done and then I look up to nature for help to do the rest. The ultimate healing is done by nature and my being a good craftsman is only some help, hence the sense of helplessness and humility. There are many unsung Viviens behind glamorous Blalocks.

The story of an ailing colleague who saw his doctor is instructive. Describing his consultation with his cardiologist he said, "We talked about my heart as if I was talking to a mechanic. That 'it', the 'pump' had a problem, a mal function, an error in its output and it needed fixing. The doctor exhibited no interest in me as a person, never made even a casual inquiry about my work, my family, or my interests in life during about half an hour of consultation. The only time he seemed to come alive during our conversation was when pointing to the mortality chart, he said, "Very interesting, there is an interesting rise in mortality in the month of December!" Describing how he would open my blocked coronary arteries by passing a wire through, clean the sludge and how he would keep them open with a stent did not seem to me much different and more refined than had I been listening to a plumber explaining how he would open choked drains of my bath! My worst fret is that Medicine alas will soon be reduced to a blue-collar job.

Medicine is a splendid blend of objectivity and subjectivity: -

1. Hard science: dealing with statistics; inanimate bone-dry facts and figures, algorithm, and generic profiles.

2. Compassion: sentiments and passions, dealing with people, their fears and hopes.

How short is the calling between the head and the heart? Our medical training instills a certain scientific objectivity—a distance from the heart. Science cannot comprehend emotions. But Medicine does not merely consist of dealing with pills, plasters, and injections; it involves the very fabric of life. Experiences of Medicine can only be felt, like falling in love. I may be well versed with the landscape of the brain but do not know how thoughts, memories, love, and hope are primed. Accomplishment of a physician is if he can dispense and instill Hope with healing. Falling ill is bad enough; losing hope of not getting well is worst; it is morbid, may even hasten demise. Medicine is a science imbued in emotions. The Science of mensuration has no Avoirdupois' scales so far to weigh emotions and to gauge Love and Hope. Surgeons know all parts of the brain, but not how and where memories and dreams are made.

Living in a culture that values efficiency and clear head, it is natural for us to want to avoid confusion of murky world of tears and emotions of our patients. Also, it is too emotionally wrenching to shuttle back and forth between detachment and involvement: between science and emotions like Dr Jekyll and Mr. Hyde.

Medical science is not science of life; it is only science of Medicine; deductions reached from observations, like Sherlock Holmes.

The qualities that are required to make a good scientist may in fact are poles apart from being a compassionate physician. As clinicians, we make use of many time-honored remedies that as scientific men we would find difficult to back up. Experience takes precedence over theory. Clinical process is fuzzy and imprecise. Science is organized knowledge but life, a lot more. Splendor of a surgeon is to combine in one person, the empathy with detachment; and make correct subtle clinical decisions with certainty.

Planning or pre-briefing is the most important part of executing a project. Before the surgery we consult books, journals and brush up on our anatomy, the surgical techniques and best of all discuss it with our team so that they are also prepared. One of the juniors is assigned to write down stepwise the salient steps in numerical order how we are going to proceed during surgery and then in operation theatre paste this paper on the wall and keep crossing the steps executed. This teaching will be indelible and of immense worth. Be ready to change plans if the situation on the ground so warrants. It is a good commander who at least in his mind has a plan for a retreat if the offensive turns sour. If you really want to excel, sit down again after the surgery with your team for a session of de-briefing with that paper in the hand and invite free criticism and ponder over the lacunae and the weaknesses and how things can be improved next time. The bright ideas from even the junior most member of the team will humble you. There is a difference between doing a right thing and doing it right. If you want your hands to be the proverbial healing hands then you should, make a right diagnosis, do the right operation, do it right and at the right time. In orthopedics the buzzword is 'right the first time,' which means someone with experience should perform the first operation when fully prepared and well-equipped. Otherwise, to rectify the wrongs done there will be, the misery of repeat operation, not one or two but sometimes many, unnecessary increase in morbidity, even mortality. This can make a difference between success and failure and sometimes between life and death. The other idyllic attributes of an ideal surgeon including a wizened head, nerves of steel, eagle's vision, lady's' delicate hands etc. are lyrical ways of highlighting the same qualities.

There are different types of surgeons, and they use different joints of the body depending upon the type of tissues they handle. For example, the eye specialists work with extreme finesse through operating microscopes. They use small joints of fingers to operate. The general surgeons operate at the wrist level. Orthopedic surgeons use hands, elbows, shoulders, even potbelly to support the patient; sometimes also the brain! The hammers and the drills, the oscillating noisy saw we use, it seems you are working in a workshop. Professor Kadri is an eye specialist and a close friend with whom sometimes I shared operating rooms. While he operates in a calm quiet operation theater with great precision, next door I am busy drilling holes in the bones with noisy machines. When he is not busy, he often walks into my clamorous operation theater to watch what I was doing. The contrast is stark compared to his serene surroundings. I would often make him an offer shouting through the din of clanging clutter of the machinery, "Do not hesitate to ask if I can lend you an instrument or two!"

The stereotypes of different surgeons are well recognized. The high achievers requiring minimal of affectations. The eye surgeons are polite, soft spoken, polished, and immaculately dressed. General surgeons are typically pictured as in "Doctor in the House." Like James Robertson Justice; Larger than life, rotund, extrovert and carefree, magnanimous, authoritative, and Lordly. Male gynecologists are basic. It is difficult to raise their sense of humor from pudendal level. ENT surgeons are opinionated, bit oily perhaps. Neurosurgeons are haughty and arrogant. Orthopedic surgeons, muscular and burly and are considered wee bit dim; nick-named orthopods.

What would be an ideal surgeon like? Tall dark and handsome, certainly we all would like to be, but then we do not control our genes, not yet anyway; A superman who single handedly performs deftly, death-defying feats? Is athletic and sporty; brilliant and furiously independent. Physical fitness for a surgeon is as important as his mental robustness. We do not want some sissy fainting and swooning over a crisis; when patient may find it necessary to cheer up the doctor, "Doc. you look after yourself, I will be all right." The optimistic demeanor, public posture and heroic mystique of a surgeon are a tower of strength that inspires confidence in his team and the masculine charisma is therapeutic in healing his patients.

Explicitly or implicitly, I cannot convince myself placing a woman in that position. I guess it must be the gender bias. While in England once I passed my FRCS examination and became a qualified surgeon my prefix changed from Dr. to Mr. The history of surgery is the history of armed conflicts and wars and I have not heard of a female military surgeon who has made a name in the field and desert conditions. So, this sensitivity is not male chauvinism alone. I would happily let ladies with their lady like hands practice obstetrics.

You cannot risk a person's life on wishy washy befuddled information, no floating in the fog; may be or maybe not, it can be and also it cannot be; is not a surgeon's lexicon. We are surgeons; we must know; we practice precision. When all the information has been presented and all aspects of the problem considered, it is the surgeon who must make the final decision. Surgery being on his mind all the time; his dreams and nightmares are all about patients. While scanning the whole canvass a surgeon must be unidirectional and focused, all his power drawn into one purpose, the good of his patient. A surgeon is immersed in a particular concrete situation with an actual patient before him. And based on pragmatic principles of many disciplines, he must reach a decision taking into consideration patient's psychological, cultural, and economic situation. He may not remember the details of everything that he had learned but he knows how and when to operate when time is ripe. After careful deliberation once the decision is made it is final and forceful and failure is not an option. There is no looking back now.

'It is better to open and see rather than wait and see.' The wait is killing for the surgeons. Blissfully, patience is one blessing; the surgeons are poorly endowed with. In matters of life and death there is no time for meditation, there is only time to do or, let die. We surgeons have a special prayer, "God give me patience, but please hurry up!"

Even under intense pressure the surgeon should be capable of making correct decisions and not shoot from the hip and create the space to work in relaxed environment in his own arena. Capacity to make continuous correct decisions under stress is woven in the warp of our professional lives. When life is hanging on a thread, the surgeon must be quick; a go-getter and result orientated. He cannot afford to just go through motions while life hangs in balance. "I saw the problem, went for it and I fixed it."

Like a commander the surgeon bears the burden of his decisions alone and the practice of surgery at times is a very lonely affair. Surgeons are known to be aloof and believe me it is dreadfully lonesome up there, only heavens above. Fire that animates them carries them to seek their own flight orbit.

The scenario, the utter submission with which the patient has laid his body before you are overwhelming and humbling; here even angels fear to tread. It is almost divine. The trust of the patient is blind and the frontiers inviolate to all except those blest, to whom medical profession gives a certain power, a surge of spiritual energy. There must be something sublime that a dignified person who cannot kill even a fly picks up the audacity to stick a knife in the flesh of a fellow human being. It has got to be an awesome experience.

While making vital lifesaving decisions, saving his hide is the last thing on a surgeon's mind. Surgeons have to take risks of active intervention and bear responsibility for errors of commission. Not surprisingly it is the surgeons who face most lawsuits, because they cannot practice defensive medicine. For sticking their necks out, they must pay a high price, the high premiums as well as high incidence of stress related diseases.

But behind that exterior, the tower of strength, style and swagger, the macho attitude and the traditional surgeon's arrogance is a terrified man with shaky legs. He finds himself very small when he stands before nature. Any complication can melt this cold steel into wax. And a believer or not, he finds solace by bowing before an invisible force with a silent prayer for his patient. The impervious, mechanical, and unsentimental face of a surgeon is a Hollywood prop like the cardboard front of cowboy's dwellings in the studio of a Western movie, where the frontage of the house is only a facade.

Becoming a surgeon is an on-job training; the peers hold hands of the protégée while he struggles to crawl and stand like a toddler. How much a cow will suckle depends on how much the calf wants to suck. Surgery is a passion and passion cannot be taught; it can only be caught.

Only those surgical apprentices are chosen who fit into traditional image of a surgeon; dynamic, confidant, penchant for action and flare of optimistic demeanor. Knowledge alone is not the only criterion. Willingness to engage in sustained training, quality of decisiveness, tenacity, and force of will are precondition to success Minions with little experience are selected and then through decades of hard work, they gradually metamorphose into first-rate surgeons. Practice, not talent makes a surgeon perfect. Skills can be taught, not the tenacity. Whenever I appeared for an interview for selection before different medical boards for the post of a surgeon, nobody ever asked me as to how many books on surgery I had read. No one measured my hands, tested their dexterity, or checked how nimble and steady my fingers were. The interviewers would converse with me pleasantly about innocuous topics, but the real motive was assessment of my resolve and it used to be a battle of nerves. They would look straight into my eyes and waited, who blinked first. Your eyes show the strength of your soul.

Tenacity and maturity come later, much later; with palpitations, with sweat, blood, and tears; burning midnight oil alone during sleeplessness nights. It comes after hitting your head against the wall, again and again, year after year; many, many years later.

"A surgeon does not slip from his mother's womb with compassion smeared upon him like the drippings of his birth. It is much later that

it comes.

No easy shaft of grace this, but the cumulative murmuring of the numberless wounds he has dressed, the incisions he has made, all the sores and ulcers and cavities he has touched in order to heal. In the beginning it is barely audible, a whisper, as from many mouths. Slowly it gathers, rising from the streaming flesh until, at last it is a pure calling."

Mortal Lessons

After my FRCS examination, lasting whole day of viva voce, grilling and uncomfortable, even painful interviews before dozens of silvery-headed professors; the result was announced publicly in a hall before the crowd of expectant, tense, and fretful candidates in just one line. "Following candidates have satisfied the examiners." Out of the scores who failed and quietly left the hall, head bowed in a melancholy silence; we a group of lucky five, were later invited and ushered into the president's chamber. I can never forget what he said. Waving the result card in the air with one hand, which he snatched from one of the now qualified FRCS surgeons, he addressed the startled, ecstatic 'surgeons' with visible contempt. "This piece of paper does not and cannot make you a surgeon. You did not have this paper in your hands an hour ago.

What has happened to you since?" Then without waiting he answered the question himself. "Nothing." This piece of paper is only an entry pass to let you in an arena full of heavy weights, top class wrestlers, world class athletes and towering Olympians. If you, who are just toddlers in the profession want to be like them, you must pass through from first to last, same rigors, apprenticeship, intensive training, toil, and hard work that they have endured. Just by holding this paper in your hand you cannot possess same strength, speed or agility and call yourself a surgeon."

Expecting congratulatory ovations, warm handshakes, pats on the backs and free flow of champagne, the occasion turned out to be a rude shock. I came out of the college edifice so flabbergasted that I had difficulty walking steady in a straight line. My head twirled faster than the revolving door through which I left the college atrium and out into freezing rain and cold winter night.

But this was not the first occasion I had passed through that revolving glass paneled door. Earlier on, during my first attempt when I appeared in FRCS, I failed. Since I had already told my parents that I was appearing in the examination, the news of my failure struck them like a blast from North Pole. There was mourning for quite a few days at my home in my native country as if someone had died. The mourning was not only for the failure in examination but was for more; that I must have gone astray in the foreign land. How else they thought it was possible that their son could ever fail in any examination?

The reason I was so confident that I would pass my fellowship was that I was a member of a professorial team in a teaching rotation in Bristol Royal Infirmary (BRI) where we were grilled day in and day out along with the medical students which had polished our concepts. There were only two Pakistanis in BRI. The other one was a brilliant student, Dr. Shah a class junior to me in the medical school. He was extraordinary. Not only ruggedly handsome and well mannered, but he was also a very brilliant student. He was the best graduate of his class. In Part I fellowship examination of the Royal college of Surgeons the world over, he had stood first and had earned a coveted distinction, Hallet prize. The two of us used to spend most of the time together discussing, reading, and quizzing each other about our surgical problems. The nurses and other female staff were at times concerned about our social behavior. The only parties we attended were the black-tie official dinners of BRI. Otherwise, we were all the time either working or were immersed in studies. Examination for us was a matter of life and death. Our greatest entertainment used to be Sunday night dinner in an Indian Restaurant and here too when served roast leg or a joint we used to go back to our anatomy. We never visited any pub or went to parties; all we did was study and quizzed each other in our spare time. Some of our teachers in the hospital were also examiners in the fellowship and their grilling had sharpened and polished our repertoire. So, we were very confident and all set for the examination.

The written paper of Part II examination consisted of just two questions. I knew the answers backwards; I therefore qualified the examination without a hitch. The real test however was the viva and interviews before a board of examiners. It used to last whole day. There were a couple of examiners on each table with pickled human specimen in the jars before them and numerous X rays. The two examiners, one at a time would grill the candidate till exhaustion and there was no way anyone unprepared could get through. There were four stations with two middle aged or very aged examiners waiting their turn to skin the candidates alive.

I started my day at first station with two examiners who seemed neutral and had the attitude that if I wanted to pass, they would let me and if I did not want to, only I will kick the chair under my feet and hang myself. None of them seemed too keen to help. With the first pair I did well. Thanks to my training at BRI, I knew how to answer most of the questions. Station two, again the X-rays and the specimen seemed familiar, and it looked I had seen them before, and I comfortably cruised to the third station. Very happy with my surgical prowess, it gave me pleasure to impress the examiners as I could answer them without any hesitation. Third station again was a walk-through. I managed to diagnose all specimens and knew answers to their questions. I was flying on a pink cloud and felt very pleased when one of the examiners instead of calling me Dr. Cheema called me Mr. Cheema, a sure indication that I was about to join that elite class. With lot of confidence and enthusiasm I went to the last station; the only hurdle left before my elevation as a fully qualified surgeon. There were two examiners, one a middle-aged surgeon and the other rather a stern looking elderly gentleman. This station was about operative surgery. The younger examiner started asking me different surgical procedures and I was so well prepared that I answered some of his questions even before he could finish. The other dour looking surgeon watched me with bored interest and kept quiet. Once the first examiner had finished, he passed me over to his colleague. I, in the meantime was feeling on top of the world that I had virtually sailed through the examination.

The examiner, the older surgeon asked me how you do a cholecystectomy— remove the gall bladder. I had assisted and performed this operation so many times that it looked a piece of cake, and I blurted out all the steps. I virtually leapt in the air. He then asked me about possible complications of the procedure. I started with injury to the common bile duct and to put some life in the proceedings, I illustrated my point with a famous name; the British prime minister who recently had cholecystectomy done. Confident of having done so well in professional matters, I thought of extolling my grasp on current affairs—the Anglo-American relations. I was hoping perhaps this may bring a faint smile on his stern face. I said, “In America, they call it as English disease.” As I expanded the dour demeanor deepened and the face of examiner went sterner. Anthony Eden had his gall bladder removed in London. His common bile duct was injured during the operation, and he had to go to America for its repair. A dark, almost painful shadow crossed his face but surprisingly a broad smile came on the face of the younger surgeon who with sparkling eyes now started showing keen interest in what I was saying, almost egging me to go on. Noticing the older surgeon’s dirty looks, he made desperate but unsuccessful attempt to hide his grin. I noted that instead of pleasing the examiner, my spontaneity had quite the opposite effect on him. Excited, with my heart thumping and sweaty palms I galloped on. My youthful exuberance, my jack in the box response to his questions did not seem to please him. A side glance at the younger examiner revealed a jubilant man, I did not understand why.

“When did you pass your MBBS examination doctor?” He suddenly interrupted my flow stressing on the word, doctor after a small pause. I told him the date. “Just over three years,” he muttered to himself; “and the Part I of fellowship?” Again, I told him the date. “Hardly a year!” He exclaimed. “How many surgical rotations have you done in England?”

"Three." I answered. Nothing seemed to his liking; infarct everything I said seemed to annoy him. "All right doctor, what are the indications of exploring the common bile duct?" He asked. I blurted out the five indications in one breath. He was not exhilarated at my speed. But since I had answered all his questions correctly, I did not take much notice of his sadistic attitude. He now seemed stuck and wanted to ask me something I would not be able to answer. "At the table doctor, when you have opened the common bile duct how do you differentiate between a spasm and a stricture?" I replied that the preoperative radiography would have given me ample clues even before the surgery. He insisted again, "on the table, doctor." I said, "The relaxants given by the anesthetist should have taken care of the spasm." "What if these have not? He asked. "I will pass a probe down the common bile duct and in case of stricture the feel of stricture would be gritty while the spasm would give me a feeling of clasping the probe." I explained. Not satisfied he now looked for my Achilles heel and dragged me in blind alleys. Seeing my helplessness for the first time brought a glimmer of glint in his eyes. Rather pleased with himself, he commented, "Obviously doctor, you have not done much surgery yet." That seemed to me like a death knell, and I now knew the end was not far. "Thank you, doctor." Saying that he dismissed me, and I knew what that thank you meant. Crest fallen I limped out of the room knowing full well my fate.

I later found out that this surgeon was an authority on biliary surgery and had performed the operation on Anthony Eden.

When the result was announced I was not surprised when my roll number was passed over and with my head bowed on my chest and a heavy heart I left through the revolving door.

A few days later when I opened the official envelope in Bristol, I knew already that I had failed in operative surgery. I broke down, failing only in operative surgery on that one silly question and failing for the first time in my life. I felt sorry for how much shame and sorrow it would bring to my dear ones back home and I made a vow that next time I appear in the examination I am not going to let anyone know; like the local boys who took the event so lightly; it was just an examination.

Formal education does not cease with the attainment of a single certificate or a degree. On-going training and lifelong commitment— to new learning are essential in the daring world of science. It is with time, effort, and hard work; pondering over difficult problems and attending very sick patients alone in the dead of the nights that you slowly, painfully clothe the bare bones of your theoretical knowledge with flesh of practical experience, bit-by-bit, fiber-by-fiber and sinew by sinew.

I can remember the night many years earlier in my medical school when after passing our first professional examination we, now the proud and thrilled 3rd year students celebrated the event by dancing around a bonfire lit by Grays' anatomy and other lead heavy medical books in the lawns of our hostel. Little did we realize then that these books were the very foundation on which our entire career would later be built.

I can also recall the ecstasy of an illiterate village woman who greeted her son, a fresh recruit in the army who was visiting home on his first leave from the military academy. The boy only a weakling when he went for training, returned with hair cropped short, skin tanned and bulging muscles filling his well starched uniform. She glanced at her handsome son with maternal pride and asked him proudly over dinner; "Son, there must not be any bigger officer than you in the army now?"

Learning is a lifelong process. More than half of my surgical work I practice today I had not learnt during my FRCS. Learning new skills is a continuous practice, and learning as you age, requires extra effort. It becomes increasingly difficult to teach new tricks to an old dog.

A surgeon friend once invited Barbara Hepworth, the famous English sculptor to his operation theatre. Her daughter was admitted to hospital for surgery. Her comments summarize it all. Recalling the invitation, Hepworth said, "When the suggestion was made to me that

I might watch an operation in hospital, I expected that I should dislike it. But from the moment I entered the operation theatre I became completely absorbed by two things: first, the extraordinary beauty of purpose and coordination between human beings all dedicated to the saving of life, and the way that a unity of idea and purpose dictated a perfection of concentration, movement and gesture; and secondly by the way this special grace of mind and body induced a spontaneous space composition, an articulated and animated kind of abstract sculpture very close to what I had been seeking in my own work." A surgical team is a dedicated group of highly trained individuals who come together for a specific and a hazardous task requiring the utmost in-group interaction and the interplay of shared responsibilities; even without a word being spoken.

An operation is an extreme exercise in trust. While the patient has reposed his trust in a surgeon; the surgeon is putting his trust in the organization; the hospital where he works, the system by which the group has been assembled and all the people, bearing even distant and peripheral responsibilities for the success of the surgery. This is a tall order, since supervising all these men and women by remote control call for highest qualities of leadership. These people may not be visible, whose duties are performed far away from the operation theatre; like the ones who sterilize or maintain equipment, prepare the instruments, or recruit the team of doctors, nurses, and the paramedics. Any lapse anywhere can result in a disaster. Surgeon is an engine; the others are wagons on wheels and even a loose nut can shatter a wheel and a broken wheel can stop the entire train. A masterpiece of a surgeon can be wrecked by just one slip down the line.

The surgeon is the captain of the ship and ultimately the buck stops at his doorstep.

In the actions of operating theatre team Hepworth saw, "amidst the scurrying movement of modern life, the conscious and articulated desire to achieve a common goal could produce movements of extraordinary beauty of purpose and coordination between human beings."

I do not think any person can appreciate the beauty of purpose in the working in the operation theatre or the harmony of machine and man, unless he or she is really involved. Watching the operation she commented, "The figure of the surgeon pointed out a way towards resolution of a conflict between beauty and hard work, between life and mechanism."

We consider operation theaters revered: like the places of worship. To keep them pristine we ourselves do not and let no one else enter with shoes on or in street clothes. Only surgeons can appreciate how difficult it is when infection converts a super technical result into a disaster.

We venerate going through rituals of ablution before entering theatres. We go to great lengths and would do anything to restrict unnecessary traffic in the theatres; even at the cost of annoying quite a few, even close friends, and superiors. We jealously and zealously guard its cleanliness, sterility, and privacy. More martinet and scary a theater sister is, cleaner the theatres are. My experience over the years has found the right person for this job: a daunting middle-aged spinster who would snipe at anyone that comes her way. Theatres are no public places, meeting points or rendezvous. Entry should be restricted as for a high security zone and its secrecy closely guarded.

Surgeons however never were as glamorous as today. They started from rather humble beginnings and were known as barbers, wound healers, and bone setters. For last few centuries, physicians carried more prestige and were considered gentlemen and aristocrats. Better hygiene, Lister's discovery and safe anesthesia, advances in every related field; physics, chemistry, in fact everything applicable in the world today has made surgery what it is today. But looks like the heydays of surgeons are over and they are going to fall from their high pedestal. Cyber surgery is reducing their God like image to the level of technicians, because of robotic touch button technology. I feel soon that would also help obliterate the gender gap. With better imagery, MRI and Robotics, surgeons will be doing just another job and they would no more be the awe-inspiring heroes. With monotony of the mundane the machines will take over our work and we will feel redundant.

In medical field one falls into one of the two categories: generalists or specialists. Generalist is the one who knows less and less about more and more till he knows nothing about everything. The specialist is the one who knows more and more about less and less till he knows everything about nothing. Yet the specialists, who want to further insulate into a cocoon, complain that they are being asked to learn about other fields, which they do not need in their daily lives and their teaching should be restricted to their own specialty. Some eye specialists who themselves suffer tube vision, say that they should specialize in only one branch of eye surgery like cataract or Retina, and it is no use learning about other subjects like anatomy of the brain. In fact, WHO has been toying with this idea and a proposal is afloat that the cataract surgery, Phacoemulsification which is entirely machine dependent may be performed by a technician who is more conversant with the machine rather than a doctor who knows little about it and the principles of the physics involved in its functioning. I am sure the ophthalmologists will not be too pleased. The story of ten blind men who were asked to describe an elephant and each one described the animal by the part of elephant's anatomy that he held in his hand, is well known. We specialists soon would be those blind men.

When I qualified as a surgeon nearly half a century ago, orthopedic like cardiac surgery was not as highly advanced. There were no scopes, cameras and endoscopic operative procedures or replacement of the joints in orthopedics. Infection was a curse we were dead scared of, and we used to be very conservative. In cardiac surgery the heart lung machine was under study. Patients, usually children with congenital heart deformities used to be immersed in freezing ice to slow down their metabolism and stop the heart. This used to buy a few minutes to quickly correct congenital defects before thawing the patient back to life. Surgeons used to be in a terrible rush, and it was a hit and run affair.

The mortality used to be atrocious and very depressing indeed and the surgeon after the death did not have the heart to face the parents and would sneak out of theatre through the back door, leaving the damage control to his assistants. Now the machines have revolutionized cardiac surgery which has become like a conveyor belt system plant. Cardiac surgeons can perform up to half a dozen bypass operations a day.

A cardiac assistant described how mechanical the surgery had become despite working with a glamorous surgeon. "Cardiologist does all the scut work and presents us the patients for surgery. First full exposure of the patient to the surgeon usually is on the workbench in an operation theatre where we, the assistants before the arrival of the great man would have harvested the vein grafts and opened the chest. CABG surgery now has become a monotonous routine," he said.

1. Split the chest.
2. Stop the heart.
3. Reroute the plumbing.
4. Bypass the choked arteries.
5. Close the chest.

The surgeon would usually leave the operation theatre long before his assistant start closing the chest and would not be seen again. The patient may catch a glimpse of him after a couple of weeks in the outpatient department or not at all!

The post operative care is left to the junior doctors and the nurses; as the principles are simple: "If the blood pressure falls start Dopamine. If the pulmonary pressure falls, start Saline and if it rises give Lasix. That is all to it." He spoke.

How would a patient come off the respirator? "It is simple, we prod the patient and if he stirs, he is ready to be taken off the machine!" he said. Once awake the same cardiologist again would look after the patient for rest of his life.

Since cardiologists had been doing all the work up and the follow up, it was inevitable that one day they would contemplate opening blocked coronary arteries themselves. With excellent equipment now available they under direct vision can now do the job very well, even better; taking over lion's share from the surgeons; like the story of camel and the tent, one freezing night in an Arabian desert. User friendly machines and minimally invasive procedures have come to the rescue of the patients, who now are spared all those macabre procedures. It was a sad day when the cardiac surgeons let physicians' fiddle with Seldinger needle and tinker with coronary arteries! Now they find themselves redundant, are at the mercy of cardiologists for work and are going out of business.

18

Why Do People Complain Against Doctors?

They do so simply because they are not satisfied; there is a mismatch between patient's expectations and what is delivered by the doctors. Patient's dissatisfaction stems from their perception that we have not come up to their aspirations. Most complaints however emanate from poverty of communication and indifferent attitude of the treating staff. If the patient and his relatives are kept on board and explained the proceedings; people understand. In the management of the patients our attitude and communications skills are as important as the medical and surgical expertise. We need to develop a talent for effective communication that should adapt to every individual in the language he or she understands; condescending from our lofty ivory towers and descend to the level of the patient. We should seek to understand patient's story in the context of the patient's beliefs, family, and social and cultural values. I strongly believe that each one of us must be a bit of a psychologist/psychoanalyst before being a specialist in one's field. We must read the patients' mind (as he reads ours) as we go along. It is the worried mind of a person that brings a diseased gall bladder or a lump in the breast to a doctor. It is therefore imperative to allay the patient's anxiety while treating the malady. Care while we endeavor to cure. Do not think big; think small and act small. While an orthopedic surgeon is thinking months ahead as to how the patient after healing of a fracture is going to run a marathon, the patient is worried most what is happening now like discomfort and pain.

Patients have only a few minutes with a doctor who should put them at ease as quickly as possible even at the risk of appearing prying and nosy; rather than waste too much time on pleasantries, platitudes and standing on ceremonies. Illness is a terrifying experience—and people do not know how to deal with it. More than cure they are reaching out for Hope. Because of their limited medical knowledge, patients who need to undergo surgery are scared and indeed scared to death. A physician must develop a good rapport with the family and must allay their anxiety. The sure sign of a patient being at ease is if we can work a smile on his or her face despite being in pain. Infusing confidence remains a skill. It is most important to pull the patient out of his gloomy world of disease, darkness, loneliness, hopelessness, and helplessness and steer him to the dazzling world outside, where the sky is blue and the day so beautiful and what a wonderful world it is where it is good to be alive.

Remember the moment you touch your patient you give the impression that you have already begun to heal him; certainly, patient takes it that way. A warm smile, an outstretched hand, a pat on the back, perhaps a hug is valued well above the offerings of modern sciences. It is an article of faith that there is a nexus between healing and state of the mind. It comes with communication, communication not only between doctor and the patient, communication between doctor and their relatives, between doctors and doctors and between doctors and wider public. Our teaching obligations should not be reserved for medical students alone; we must educate everyone we work with; nurses, paramedics, patients and their dear ones. That is the difference between science and humanities.

We should have an impact on the patient as to how we aim to heal him. A crisp sense of humor is a gift. There are not very many secrets between a physician and a patient. A wry comment about an obese woman to share some of her rations with a toothpick like husband will quickly annul an alien situation. Or advise to a person who has arrived for the treatment of a painful stiff back, "Your body is trying to tell you something, do not bend before anyone in life." How much liberty you can take depends on where you are working, as the geography of thinking and behavior stems from different cultures? East is East and West is West. It is best to stay formal and purely professional if you are not sure of yourself, are not at the same wavelength or are meeting the patient and his family for the first time. One must use all the skills of good salesmanship but if you have the slightest doubt that with any snooping remarks you may muddle an already gloomy situation, stay shut.

In America it was headline news that an obese lady dragged a doctor to the court for his polite advice to get rid of some extra luggage that would be injurious to her health and may decrease her longevity. She felt offended for just being labeled fat, whereas we in the subcontinent can get away even with a quite a few rags.

A disgustingly fat middle-aged man with a pot belly and thick bushy beard came to see me complaining of pain in his knees I asked him to stand on the weighing scales. The needle moved as far as the scales would let it—-200 kilos.

I started a sermon on the disadvantages of carrying so much dead weight, enumerating different obesity related diseases that he was likely to suffer from in the future: but to no avail. I gave him an example, that a mini car cannot pull a truck however hard it may try, still no effect. Thinking that fat perhaps had also infiltrated his brain, I was blunt and told him that God did not design human knees to carry an elephant.

But soon I felt sorry for my unkind remark and to soften it I said that if I carry a sack of potatoes weighing fifty kilos on my back the whole day my knees would also ache. Still no signs of guilt or remorse!

In the hospital I work in, we have arrangements for our congregational prayers in front of my office. The time for prayers arrived and since he looked a religious man. I invited him to come and join us in prayers. He seemed pleased and we prayed together. During the prayers I was dismayed to see his attitude; complete lack of interest in what he was doing. Most of the time he was either yawning or kept scratching his beard and did not seem serious in the sanctity of the prayers, He just went through the motions. Then we came back in my clinic to continue the consultation. The man was now full of beans and in a very patronizing tone said, "Doctor, you look to be a good Muslim, why don't' you grow a beard?" Connection between Hirsutism, music and religion has always baffled me. I took some time for this advice to sink in and then asked, "Why?" "Your profile will look more like that of holy prophet," he answered, kissing his knuckles a couple of times as a mark of respect for the name of the prophet "Don't we work all our lives to emulate him?" He asked. I looked at his ugly potbelly and thought of playing a dirty trick on him. "Right," I said, "let us make a deal. I will grow a beard to improve my profile on one condition; that you also do the same." Very pleased at my rapid conversion he asked me enthusiastically what he should do. I said, "Your profile looks like that of holy prophet above the neck I want your middle section also like his. Remember the holy prophet did not have even an ounce of fat on him." Growing beard, I thought did not entail much of an effort, I will not shave for a couple of weeks; but this man will have to kill himself to lose that extra luggage.

I have not seen him since!

I am sure no sane doctor can afford such consultation in the West!

I was very politely trying to ask a smoker patient to quit smoking. I warned him," Mr. Smith, smoking is a slow killer." "That is OK with me doctor," replied the patient, "I am also in no great hurry!

How do people give up smoking? Not on the advice of the doctors.

The doctor's advice does not cut much ice and they continue smoking. People never learn anything by being told, they must find out for themselves.

An old man was playing with his three years old grandson who said, "Grandpa, I want to grow up into a big man like you." And the grand dad said OK you put on my hat, and you will look big. After the child had done that, he asked his granddad to put his glasses also on the boy's face. The grandfather obliged and asked him now what? The child said, "Put also your cigarette in my mouth."

While in the army, either because of rank structure, strict military discipline or blind faith in their superiors, some soldiers used to astound me. A soldier when brought to a military hospital with severe abdominal pain would be taken to operation theatre and operated upon. After convalescence on discharge, despite a foot long scar on his abdomen extending from pit of stomach to his pubes; he would not even bother to ask what was done to him!

Our job in the Third world is easy, in the West due to access to medical knowledge and the Internet, patients are loaded with information on the malady they suffer from, and the doctors have to go an extra mile to remain current and to satisfy an informed public. There the source of danger is not ignorance but knowledge; but information without perception is a higher level of ignorance. Patients may be flooded with information but without an appropriate insight.

In the Medical school we were taught, and we continue to teach our students diseases in an abstract manner; isolated and cut off from live human beings who have fears, hopes and emotions. We consider relatives of the patients only a nuisance who unnecessarily meddle in the management of the patient. Whereas medicine is deeply involved in social organization of our life, if there is a meaning in the phrase "doctor- patient relationship." This implies the recognition of a patient as a social being who lives in a network of relations and not in the mere chance isolation of sickness. We need to connect intimately to the life around him. To a large extent the course of healing in any individual also depends on what takes place in the mind.

What is spoken of, as a 'clinical picture' is not just a photograph of a man sick in bed; it is an impressionistic painting of the patient in his home in front of a warm fire with glowing logs of wood in the hearth, surrounded by his family and friends or place of his work; his joys, sorrows, hopes and fears. At the end of a consultation, patients and their loved ones must feel that they have been heard and understood and their self-esteem ought to and appear to be enhanced. Patients should be awed by our presence, with the charisma of our person, depth of our knowledge, compassion of a noble being. The consultation should become an occasion, indeed an event to remember for rest of the patient's life. Even without words, their body language should beam that they have met a compassionate and a competent doctor, in whom they can repose full confidence where the health nay their lives would be in safe hands. "Cure occasionally, Heal sometimes but Comfort always."

But in the end, it is our professional knowledge and experience that will deliver. Public relationship being confidence builders alone cannot bail us out. One may get away with bad behavior and good treatment, but not with bad behavior and bad treatment. Many patients could sue a doctor because of a bad outcome but don't because they have a good relationship with him.

Technical competence cannot be compromised. The hype created by the media and the web due to the glorification of medical miracles has set people's expectations very high.

Professional negligence is a serious business and genuine complaints must be handled with extreme care.

A young, over-enthusiastic and semi-employed surgeon can be a dangerous man, for he may become knife-happy, like the trigger-happy villain of the Hollywood Westerns. To show his prowess he may cut open anyone that comes his way. To keep his skills and scalpels sharp he would resort to doing unnecessary surgery like removing normal appendices or tonsils and operating on un-displaced fractures. He belongs to the 'AO' set—-always operate. Senior surgeons will be failing in their duty if they do not keep an eye over such juvenile delinquents and hold their hands when patient could get better without surgery.

A fully employed 'commercial' surgeon can be an equally dangerous menace. Unfortunately, unethical practices have crept in surgery. Once a physician and a surgeon were examining a patient jointly, trying to figure out a diagnosis of a rather baffling case. They had not arrived at any definite conclusion when they left. That night the physician could not sleep: the sense of curiosity kept him awake, as he raked his brain to reach a definite diagnosis; but as he left his bed early in the morning, he was as far from identifying the cause of trouble as he was the night before. So, the first thing he thought of that morning when he reached hospital was to go and re-examine the patient. To his surprise he found out that the patient had already been operated upon. For his own education about the previous night, he asked the surgeon who had also arrived there. "What did you operate the patient for?" "Five thousand dollars," answered the surgeon coolly. Feeling a bit embarrassed the physician who was interested only in operative findings thought he was perhaps misunderstood. He rephrased his question, "I did not mean that, I wanted to know what he had?" "Five thousand dollars," repeated the surgeon nonchalantly.

Morbidity and mortality can occur at four levels and in that order: -

1. Post operative period.
2. Preoperative period.

3. During Anesthesia.
4. During Surgery.

Essentially the problem is either with the: -

1. Diagnosis
2. Technique or
3. Judgment.

Taking a good history is essential in diagnosis of a disease. The questions put to the patient should be open ended where instead of answering just in monosyllables like no and yes, he or she would have to explain. Keep adding the continuers, so that the patients get the feeling that you are interested in his or her describing the symptoms. Spicing with elaborators will further help develop a rapport with the patient. Armed with the understanding of patient's psychosocial-economic strata and the understanding so developed we can now size up each other. Clinical medicine is much more than heuristics where 2 when added to 2 make 4. We unfortunately are in such a hurry that we have already made a diagnosis at the door before the patient even steps in the clinic.

The physical contact and the intimacy shared during physical examination will further strengthen the bonds between the doctor and the patient. A warm handshake on arrival, a captivating smile, may be a hug later will soothe the ruffled feathers of a frightened patient, who with pseudo-knowledge from internet is trying to take control of his robbed health. It is empathy that the bewildered, brash, and difficult patient is pinning for. Inspiring confidence in a patient remains a gift. Despite the media hype, the world of medicine and the hospitals for a common man remain forbidding, foreign, almost mysterious institutions with strange powers, distant and out of his reach.

Scenario that any physician dreads most is, to appear before an inquiry committee or a court. If the patient or his dear ones are not involved, even a minor mishap can have a snowballing effect and there are bound to be serious repercussions. Only one unsatisfied irate patient is enough to mar an otherwise brilliant professional career. It is no consolation to the orphaned children or a widow; that your other 99 patients got well. In death or damage to children medical insurance companies usually do not stand much chance and would like to pay compensations avoiding any lengthy trials. No logic can stand before tears. Surgery may be a routine for you, it is not for the next of kin and dear ones, who sit outside the theatre, worry, and pray till the operation is over. Patient must never feel like a pack of lumber staked outside a sawmill.

We the clinicians, who are widely read and broadly educated, who have grappled with research as part of our training, should be able to converse intelligently with anyone. We should do this better than our equally talented colleagues who restrain themselves intellectually to the confines of their profession. As a doctor I come across cross-section of populace: from farmers, mechanical and electronic engineers, barristers, judges and generals. I can apply my diverse knowledge which can work as therapeutic in confidence building and it is incumbent upon me that I should know enough to be able to converse with everyone and engage him or her in an intelligent and meaningful conversation at his or her wavelength. I should be looked up to, like a father, who should be able to answer the children's queries to their satisfaction. One mark of a good surgeon is the power of making lasting impression on a patient and his relatives he meets during consultations. We do it through our physical presence, strength of intelligent conversation, crisp sense of humor and depth of our knowledge. It is a poor doctor who cannot communicate with a patient at his or her level, at his wicket; or involve the patient by explaining the malady he suffers from, in the language he understands.

Why do people consult doctors? They do so because they are worried and perceive that there may be something threatening to the quality of their lives; they fear that the symptoms they are experiencing may be injurious to their health or decrease the span of their lives.

The diseases may originate in the genes that change the chemicals but manifest themselves due to mechanical malfunction, like narrowing of a tube. The person may not be conscious of it yet. When he does, only then he experiences symptoms and then the awareness of those symptoms will bring him to a doctor. As is the physics so being the signs. Doctors detect a disease through signs, because of altered physics and physiology. People vary; some have low degree of perception, and they would drag on; others will report much sooner. The management is either preventive or curative. Mostly the patients consult doctors for the following reasons: -

1. There is an acute symptom like pain, or a fever and the patient want immediate relief.
2. There may be a lump say in the breast. It is not affecting the activities of a person, but fear is it may be harmful for her health.
3. There may be neither symptoms nor signs of any disease, but the parents or family has history of say diabetes, heart disease or cancer and the lurking fear in the back of the mind of the patient is he or she may not inherit it.
4. The patient is in good health and wants to stay that way. A thorough physical examination, some tests (these work as Therapeutic) a confident reassurance and a pat on the back will put a worried patient at ease.
5. Then there are diseases that the patients do not have, but laboratory or Computers tell them; that they have. In this age of information technological blitzkrieg, it needs a very well informed and a confident doctor to satisfy or manage such patients.

Why doctors and nurses are bad patients? It is because our medical knowledge makes us more susceptible to fear, we dread any illness and presume first, the worst—cancer; not common cold. Fear can counterfeit any disease in the mind.

To a large extent the course of healing in any individual depends on what takes place in the mind. The challenge is to realize ways to harness the awesome power of the mind in the recovery of the body and to find a way to the patient's mind, converting fears into an opportunity. The death of heart precedes the death of man.

I have a friend who practices medicine in Germany. A patient consulted him for indigestion of a short duration. My friend prescribed some medicine and told him to come back if he was no better. The symptoms did not abate and in the meantime the patient on a business trip traveled to America where he consulted a gastro-entrologist who immediately passed an endoscope in his stomach and diagnosed a Peptic ulcer, started a full regime of treatment, and left an impression on the patient that if untreated, the ulcer might have perforated. When the patient went home, he beleaguered the doctor for not doing an endoscopy. My friend tried to explain but the patient was not satisfied. My friend learnt his lesson the hard way and now he scopes every patient of dyspepsia; even for a minor belly ache and charges them for the unnecessary procedure. He says this has been the most 'profitable' lesson that he has learnt in defensive medicine.

19

'Till Death Do Us Part

The concept that——Life is finite does not seem to have caught up public or even professional imagination. Students in Medical schools are not trained as part of their curriculum to expect and accept death as a real possibility. The topic is considered a taboo, not to be spoken; look the other way and best avoid it. Life to a medical student looks so rosy when he enters a medical school, full of noble ideas with enthusiasm to serve humanity and cure the world. In daily life we fight disease like our enemy that must be defeated every time. No one appreciates the fact how doctors pay a price for their failures and that price is the ultimate basis of our distress. Death, when it wins, hurts deep.

Most people take surgeons to be cruel and callous lot. How else can they do the grisly things they do to human flesh, akin to butchers? Cruel to be kind, is not quite the sentiment people would comprehend. Whereas I have found some surgeons, the most compassionate specimen of humanity. Being a surgeon myself I know how it hurts when one of my patients unexpectedly dies, or even has a complication. Caring takes a terrible toll and no one can possibly experience the distress that we live through.

To enlarge my horizon and to gauge their mind-set I thought of probing my colleagues on post operative deaths; how they coped with death. But as is their wont, I found them mute after such tragedies, wearing a mask of professional detachment with the result that it was difficult to draw them out; one could only peek through a chink. They had cowered into a shell, a private cave for mulling over their pains on their own; grief being such a personal and private affair. The doors were tightly shut. Most kept their pains locked under the lid; let the pressure build up as in a pressure cooker and corrode their inner lining. Underneath the ice cap a simmering volcano.

As I thought, each of my friends had serious problem with death. How much it hurt them and how long the misery and sorrow lasted? The predicament was perplexing.

The silver lining of pain is what Aeschylus said centuries ago: -

"Pain, bringing wisdom against our will through the awesome grace of God."

If death does not defeat you, it will only make you better. The pragmatic way to perceive a tragedy is to wring from it the truth and a lesson. Suffering will then divulge a purpose in life. I remember while working with an English consultant, when a patient would die a mysterious death, he would make sure I attended the postmortem examination. And even then, when we could not figure out why the patient died, he would be very cross as to why we could not pinpoint a diagnosis and not learn from our mistakes. "Mr. Cheema did the patient die in vain?" He would ask. Motui vivos docent: the dead teach the living!

Life holds a potential significance under any conditions even the most miserable ones.

People cannot appreciate how severely a surgeon is afflicted by tensions during difficult surgery. If one were to tag on the same monitors to the operating surgeon, that are attached to the patient during surgery to read and monitor patient's oxygen, blood pressure, pulse, and other parameters, many a time the readings of the machines tagged on to the surgeon would be alarming. When a patient misses one heartbeat surgeons miss a couple.

It was amusing to read in a book on history of medicine as to how the operations were performed in the past. In earlier days the anesthesia was not developed as a specialty and the unfortunate patients had to undergo surgery fully awake, feeling all the pain. Both the surgeon and the patient before the operation used to chew coca leaves to 'harden' them. This, it was believed would give the surgeon the strength to cut human flesh and the patient, fortitude to undergo the ordeal. I am sure the surgeon needed double the dose than the patient!

A famous urologist when asked how an unexpected post-operative death affected him and his daily routine, was rather candid, "I feel I am in the wrong line, and I keep on wishing that I had not chosen surgery as means of my livelihood. I feel certain there must be easier ways for earning one's living." He said, "After the death of a patient I very often wake up in the middle of the night, drenched in sweat, heart pounding, remain very disturbed and cannot fall asleep again." He would analyze the situation again and again and curse himself, sometimes for doing too much and some time doing too little, too late. "Then I raise my hands."

"God grant me courage to change this world and the serenity to accept the things I cannot change; and the wisdom to know the difference."

Surgeons love to play God but the efforts and expectations need to be balanced. The wisdom of getting things done is, knowing what to leave undone. This applies particularly to the old and the frail. Just do what needs to be done; tighten a loose string or turn a nut, quick and fast. To err may be human; to err here can be fatal. No heroics. One who underestimates himself is perpetually being surprised by success, whereas the surgeon who overestimates himself is just as often humbled by failure. Accept the limitations of the patient; and also, yours. You may behave like God, but you are not.

Our march towards progress however depends upon how far we are willing to touch and cross beyond our frontiers. But before breaking or bending the rules one must know the rules. For surgeons and craftsmen, daily exercise of skills can become a matter of course and then a routine. The death of a surgeon is to live with status quo; stop thinking, carry on with the mundane and continue to limp on the old beaten track. One must not let that happen and always keep trying, persevere and try to excel; till your good is better and your better, very best. We must keep touching the frontiers of possibility. If we are not sweating—and panting that means, we are not going uphill.

Tension is a professional hazard, and it is necessary for any creative work, and it is natural reaction when we face a crisis. It is only harmful when we are more concerned about it than the crisis that we must deal with. The fire should be in the belly not the ass. We tend to work best when stretched: but not over stretched.

A surgeon I spoke to was more religious. He pointed at a number of patients. One had traveled from as far as Tora Bora, some from outside the country. He spoke. “God sends all these patients to me from far and wide and I try to do my best. Some get well and others do not, I pray daily that Lord, please do not send me the patients who are going to die. They can go elsewhere. I keep wishing that I had a way of telling, a premonition.”

As the story goes, a surgeon once prayed to God for granting him this premonition. His prayers were answered. He was told that when a patient would be admitted under his care, he would see an angel standing on one end of the bed. If the angel was standing at the head of the bed, this patient was going to get better. So accept that patient and treat him or her, even operate if you like because, even you would not be able to kill him! But if the angel was standing at the foot of the patient's bed, that patient was bound to die. That patient should not be accepted. Send him or her someplace else preferably to your enemies! The doctor followed the practice and things went very well. His practice flourished and patients came from far and wide, and everyone got better. The miracles of his healing hands were talk of the town, to the great annoyance of his competitors.

One day it so happened that this doctor himself fell ill. When he was lying in bed, he saw the same angel standing at the foot of his bed. The doctor was horrified. He jumped and changed his position so that his head was now on the opposite side of the bed. Soon he saw that the angel had also changed his position and was now standing towards his feet. The doctor dashed and changed his position again; the angel did likewise. These maneuvers went on till his friends and relatives seriously got concerned about the doctor's acrobatics. They feared the old man had gone crazy and might hurt himself by these unexplained gymnastics. A couple of strong fellows got into his bed and grabbed him, till the doctor could move no more. The angel quietly moved to the foot end and the poor doctor breathed his last. After his death, the angel confronted this doctor in heavens, or may be in hell, wherever he was destined for and said to him, "I got you in the end. Didn't I?" The doctor still defiant said, "With friends like mine who needs enemies!"

A leading neurosurgeon who spoke his mind on unexpected post-operative deaths took refuge behind the fact. "The patients with brain lesions report very late to us. If I can send home a patient in a wheelchair, after an operation that earlier on had arrived on a stretcher, I feel good. If the patient dies, although it hurts, I lean on that comfort of the inevitable. The harsh reality I hide behind is that the dear departed is rid of the misery of pain or a vegetative existence."

All our lives we ride the surgeon's roller coaster, soaring to dizzying heights one day and plummeting into valley of depression the next. In our profession it is not possible to separate chance of good from risk of harm. The physicians can only commit errors of omission whereas a surgeon suffers both ways, due to errors of omission and worse; errors of commission, which are much more painful.

Complications and cure come from God. Test and try everyone He will; that is why you are here in this world in the first place. I can only ask to rescue me from tribulations others have suffered. Everything in life is destined and man functions through chemicals—-enzymes and hormones. Because of them man will do what man has got to do. No wonder that despite the rigors of medical training, the suicide rate in surgeons without faith is ten times more than the average public and drug addiction a thousand times! Faith can be a wellspring of comfort and a great strength.

For the unexpected post-operative death, a surgeon has no quick fix. Wounded healer can crack and drown in a sea of misgivings. Death gives palpitations, loss of appetite, depression, and insomnia. One tries to put up a brave face, but the loved ones somehow get to know that something is amiss. This is even though surgeons try not to involve their families in their qualms and try to portray a confidence they do not possess. Most surgeons find solace in discussing such patients with their friends and colleagues. What should have been done, less or more and when? By trying to put up a brave face before one's colleagues and adversaries only help to keep up the exterior. One tends to take refuge behind medical jargons by giving death a name, Pulmonary Embolism, Septicemia, Cardiac Arrest, D.I.C and Multiple organ failure. I do not believe that a surgeon howsoever steel nerved or as some people may call—callus can get desensitized.

"No man is an island, entire of itself;
Every man is a piece of the continent, a part of the main.
Every soul is part of me. I am part of every soul.

The death of every man diminishes me,
Therefore, never send to know for whom the bell tolls; it tolls for thee."

John Donne

Meditations XVII

People who think surgeons to be insensate and callous do not know them well enough. Stories like surgeons asking for more money after opening the patients in Operation Theater seem exaggerated. Whereas, I have seen many surgeons after hours of back breaking surgery to save a patient's life not charging anything. In fact, I know a lot of surgeons who on the quiet donate to the poor patients from their own pockets without beating any drums. I know several doctors who regularly donate blood.

You can be useful to your fellow men, by what you can give to society in cash or in kind, and sometime tears. And where opportunities for service are concerned, there is no endeavor compared to that of a surgeon. If I were not a surgeon, what would I be, I keep wondering? Veterinary surgeon perhaps; that seems the only other profession that yields gratitude where your patients cannot express, cannot even say 'thank you,' once they are better. It is that look in their eyes that says it all and there is no device or scale to measure gratitude and emotions.

Cardiac surgeons face sudden death much oftener than the rest of us because they deal with such a vital organ and death is always lurking around. If anyone needs the nerves of steel, it is them. On the table deaths are devastating for the relatives and surgeons alike. I can only pity their plight. To minimize the trauma a famous heart surgeon said, "With the patient, scheduled for surgery I make a deliberate effort to have as little contact as possible before the surgery. Cardiologists do all the preliminary work and I hardly know what is coming up until the conference. The first time I see a patient is on the day before the operation. Even then I keep my examination as short as possible." This he does, lest he gets involved too much with the patient, because in case of death the pain and grief is going to be directly proportional to the degree of involvement. Some would say this is a very selfish attitude, but surgeons are also human. It is important not to get so attached to the patient that one's faculties to help are affected. To mitigate human sufferings and to survive, surgeons must build fortresses around their feelings to withstand the assaults of emotional involvement. Fear of suffering is worse than the suffering itself.

To bear misfortunes well, one must seek diversion and diversity. It is wise to have cultivated in happier days a certain width of interests, so that the mind may find some undisturbed cove leading to other associations and emotions than those, which are making the present difficult to bear. Build a shelter against rainy days. It is critical that our lives should not have that narrow spectrum that puts the whole meaning and purpose of life at the mercy of accidents. Thank your stars that things are as they are; these could have been lot worse.

To face a tragedy boldly it is counseled: -

1. Keep up your daily routine that should include outdoor exercises.
2. Continue working at same pace, as far as possible. Lot about life is just showing up.
3. Develop a bit of selective amnesia.
4. Be realistic about concept of life and death.
5. Firmness of faith. Agnostics have nowhere to turn to.

We have no constant cohort other than death and in death we deem a defeat. But if the defeat does not destroy us, it will only strengthen us. Failures are sad but the greatest sadness is not to try and fail; rather to fail to try at all. Failures certainly confer courage; take you up a ratchet higher. Without risking failure there is a zero percent chance of success.

Life is a roller coaster and ups and downs are part of it. Only if you have been in the depths, you can appreciate the exhilaration of heights. Do not give up after a catastrophe; the pain will only lessen when you meet next success and if you shroud yourself to mourn your loss the success has no chance to come. It is mere sentimentality to squeeze the last drop of misery from misfortunes. If you want to perceive something out of misery then try to learn the truth and a lesson from the tragedy. Ask yourself where you went wrong and how could have the patient be saved; no patient should die in vain. Here dead can teach the living.

One feels sorry for the nurses working in post-operative and intensive care wards. In case of death, they must suffer similar misery, the same sad sentiments and for no fault of theirs. Unlike us some of them have not yet been exposed to the rigors and the hazards of the medical profession. No one can ever get used to death. Medicine is not like any, nine to five job or working on an assembly line or a conveyor belt. The involvement with a living human being, one who has died in your hands, is an emotionally traumatic affair.

Success of an operation depends on skill and care exercised by the surgeon. Unceasing supervision and scrutiny of every procedure. A surgeon I know said, "After a post operative death I sit down and ponder over all the facts, adding pluses and subtracting the minuses. I feel that I should be wiser after this death and with my next patient; hopefully things would not go wrong." Medicine after all is a science: An eternal quest for reason—affects that point to causes.

But death does not strike like a lightening flash. There are always forewarning and tell-tale signs and if one is discreet, pre-emptive measures may thwart a tragedy. In a Morbidity and Mortality conference a befuddled surgeon was waffling the cause of a complication; a neurosurgeon who had to reopen a craniotomy because of hemorrhage, "When we had opened up the skull, there was blood everywhere and I could not figure out as to where the blood was coming from," he said. The chairman of conference a seasoned surgeon interrupted, "I will tell you where the blood comes from; the blood comes from blood vessels!"

That is Sutton's law.

Willie Sutton was a robber of Brooklyn who became very rich by breaking in banks till his luck ran out and he was finally caught. He was produced before a judge for trial. I do not know what was in the mind of the judge when he asked the robber, "Why do you rob the banks?" "That is where the money is, my lord," replied Willie Sutton. Ask a stupid question!

We tend to hide behind technical jargons to diffuse the situation. This muddling may be beneficial for the layman or uninitiated public but deep inside I know very well what a mess I have made in this case. The experienced surgeon has not only done more cases he has also made more mistakes. The comfort comes from reflection; that only way not to make any mistake is not to work. The consolation most surgeons seem to have is that, so many patients get well after surgery and it gives them strength to carry on and operate after tragedies and catastrophes.

When deaths after surgery come in clusters the feelings of the surgeon are intense. First death is a tragedy, second a mystery, and third is perceived a coldblooded murder. I once faced a series of deaths in a row following operations on three dear old ladies whom I knew wellbeing grannies of my friends and colleagues. They all had fractures around the hip; a potentially fatal condition even if energetically handled. If you do not operate because the patients are usually very frail and you chicken out, you can be sure that death from complications of fractures is certain in ensuing weeks if not in days. The misery of nursing a patient with a broken hip is extreme. Even simple chores like using a bedpan can become an ordeal. Even to keep them clean, for the relatives who want to be helpful to their elders in the hour of distress becomes impossible. Bedsores, chest complications, urinary infections; one complication will follow the other like dominos, the old grandma or grandpa will melt away before your eyes. If you do not operate, you are doomed. The only chance of survival for the dear old granny is to be on her feet with the help of surgery. Operate and mobilize the patient quick, out on a chair following morning and, on her feet the next. If the patient still does not make it, one should have the satisfaction that no stone was left unturned. Still, the social connections with the patient will make you feel very uncomfortable, and you will keep cursing yourself, as to why on earth I undertook to operate and took the blame, where a prudent surgeon would avoid such a situation. Once operated, people tend to forget the fracture and the frail nature of health of the deceased. Death is the final milestone in anyone's life. Everyone is going to bracket your name with the cause of death. Attend a funeral of such a post-operative death and then you will find as to how many times your name is mentioned. Many funerals discredit a surgeon.

So, when these three dear old ladies died in a row in one week, I had difficulty facing my colleagues. I felt those deaths were attributable to my poor judgment. I wondered as to why I always undertake such surgery and suffer such humiliation for my acts of commission where more pragmatic surgeons would have passed on the buck. Once you have stuck a knife in a patient all the previous ailments are washed clean from the slate and death becomes attributable to the surgeon of the last operation. Feeling very low, I went over to one of my sincere friends and poured out my worries on the poor fellow; he is a prudent person, his analysis of the situation gave me some comfort.

He said, "Leave aside all the emotional factors for a moment and answer just two questions. Number one, was the operation essential? Number two; was it properly performed to your satisfaction? If the answer to both the questions is in the affirmative, stop cursing yourself. It would be a coward, indeed an unethical surgeon who would shun his responsibility. Remember you are a surgeon and not a skin specialist. Very sick patients will come to you, several of them are bound to die and if you can salvage a few, even one you have saved the whole humanity." It really is a duel between head and heart; there is no rationalism before tears. So, at the end of the day, it seems ultimately one must fall back on faith; as the time, place and circumstances of every person's death is predestined. If your time isn't come even a surgeon cannot kill you. Yet I would be glad if I am left out of such situations. Finally, only time will dull the pain and there is no short cut to it. A death will haunt you for a very long time and wake you up in the middle of the night.

Some comfort can be taken from the fact that death can never be due to fixing of a bone with a metallic implant. The anesthesia can start a cascade, in disturbing the normal rhythm of the body, the natural functions of human body like respiration, the cardiovascular system and the brain. It is the anesthetist who tinkers with them. If you put a patient to sleep in an operation theater and then wake him up without any surgical procedure, he won't be the same for some time. It is then fair that part of the blame should be shared with the anesthetist. Over the years we tend to develop such a team as surgeon and anesthetist, that there is complete understanding about the way that we handle a patient. We are both fully involved. The anesthetist without your asking will change his technique according to the state of the patient. He may decide on his own or with your consultation to change the mode of administering anesthesia.

In any case it would be very unkind to shift the responsibility and incriminate the anesthetist as some surgeons do. I know it as a fact that I have practiced surgery for decades entirely due to the goodwill of the anesthetists. I have had the good fortune of working with some of the best in the country. They have stood with me like a rock in difficult situations—that are commonplace in the life of a surgeon. A cool competent anesthetist is worth his weight in gold. One should never forget that it is as much his patient as that of a surgeon and surely he will put in his best. My mistakes may be retrievable, his or hers may be not.

Another weak link, certainly in our set up is the post-operative care. What happens to the patient after the operation is over is as important as what goes on during surgery. Unfortunately, this branch of medicine is very poorly developed in the developing countries like ours. One may do a miraculous job in the Operation Theater, only to be dismayed post-operatively. Again, it will be unfair to put the blame on a poor nurse who has not had as much exposure as we did. We should take extra pains to train them.

Unlike European or American systems where we were trained and everybody is conscious of his or her duty here, duties are not designated in watertight compartments.

For as long as I have practiced, I have stood by wherever I found weakness in my system. I have been a consultant, at times my houseman and a nurse; certainly, a physiotherapist and at times a janitor. If you do not want to be disappointed, you will have to learn the hard way; that the degree of responsibility will be determined by the degree of involvement with the patient. Success is the accumulation of attention to details, but while tending to each tree you must perceive the entire forest.

The patient does not come to any other member of the team for treatment. He or she has put the trust in the surgeon for an operation, in good faith that he will look after all other departments. The credit or the discredit will also be of the surgeon.

I have worked abroad for a long time where surgeons train themselves to remain aloof and detached. This emotional restraint becomes a necessity when caring for seriously ill patients. Surgeons tend to avoid overt communication with the patient to distance themselves from their own emotions and shield themselves from the patient's sufferings. The isolation and following rituals in operation theatre, including not seeing the face of the patient while operating and wearing masks themselves, surgeons try to distance themselves from distressing emotions of their patients and depersonalize the patients, they protect themselves from the experience of empathizing with the personal anguish of the patients. While working in the West I found this detachment and fragmentation of the responsibilities soothing, where the duties of each member of the team were well defined and demarcated. In the event of death, the system and not one individual would carry the burden of guilt.

But we must ponder; how far it is apt for clinicians to try to enter the personal world of suffering of the patients. It may look like a mark of an amateur actor and amateurs would exhaust themselves after a few performances and then would not remain fit to help the sick as happens during our formative years; in Residency programs. Experienced surgeons understand and can detach themselves from the patients and at a quieter moment can in their reminiscence watch their own performance with detached objectively; learn something for self-improvement and perhaps at times also 'enjoy' their performance as we orthopedic surgeons do by musing at good post operative films.

In a theatre, performers create the right impression night after night only by detaching themselves by not undergoing the emotions of the character. We need to try to do the same in our workplaces—theatres?

Peter Sellers the famous English actor of Pink Panther fame who used to get so involved in his performance that at times he would cry out, "Who am I?"

No wonder he did not last very long!

While working as a resident in Bristol Royal Infirmary, a middle-aged patient was admitted in the hospital with an abscess in the perineum, to be drained under a general anesthetic. After a thorough physical examination I ordered the relevant investigations. All were within normal limits. I therefore, proceeded to drain the abscess right away as the patient was in agony.

Foul smelling pus was drained, and it was ensured that no pocket was left. All went well and the procedure did not take more than half an hour in all. The patient was then placed on antibiotics currently in use those days i.e., Penicillin and Streptomycin. The usual post-operative care was followed for the next couple of days. The patient had fever before the operation, which started settling down after the drainage.

On the third post-operative day the patient started running low-grade fever again and became drowsy. No cause could be found. The culture report had arrived in the meantime and same antibiotics were found suitable and were continued. The patient, however, went from bad to worse, despite all the negative investigations, including an x-ray of the skull and a diagnostic lumbar puncture.

This was back in 1965. CT scan was only a dream. MRI was unthinkable. All the wizards of the teaching hospital saw the patient, but nobody could make anything about him, except to help in carrying on supportive treatment. The patient died on the tenth day in deep coma. The postmortem revealed that the perennial abscess had dried up. There was a small inter-atrial septal defect, the size of a pea, probably non-functional. However, when the skull was opened, deep inside the brain there was an egg size abscess, which was thought to be the cause of coma and death. The pus was sterile on culture.

In such settings the consultants take over responsibility for the fallibilities of the juniors, and 'I' become 'we.' The coroner asked my consultant if the resident could have diagnosed foramen (ovale) of this size pre-operatively. His answer was in the negative. "Was there a way to save this patient by any other means?" The answer was straight. "Had we been able to diagnose the cerebral abscess and drain it, may be the patient would have survived." Which with investigations available in British hospitals those days, we could not have. This satisfied the coroner.

Since, I had managed this patient the coroner sought permission of my consultant to question me, and he readily agreed. "Why was the patient not placed on antibiotics on admission?" He asked me. I stood up and boldly in a very authoritative tone said, "The treatment of an abscess is drainage. Not antibiotics." My over-confidence, confidence of an ignorant and enthusiasm of youth bemused the coroner. There was visible tightening of humorous creases around his eyes and even in such somber settings he allowed himself a faint smile. But I learnt my lesson that inexperience and overconfidence were a lethal combination.

Unlike physicians, surgeons are not overwhelmed from the rows of patients in the wards. What big contribution to humanity is being made by giving them a pill here, an injection there or intravenous infusions? The body being a self repairing machine, surgeons consider that the diseases that do not require surgery are not much to worry about and are contemptuous of their physician colleagues whom they banter that they, by giving the symptoms of the patient a name, think they have done a great favor to mankind; and that there is a 'pill for every ill'. The surgeons believe it is a bad doctor who writes too many medicines, a tablet to draw the breath in and another to blow it out. The coroner who was a physician also thought that I should have put the patient with an abscess in the bottom on antibiotics long before his arrival.

A very concerned nurse once came running to a resident and said, "Sir, the 'Cholie' is still vomiting. What should I give him?" "A bucket, I should have thought," answered the irate House surgeon contemptuously. Wrong we may be, in doubt——never!

Doctor-patient relationships unfortunately have fallen from grace. The patients have become figures and syndromes; 'Cholies', MI's, IVDA, in fact inert; and the doctors desensitized. Crop of middlemen have made our affiliation sour, the unemployed lawyers, the managers, and the media. To ward off any unpleasant eventuality, the doctors in the West must take up memberships of the Medical Defense unions. It is a legal requirement before the doctors are allowed to see patients. Medical lawyers keep sniffing the hospitals, looking for trouble; coaxing the patients to sue the doctors. If a case is won, the loot is divided and if the case is lost the patient or his relatives do not have to pay anything for the 'services' rendered. This has made medicine defensive, and the doctors weary in an area they have little knowledge and would hate to deal in. The premiums have skyrocketed. When I went to England for my FRCS, in early sixties, the fee for Medical Defense Society membership used to be one pound sterling. Now American surgeons must pay enormous amounts, hundreds of thousands of dollars as premium. Medical treatment therefore in USA has become very costly.

Little do people realize that all this money ultimately must come from the taxpayer's pocket. In fact, the health service is a major election issue in American politics.

Sadly, the American fall out is reaching the British Isles. The fee for the defense unions has increased manifold, although mercifully not to the level of USA. For us in the subcontinent, because of illiteracy, poverty, and the low expectations, blissfully patients leave everything to God and the doctor. This enormous confidence of the patients in their doctors is a humbling experience. You are not only their doctor but also a godfather. Under the pressure of this heavy mandate, you must make not only your professional decisions, but also on behalf of your patients——solicited or unsolicited paternalism. The weight of the responsibility is humbling as well as daunting. Perhaps this is the reason that death hurts so much more. When medical defense unions cover you, you are only thinking of saving your skin.

A representative of a Medical Defense Union stationed in London visited my alma mater way back in late fifties when I was a student in King Edward Medical College. He wanted to speak on the advantages of membership of his union. All the junior doctors and final year students were huddled in the great lecture hall for his address. He spoke at length about the advantages of membership. Most of us did not understand what he was talking about. Naïve as we all were in those tender years, we could not conceive that a patient could sue his doctor. He then narrated a story.

He said, "There was a patient in an English hospital suspected of Leukemia. All the tests were negative. It was therefore decided, to do a bone marrow examination of his sternum. Unfortunately, the trocar of the doctor doing this procedure slipped and punctured the patient's heart. There was torrential hemorrhage, of which the patient died. The patient's relative sued the doctor and my union came to the rescue of the doctor." There was a pin drop silence in the hall. But before the speaker could cash in on this crescendo; the punch line, one of my friends, now a professor in an American university, who was sitting in the last row stood up and with a poker face innocently asked, "Sir, what was the result of the histology report?"

The speaker was bowled over completely at our naiveté, mumbled some perfunctory and decided to give it up as a bad job when another student asked, "But why should a patient sue a doctor?" The speaker must be cursing himself that he had wasted a return ticket from London.

But perhaps these were cultural differences that make our thinking very different. Reminds me of a thin lean undernourished African, who was paddling uphill with great difficulty under a blazing hot sun one afternoon. Drained, hungry, and exhausted he was returning from work on his old rickety, noisy bicycle on a dirt track. He saw a big fat American of Peace corps posted in the depth of black Africa as an aid worker, jogging up the same path; trying to lose some extra kilos and gain some tan on his fair skin. The African stopped in astonishment and wanted to know why the American was in such a hurry and could not help asking, "Oga, (sir) why do you run. What is the hurry?" Black man, white science!

While working as a resident in an English hospital, life used to be extremely busy as I was on call almost every night and the emergencies never let me rest. To top it all once or twice a week I also had to man the ER where all sorts of patients thronged at night, and one could not get a wink of sleep. One night after having been woken many times, having attended to innumerable so called 'emergencies,' so petty and trivial that I was sure these could have waited till the morning I returned to my room and tried to snatch a few moments of sleep because following day was going to be grueling. I was called again to see a couple that had come to hospital probably after seeing a movie or from a pub. The young girl, stinking of alcohol had some irritation in one of her eyes and wanted me to have a look at it. When I asked her how long she had this problem she said for three days. I held my ire that she had managed without seeing her own doctor or an eye specialist for three days but has decided to wake me up in the early hours of the morning on the third day. With a poker face, robotic actions and without trying to show any emotions I treated her. But I could not hold it much longer and next day narrated the incident to my consultant during an operation. A kind noble man who was the father figure I had seen in the paintings exhibiting love and care. Expecting some sympathy, he said instead, "The girl woke you up because she must have been very worried." When he saw my blank face, he knew that I was not convinced, he then asked me, "Would you wake me up at the dead of the night if you were not worried? Remember the Hippocratic advice, "do not treat the disease; treat the whole patient."

Fortunately, in our practice so far, the patients and doctors are on the same side. That is the reason it hurts to see a patient die. Once we are civilized enough, the medical defense unions will come in and the doctors will always keep their interest above that of the patient. It then perhaps will not hurt so much if the patient died. Your skin will be more important, than that of the patient. The 'Informed Consent' that the patient is asked to sign before an operation is a modern invention of the medico—legal science. When a patient is signing a consent form, he is being asked to agree to accept any wrongs to his body that the surgeon might do. This is a defensive approach so that if things go wrong the surgeon can turn around and tell the patient 'I told you so!' The approach if not cruel is mercenary and not holistic. Poor patients are expected to make decisions that are beyond them. We have no right to undermine the hopes of the patients.

This was not the medicine practiced by our forefathers. Starting from Confucius 600 B.C it had been, 'do unto another as they wouldst be dealt with thyself;' with the same skill, the same judgment, and above all the same compassion with which we would want something done unto us, and that without being told by anyone, particularly the Defense unions. Complications and cure both come from God. Despite all the pangs, life here is much fuller, as it is. I will want it to stay that way, the holistic way.

The image of a father figure caressing and comforting a sick child or a woman in a country home during a snowy night depicted in the paintings, hung in the modern skyscrapers of hospitals is the real picture of medicine; though it looks so out of place these days. While we are all children of God, sick patients are our children first and we should treat them—-like we treat our children. The good doctor concept left by our forefathers is what we are still thriving on. That was the medicine in the good old days depicted in the paintings.

But that alas is only a dream, wishful thinking, as the hospitals now have changed beyond recognition. In the early sixties while working in an English National Health Service, the county hospital used to be run by an invisible hospital secretary. It took some time for me to see his face as the system worked so smoothly. Now there are so many scavengers and buzzards filling posh offices in hospitals that it is difficult to locate a caring physician.

Deep personal dissatisfaction and diminution of prestige in medicine is because it is no more holistic. Pretentious administrators drawing fat salaries and the fringe benefits run the hospitals. Bureaucracy has plagued dissatisfaction in medical practice; the authority is no more in the hands of medical men. Administration is mightier than Academics. There are now more boardrooms and committees buzzing with conferences and seminars. With hierarchical and institutional rigidity, the atmosphere is that of a five-star hotel, an industrial conglomerate; where money dictates everything, and the poor patient is only a commodity. Men here are MBA's, who practice Economics, not Medicine.

In modern medicine businessmen weigh services rendered against dollars. There are agreements to provide and to receive. The language one hears in hospitals is same as in a supermarket customer, clients! Such medicine is a trade and not the noblest of profession. The difference between a carpenter and an orthopedic surgeon, or between a urologist and a plumber; worst still a butcher and a surgeon is fast disappearing—no wonder both wear the same white coat!

The contract between the doctor and his patient is sacrosanct and is that of trust, and there are no scales in the super stores to weigh reverence and measure compassion. A laborer works with his hands, a scientist with his head and hands whereas a surgeon should work with his hands, head, and the heart. He is a scientist, sculptor, and an artist. He must perfect the art that nature sketched in raw. These are the attributes of an artist where medicine is not a labor but labor of love—a sheer joy.

> ***Choose a job you love and then you will not need to work for a single day.***
> ***"To each one of us the practice of medicine will be very much as we make it.***
> ***To one, a worry, a care, a perpetual annoyance***
> ***To another a daily joy and a life of as much happiness and usefulness as can well fall to the lot of man."***

20

Farewell To Arms

After the dining out parties had dried up, a recently retired general looked rather forlorn in a marriage party. An old friend approached the lonesome general and to start a conversation asked him, "General, how are you killing time these days?" "Right now," said the general sadly, "the time is killing me." That is called stress of no strain.

There are two very important milestones in a man's life. Entry into and exit from service. Both should be occasions for rejoicing. In most civilized countries people look forward to a dignified retirement as a welcome relief. Reason is perhaps their social security and diverse interests in life. Most eminent professors abroad work as Emeritus and following generations can learn from their vast experience, while they are no burden to state or hindrance to their juniors' march for a place in the sun. Most have hobbies they can look forward to. Almost all travel, living their dreams, which while in active service they did not have time to fulfill. Travelling, also called newness is the most rewarding compensation of retirement. Retirement therefore is welcomed and is an occasion for celebration.

At retirement it is not the money alone that is wanting, it is the loss of exaggerated fringe benefits that bring the retired person down to earth. While in service most bureaucrats carve out their pound of flesh by reversing the famous advice of President Kennedy, "Ask not what you can give to the country. Ask what you can plunder of the country." With every promotion to the next grade or posting, their houses and offices must be again renovated, and perfectly roadworthy staff car must be changed to the latest luxurious expensive model. What it costs to the exchequer, authorized or not or where the money comes from is not their problem. If some of the senior officials may try to show some dignity and self-respect, their families would stop at nothing. In fact, the wife of an old 'C in C' was known as 'She in C.'

I have visited Tehran, after the Shah's era and there was great talk about the luxurious living of Shah, drummed up by the new regime. The palace of Shah now is a museum, where the visitors are taken around showing his lavish lifestyle in stark contrast to poor people whose pictures show that they did not have even water to drink. I saw the Shah's bedroom, supposed to be very rich, luxurious, and plush. After having seen some even better furnished houses back home, I quite honestly was not impressed, because I can show you in our capital or any other provincial metropolis not one or two but many even more luxurious palaces than the Peacock palace.

Retirement does not bother much to persons who do not change themselves and their lifestyle with the grade or rank. It certainly hurts much more to the persons who start behaving differently with each promotion. One should never forget a time-honored axiom; the higher a bamboo grows more it bends. If people change in the process, they keep on losing friends, nurtured over lifetime just for temporary affectations. I know a number of senior officers who rose to the top of the ladder and their behavior got worse with each grade. For a wise man, the days in the office are the best times to make new friends and consolidate old ones, rather to lose them. Be nice to people climbing up you may need them coming down.

Every new star is a challenge to grow in stature, to fill the exalted position rather than drag the rank down to your own small mind. Soon to some people the chair they sit in look too big.

With each addition of grade or a rank the attitude of such people changes even towards their bosom pals as they gradually start pulling away. What in the past used to be warm triple embraces, with change in luck reduce from double handshake to a limp stump of hand as they slowly drift away. With further addition of a grade, the hand becomes unresponsive, the tone of muscles of the hand vanishes and for a handshake you are offered only a lifeless stub. Whereas the tone of hand muscles diminishes, that of neck muscles increases with each addition of grade till the neck becomes porcine, inflexible, and rigid. These differences in tone of different muscles of the body worry close friends, lest the fellow has caught some strange neurological affliction, something in between tetanus and an impending paralysis due to toxemia of brass.

It also goes for their attitude of addressing old friends. First it used to be your pet name. With addition of brass, it changes to your surname, then either 'Doc,' 'Major' 'or 'Colonel'. There is deliberate attempt at keeping a distance. You are ignored in public, your calls are not returned, as the boss is busy; the scheming possessive staffers will dispose you off leaving you guessing. Soon friends will start to shun such person and retaliate in the same coin. With further shine of stars, the response will be interestingly muted as if you were a poor relation. They used to enjoy hilarious jokes together. From warm and friendly laughs, the laughter will change to a sardonic smile. With further increase in position, the most hilarious jokes of friends would manage to bare only his canine teeth on one side; the type you see in cartoons, the canine smile! Friends may get concerned, lest the poor fellow has been struck with a facial palsy or Parkinsonism.

To improve the pedigree, the family tree also changes with the promotion. Close friends knew all along that their dear friend, who now is vying for top post comes from an obscure rural village. Once more stars shine the ancestry moves to some other part of the world, Iran, or Turkey. If the next star comes along, there is further attempt to improve the dynasty. Even the very close friends are blatantly informed to their utter disbelief, 'actually our ancestors hail from Hamadan.' If luck keeps pace and more brass is added such people would not mind digging out a connection with the Peacock throne!

Ours must be the only society under the sun where it is fashionable to behave like an outsider in your own country, abuse it, eat, and spit in the same plate and regrettably also get away with it.

Most exasperating fact is that this attitude also gets into the heads of top brass of supporting arms, a second-rate entity known as the Services. They may be better qualified but hold rather impotent titular posts. Instead of raising the medical corps to its past glory, during a year or two of their tenure they waste this time, at the cost of their self-respect and dignity of the Corps to extract petty personal favors and to please the combatants. Services are a second fiddle and are completely subservient. The authority in the armed forces vests in the hands of the combatants. Such persons can now author books like, "How to lose friends?" or "Crawling is the best form of locomotion!" It is my considered opinion that we, the physicians whose profession demands appeasement, which we have practiced all our lives, suddenly can never become good commanders. The line between appeasement and sycophancy is very blurred. The pre-requisites and requirements for leadership are far, far different than for a compassionate physician.

With all these affectations, conceit, and contempt if the retirement does not hurt, what else is supposed to happen? It would be a shock of their life when the rug is suddenly pulled from under their feet and the friends are no more there to support them, because they all had been alienated. Now this fellow would go out of the way to revive old connections and look around for the friends in need. When you are on the rise friends know it but when you are climbing down only you know your friends. A person who was not willing to return your greetings while in office will try to embrace you and the hurt friends will retract. He will now return the long past telephone calls saying, "It was my moral duty to ring back!" Superannuation is a splendid equalizer.

All this transformation in a few days after retirement, but it is too late. The damage is already done. Perhaps all such people on their promotion should spend a day with their predecessors to see how life was treating them after retirement, when all the conversation of old timers starts with, "my days, oh those were the days…" and there would not be a receptive listener. History is the record of man's steps and slips. It provides us with the opportunity to profit by the tumbles and stumbles of our forerunners. But the tragedy of history is that no one learns from history and therefore is condemned to re-live it.

The retirement in army hurts a lot more, because even your exterior changes once you cast off the uniform, a symbol of authority, which in civilian life does not happen. The effect the uniform has on other people is obvious, but it also affects the psyche of the man who dons it. Everyone diminishes after retirement, more so men in uniform. While in the chair one should cultivate human relationship rather than base them on rank or position. Lead by example rather than drive with rank is a sound advice. Lasting relations are man-to-man, irrespective of position or uniform. What really matters is the person within the hulk and the hide.

If one were to strip a senior officer and his same age subordinate as a JCO, it would be difficult to tell them apart. A dashing general was once invited to a function at the embassy of a friendly country celebrating their national day. Trim and buoyant he liked driving his own staff car while the driver sat nervously behind. When the car stopped in front of the embassy porch, the driver who was sitting in the rear seat rushed out to open the front car door for the general. Before he could reach there, the waiting affectionate ambassador grabbed the stunned driver, hugged him profusely and kissed him passionately on both the cheeks. The ambassador soon discovered his mistake. The general has not driven his staff car since!

Life would not be so painful on retiring if one very important lesson is learnt. That nothing in this world is permanent and whatever goes up must come down. The rank will go, and no chair is durable enough, so do not let it get to your head. Unfortunately, nobody learns from history and his predecessor's fate and would again go through all the motions personally till retirement brings him down to earth. It was therefore not surprising when I saw a very senior officer break down and sob unashamedly when he was suddenly sent home. Numbers of lesser mortals are on record those, who fainted and have had heart attacks when they were abruptly retired; though while in service they may be bragging, "can't wait for the day of retirement." Soon they would not be able to stand it.

The intense depression that follows retirement is, like the fear of death, the inevitable result of refusal to accept the inevitable. One has to die whether one likes it not, and die at the appointed hour, not a moment before it, nor a moment after it. So, death is the best protector of life, and should inspire confidence, not fear, that nothing can deprive us of life before the expiry of the allotted term. Of course, nobody knows when the angel of death will visit him, for he does not make appointments, but he knows his schedule, and does keep his appointments. Arrival into this world is in chronological order exit is not. This is why we should remain prepared for death and keep our accounts straight. Blessed is the man, who in all circumstances is at peace with himself and happy in the will of the Lord.

Retirement is as natural and inevitable as death. One may put it off by flattering his superiors or convincing them of his indispensability, but he has to retire someday if death does not claim him before that day. There should be no reasonable excuse to be depressed at the prospect of death and retirement.

I know of an eminent senior military surgeon who 'became' indispensable; he was given one extension after another. His would-be successor by tacit understanding in the meanwhile, became desperate. He would lose temper easily and was becoming paranoid. After yet another extension to his chief, he was a mental wreck. Following day, he was operating in an operation theater, struggling to remove a big abdominal tumor through a small incision. He tugged and pulled without success. His assistant, a junior surgeon was trying to be helpful. He meant well when he very respectfully suggested, "Sir, perhaps the incision needs extension." The surgeon stopped the operation in the middle, pulled his hands out of the abdomen, turned livid, blew up in rage and shouted, "Don't you dare talk to me about extension!" The army is a very strong institution. The sudden death of a planeload of generals, when the C130 plane crashed over Bahawalpur only caused a ripple. Graveyards literally got filled with the indispensable. Life went on as usual. In armed forces one cannot afford to mourn the dead and departed for long. Subaltern and captains are friends, Majors and colonels are colleagues, Brigadiers and Generals are sworn enemies. People in the wings are waiting eagerly to replace you. So went a popular old toast in the British army:

"To bloody wars and sickly seasons.
Two quick ways to gain promotions!"

In England I used to work in a surgical unit whose head of department would wangle one extension after another every year. His would-be successor a Senior Registrar in the meantime lost most of his gray hair and patience, still waiting his turn for promotion. He was so fed up that he would not mind sniping at the old man. Once, while seeing patients in the outpatient department, an elderly farmer walked in with a swelling in his right groin. He said, "I want this 'rupture' repaired on my right side." Pointing to his other groin he continued, "Mr. Abraham did this many years ago on my left side and made a good job of it, he did. He is still alive. Isn't he?" The Senior Registrar was up to his brim but kept his English composure and in a matter-of-fact tone said, "Actually, Mr. Abraham still claims to be alive!"

Churchill at the age of 80 reluctantly relented and finally allowed his heir apparent, Anthony Eden to succeed him. "I must retire soon," he said. "Anthony won't live forever!"

The founder Principal of our Medical College, in his seventies established Army Medical College with a lot of hard work and dedication; with the result that in a short time the College shot up in prominence. Students and teachers came and went he seemed irreplaceable. He was Principal of the college for umpteen years. In fact, the President of the country would proudly introduce him as the life Principal. Everybody had come to accept the fact that the college would collapse once he was retired. The politics of the country changed and one day he was unceremoniously sent home, I am sure without the concurrence of the President. He had crossed the superannuating age many years ago and someone must have thought of applying the rules in the book.

It is said that he went to the President complaining that he had been given to understand by the President himself, about his being Principal for life. "Why this sudden change of heart?" he asked. So, it is alleged that the late President after paying rich tributes to the efficiency of old man, complimented him about his robust health at that age and said, "actually we never thought you were going to live that long!" The grand old man died at the mature age of 85. He was a great man; transparent, utterly predictable and a man with a very clear head. For him, a spade was always a spade. He could never tolerate affectations or stand on ceremonies. He would go straight for his point without any prelude. While still in office he once approached the President for some odd favor for the college. The President very diplomatically declined, whereupon the old man lost his poorly endowed patience and blurted out, "If you cannot do even this little job for the college, how do you manage to run the country?"

The intense depression that can follow retirement is due to lack of acceptance of facts. If like a good faithful one remains prepared for death, the rest looks easy. There are lots of definitions of depression, The American, the British, and that of WHO. There is no better definition than that prescribed in the Holy books, which is; If you do not accept the will of the Lord, you will suffer mental anguish and pain and all in vain. But if on the other hand one resigns before the will of God, the events will be taken in their stride. For a believer everything turns out to be right in the end. The things I have no control on is called, fate, destiny, or kismet.

Nothing will be gained by hitting your head against the wall except a bloody nose. If you do not accept the facts today, time will make you accept them tomorrow, may be day after. Ultimately only you will suffer. Nothing will change by your reaction. All the unnecessary anxiety leading to sleepless and sweaty nights, the palpitations, hypertension, and the peptic ulcer, may be a heart attack, in retrospect will appear self-inflicted. Happy is the man who is at peace with himself and His Lord. In the end His will reign supreme. The retirement is part of destiny and in the history of cosmos this event is not a big event. Instead of sulking about the past, one should look ahead and look forward to something more exciting. There is a whole bright world outside if you care to see.

We the doctors are lucky in a way that the ground realities of our profession keep our feet firmly planted on the ground, being constantly exposed to death and disease. We at least should not have that arrogance that others suffer from. If one looks at the atmosphere in a five-star hotel, the luxury, the exhibition of wealth, the rat race, and the atmosphere in the air; as if one was going to live forever, the mental makeup will be quite different. In stark contrast to that in a hospital where there is pain and misery, and you see people dying every day.

Another lethal mistake is to keep on visiting your old working place after retirement. This should be avoided, even if specially invited. Only offer advice when specifically asked for. Do not overstay your welcome and hospitality. The impression people may get can be misconstrued, that your presence here was to cash in on old connections. Let your successor grow up, enjoy his honeymoon, live it up and make his own decisions. Do not hinder his progress by becoming a banyan tree under which nothing grows. Do not deny your juniors a place in the sun and do not interfere in their affairs any more after your exit. The applause was the loudest when you left. Savor and reminiscence it's resounding. Do not let it peter out.

Warren Christopher, chief justice of America when he voluntarily put in his resignation from the post, he held for sixteen years was asked why he was opting to retire at this stage said, "Because I have never felt better in my life."

A JCO who had recently retired after a long-colored service was being dined out. In the after-dinner speech, the JCO summarized the whole philosophy of service in uniform, in a nutshell. He said, "Just for this hour of my life—this day of grace and pride that I stand before you on my send off, I have endured heaps of insults of my superiors almost every day of the thirty years of service but today I stand vindicated as a proud man for an honorable farewell to arms."

The retirement may not hurt as much if people around, particularly your wife and old staff would not make it look so morbid.

An old soldier went to his bank for drawing of his pension every first day of the month. This time when his turn came, he reached the counter and asked as usual for his pension from the teller—a young girl.

She asked him for his pension book. The soldier put his hand in the pocket; it was not there. He could not find it and it dawned on him that he had forgotten it at home. He asked the girl to help him, since he needed the cash badly and his home was a long distance away. The girl insisted for the Pension book. Quizzing at the fit healthy soldier with thick crop of black hair she could not help commenting, "But you do not even look like a pensioner; all your hair is black!"

Sheepishly, he confided in the girl that he had dyed his hair but to prove his retirement age he opened the buttons of his shirt to show her the grey hair on his chest. Out of respect and in a patriotic fervor for the veteran the girl relented and gave him cash on the condition that he would bring his Pension book next time for the entry. He readily agreed and thanked her for the courtesy.

When he reached home his wife was having tea, so he joined her, and sipping tea triumphantly narrated the incident to his wife that how by opening the buttons of his shirt the good girl had given him his pension. The woman was not impressed. "Had you opened some more buttons down below she would have given you even disability pension!" she said.

When an old faithful who has worked with you while in uniform suddenly bumps into you after a long lapse and wants to know whether you are still '*hazir*' (active) service and when you tell him you are not; the expression on his face, the look in his eyes and his demeanor change but says it all. "Are you still alive——Sir!"

21

Is There Life After 'Death'?

Retirement should be taken as a transition and not end of the world. At retirement one should sit down and think hard; reassess the priorities and ask oneself a question. What is it that I am living for now? Am I living to count the days to my funeral or there is still a purpose in my life? As Voltaire said one who does not have a purpose in life is already dead and can head for cemetery. As for dying one should always remain ready to go at a short notice; any moment and keep one's accounts clear every night before going to bed. Entry into this world is chronological, exit is not.

There is a purpose in life.

The purpose for living is in: -

1. One lives for love of the loved ones, friends, children, and grandchildren.
2. Opportunity to take pleasure in spare time, to reflect and enjoy solitude. Look back and ponder over the past; to reminisce and to philosophize. And enjoy nostalgic memories of happier times.

3. To use the talent not utilized so for.

Retirement, certainly from the army, when one is at the peak cannot be taken as end of life. After reaching prime of physical life, when hair start thinning and turning gray, the mental faculties however continue getting better all the time, due to accumulating experience. As the physical side of life is on the vane the mental, intellectual, certainly the philosophical side is on the rise. There is no moratorium on thought process. Physical appearances alone can be deceptive.

In the busy clinic of a middle-aged surgeon, a similar aged lady was waiting for her turn to see him. The surgeon would peep out now and again, either to see a patient out or to ask the next one in. The lady thought that the face of the surgeon rang a bell. It seemed she had seen him some place, where, that she could not figure out despite raking her brain. When at last, it was her turn she went in and could not help asking him, if he was in so and so school, which she had attended. The surgeon replied in the affirmative. The lady looked at the shining bald scalp of graying surgeon but could not place him. "He cannot be my class fellow,

He looks far too old," she thought to herself. She again asked him, "Were you in so and so class in so and so year?" "Yes, I was in that class. Why do you ask?" Queried the surgeon, trying to identify her he asked, "Were you a teacher of that class?" Still inquisitively searching her face! The odd thing about old age is that you do not feel old. Old person is one who is older than you. As you grow old, old age keeps rising from sixties to seventies and eighties.

Solitude, the time you did not have while busy in the humdrum of life; Solitude to reflect and count your blessings. Pleasure of appreciating the beauty of nature as in a forest where the pines are tall and green, where sparkling clear springs flow on the fall and you can picture 'books in brooks and sermons in stones,' watching silently emptiness of space and the silent mountains. One can keep on wondering about the eternal mystery of birds in the sky flying in an aerodynamically V formations, snow-white swans sailing gracefully in the lake, bees in the sun and flowers carpeting the green hill side. If you lie down and stretch on the green grass, with fingers intertwined, hands cupped behind your head, forearms covering the ears and eyes closed you can get lost in a reverie, journey back into memory lane. Silence interrupted only by the musical chirpings of the birds, the air full of smell of sun on pine trees and the soft sound of singing brooks.

These are some of my favorite things. Like: -

Throw a stone in the pond and watch its ripples grow bigger, while the stone skips the surface of water.

Holler in the woods.

Rain drops keep falling on my head.

The sort of things your grandchildren enjoy!

Orchestrate your ideas and reflect. For thinking even sky is not the limit. Thank God for His bounty. You will not be able to count His blessings. Think of all the great men who when disturbed used to retreat into solitude; Buddha in a forest, Moses on Mount Sinai, Jesus in the desert and Prophet Mohammad in a cave, where he could hear himself think. The troubled minds of all the great thinkers found peace and solace in solitude particularly in the morning calm. Mystics found that out long time ago through meditation. One can relive the trysts with dreams which one did not have time for while running the rat race.

The soothing effect of music can be medicinal. Listening to Beethoven, Mozart or the favorite melody of your youth is a conduit to heaven.

Joy of Reading; everything you have been saving to read at leisure. Like an amateur you will be pleased that you had not read before while you were busy curing the world. Amateur is defined as one who loves quiet recapture of heart, awe, and wonder.

You are as old as you think is a famous axiom. Life is what you make of it; age really is not a question of how many years a person lived but how much of them did he really live.

Recently an elderly gentleman for whom I have great reverence suffered a heart attack at the age of 88. He had been having chest pains off and on but never had the time to take the symptoms seriously. He was too busy doing lots of good in trying to help people. He had his hands full and would not think much of these little 'irritants' which the doctors named 'Angina.' He has had several surgeries and his body looked like battleground of surgeons.

A time came when this angina became unstable, meaning he would get severe chest pains even at the slightest exertion. Now this was bit too much as it prevented him from doing his daily chores and following his very busy schedule. He had single handedly collected ten million rupees that he distributed to the widows, orphans, and the refugees. He had helped establish numerous social welfare projects for the poor and needy. These pains were now letting him down. Now he was stuck and had to consult cardiologists. One cardiologist saw him after the other and all were unanimous that he should call it a day, stay in bed and wait for the appointed hour at home as he was too old for any surgical intervention. They could not pick up enough courage to perform even an angiography on him and thought it too risky while he had no qualms about death. Not in so many words but the doctor's body language suggested, 'you have lived up to eighties, not many of us will reach that mature old age, what else do you want in life. Isn't that enough?'

I have no doubt at all that while one is serving His people; his personal needs have already been taken care of. He was invited to come to a state-of-the-art hospital in Riyadh, where an Angiography revealed that all the major arteries were blocked. His Angiogram was flashed in an elite gathering of super stars consisting of top specialists. Being a doctor, I invited myself to be there in that conference. Surgeons thought they could find some way to salvage and overcome the multiple blocks till they were told his age; 88 years. Every one's face dropped except that of a physician of great repute. God bless him who knew this patient well. I remember his emotional plea. After enumerating different projects this patient was involved in, he said, "The real age of a person is biological," then he said, "I can assure you that this patient is more alive than some of the people sitting in this audience who claim to be alive! I suggest we interview this patient before discarding him." Surgery although difficult and prolonged was entirely successful, the patient never looked back and he was back in his hot seat within a month, thinking all the time how to pay back to this world for this extra lease of life.

Life of a hundred years or more can be useful only if it has a purpose. If one lives only to churn good food into bad manure, a lot of animals do it better; reminds me of a patient who was keen to complete a century.

There was an elderly man who woke up early one morning. Alarmed, because he felt a flutter in his chest and noticed that he was missing heartbeats. His pulse had been irregular, and he sat whole night counting his pulse. Early in the morning he went to see his doctor, for a thorough physical. The doctor, a man of few words examined him in detail and did an ECG but said nothing. This fellow was very worried. He found the atmosphere very disconcerting and broke the eerie silence, "Doctor, my father lived up to hundred years." "Oh, yes," grunted the dour doctor and went on reading the ECG. Some physicians have demeanor eminently suited to lead funeral processions, drawing of wills, and writing obituaries. They are at their best at bereavements and tragedies.

The patient was now nervous due to the demeanor of the non-committal doctor when he volunteered further information. "Doctor, my grandfather also lived up to hundred years. Do you think I will live up to hundred years?" he implored. The doctor was still pondering over the ECG. Without lifting his gaze from the ECG when he suddenly asked, "Are you fond of women?" Startled, yet the patient answered honestly. "No doctor, I am happily married to my Mrs." "Do you drink?" Quarried the doctor again. "No doctor; never touched the blooming thing in my life. I am a teetotaler." The man proudly told the doctor. "Do you smoke?" Asked the dour doctor for the last time, still scrutinizing the ECG very intently. The man was really getting concerned now. He thought there must be something terrible in his ECG and was bracing for the worst, he answered, "No Doctor, I hate the smoke." The grim doctor finally raised his gaze from the ECG, looked up and implored, "Tell me then why you want to live up to hundred years?"

The bewildered patient took some time to absorb the rebuff but soon recovered his composure. He was not the one to give in so easily and thought it to be the right occasion to seek doctor's advice. Fired by newfound ardor he asked, "Doctor, if one abstains, from wine, women and smoking, do you think he can live up to hundred years?" "Yes," replied the confident doctor. "It sure will seem so!"

During the depths of world war depression, walking down drab counsel houses in Manchester, Churchill commented to an aid, "Fancy living in one of these streets—never seeing anything beautiful—never eating anything savory— never saying anything clever, not even hearing anything interesting!"

These are the small joys that make life manageable; like if you have managed a smile on someone's face who was in pain; especially the joy of having helped someone from whom nothing is expected in return. It is in giving that one finds peace and can reminisce wistfully. It is not the conferring of a Noble Prize alone that can bring happiness which cynics say is in a way, a death sentence—final seal, the end of intellectual pursuit. It is the small things in life; of which one does not even take notice. If nothing else comes to mind while counting one's blessings, just marvel at, how without proper maintenance. In fact, despite gross misuse of human body, we are still alive and well. How the simple act of breathing for instance, is a blessing? Just by watching a patient in an acute attack of Asthma one realizes that what an effort it becomes; struggling, in fact fighting just to draw in a breath of air; which despite its abundance in the atmosphere, looks so scarce to an asthmatic and yet we take the process of breathing for granted. Covid has showed us the value of abundant free oxygen in the air. How much a cylinder of oxygen in a ventilator cast?

Similarly, you do not have to be able to avert a World War Three to feel that you have achieved something to feel good about; these are again the simple things in life. Like helping someone in need, like bringing succor to someone in distress, even a pat on the back of an animal that starts waggling its tail; saving a plant from being trampled. The pleasure one derives to see a seed sprout, grow into a live plant that sways in the breeze and then becomes a shrub or a massive tree that gives not only pleasure but also the flowers of different hues and the fruits. It is like watching a baby grow. The salvation of man is through love and in love.

The process of scientific discovery is a continuous flight from wonder. There is a single light of science and to brighten it anywhere is to brighten it everywhere. Any advance in technology, a discovery or an invention is indeed a miracle; and it brings man closer to his creator by tearing down another curtain of darkness between him and God. The innovations cannot remain provincial; the whole world is the beneficiary. The electricity, so essential for the civilized world today without which life looks impossible, the telecommunications, the computers, the advances in medical and engineering are no more the property of one nation, a country, or the continent. There is wonderful universal interconnectedness of science and all life on Earth. The scientists who discovered antibiotics, vaccines, and MRI have improved the quality of life of all humanity. Wright brothers who made history in flying, the communication explosion, and so many other modern tools that have made life pleasant and enjoyable today belong to every man on this planet.

For lesser mortals like us who cannot contribute as much it may be enough to know that such giants once walked this planet and just to remain current and interested is a very useful past time through Computers and the Internet. A relatively new arrival, we the senior citizens can learn it from our children and grandchildren as they learn and they learn it faster; their curiosity index being higher—-ten times in contrast to us, which with age shrinks to a single digit. It is amazing how quickly the children pick up; and outsmart our generation. This opens new vistas of information that one can use it in many spheres of interest and for professionals' sky is the limit and one soon finds the exercise not only stimulating but also extremely rewarding. At our age our children have spread all over the world and so have our friends. Internet is an excellent way of communication and one can spend hours and have an enjoyable time. Like an old dog, one feels shy of learning new tricks, but this is the language of future, and no one can do without if one must converse with those around; specially the young generation. Without it the generation gap is going to increase into an awesome gulf. The world today has shrunk and there is information explosion, and one will have to keep pace with at least part of it. A person who does not know computer skills would be considered an illiterate. The day one stops learning he or she is dead that day much before the physical death.

A searching mind is an alive mind; children have a far higher index of creativity; till they are curbed. The people and the nations that are inquisitive are creative. Just as the necessity is the mother of invention, a dose of insecurity is a stimulus to look for alternatives. A secure person soon loses curiosity. The people who have progressed did so because insecurity had been a catalyst. To be overprotective and to over-provide one's children is the best way to stunt their growth.

"Knowledge of all things is possible."

Leonardo Da Vinci.

With the mere notion that one cannot learn everything, one has already accepted defeat even before a start: nothing can be more slighting to human mind, his brain, and its Maker. There are 100 billion neurons in our brains; each cell can develop up to 10000 connections; all told we have 1000 trillion connections. The brain is not mere collection of cells; it is all connectivity and plasticity. For learning even, the sky is not the limit it is far beyond.

"Sabaq mila haiy miraje Mustafa sae mujai
Kai alame bashriat ki zad mai hai gardoon."

Iqbal

That even cosmos is within the reach of man.

The potentials of our learning are unlimited. We waste half of our life in sleep; similarly, we waste most of our brain by not using it. Do not leave this world carrying an unused brain in your head: use it. More you use it, more you will know that how much more there is to learn and how little you know, like Newton realized picking pebbles on the seashore. More you learn, more you learn to learn. Brain has vast unused and uncharted areas. There is special fuel for every tissue; for the muscles, physical exercise and for the brain mental exercise is food of thought; brain really is like a muscle; more you exercise more it will develop.

So, by saying you cannot know everything you are putting a brake on your intellect and shutting off your mind. Human mind has tremendous potentials, the only condition is you should be receptive and do not close your mind. It is only by thinking and striving to learn that you will appreciate God through observation of this stunningly wonderful world. How He created it with its beautiful colors and splendor. The worst thing, the death of a man is to close one's mind and then accept defeat that we cannot learn everything. Diverse learning also helps cushion the failures in life through assorted armamentarium.

I know several physicians who were philosophers, statesmen and entrepreneurs. I also know several doctors who were Olympic athletes and excellent sportsmen. Isaac Newton was conversant not only in Optics, Astronomy, but also in Physics and Mathematics. Leonardo Da Vinci was a master's in art, Anatomy and Aerodynamics. Albert Einstein excelled in Physics, Cosmology and Music. Mozart was a genius in Mathematics.

Knowledge is not the property of any individual, a person or belongs to a nation or a race. It is neither Eastern nor Western. Knowledge is a link in unending chain of intellectual endeavors that embrace mankind. All knowledge is built on the foundation supplied by our predecessors on whose shoulders, the successive giants stood; be of any race, religion or nation and this process of building knowledge goes on and on. At one time one nation is more vigorous than the other, can contribute more to the general fund of knowledge. Jabir bin Hayyun's fundamental discoveries in chemistry did not make chemistry an Arabic science, nor Algebra and Trigonometry a Muslim discovery. Just like theory of gravity formulated first by an Englishman does not make it British. All such achievements are common property of human race, and everyone is welcome to benefit and participate. How can we put a limit?

We professionals are lucky that we can remain useful by practicing our craft at the pace we like after the retirement. At this stage we do not have to prove ourselves, no reputation is at stake, and there is no practice to be built. No bosses to please or time limits to meet. The freedom, like a bird in the sky is exhilarating. With lifetime experience we have learnt a number of technical skills, operative short cuts and simpler ways of treating complex problems, gimmicks and tricky maneuvers. These gems can be passed on to the younger generation.

I believe we, the physicians with our training, grilling and professional brought up can excel in anything and everything. How can you ask a person to be less than what he or she is?

Why visions flash only to other people? Why do not these come to me? The answer is, 'First you have to be a dreamer and then curious enough and then apply yourself with same dedication, motivation and tenacity, as the legends did. Once you have done your homework right, only then you are ready for an intuition. Like all prophets, Prophet Mohammad mulled and meditated for forty years in a cave before the revelation.

But unfortunately, we set our goals low by accepting, we cannot learn everything. If we aim at sky only then we will be able to shoot the top of a tree.

We restrain our children and do not want them to think on their own and expect them just to obey us. Nothing can be more harmful than by trying to bring up your child in one's image; let him grow in the way Lord has designed him, in His image; a creator. Most of the inventors and great thinkers were non-conformists. Some were not good in studies; others were truants and some outright rebels. They were what their parents called unreasonable or problem children; refusing to accept status quo and they set their minds to work in a direction of their choice. Only such people have left a mark in history. As Bernard Shaw said,

"Reasonable people adapt to this world.
Unreasonable people attempt to adapt the world to them.
All progress depends on unreasonable people."

One should not only learn as much about one's specialty but much more, about the rest of medicine, in fact other sciences and the world at large. The excuse given is that there is so much knowledge in one's own specialty now that there is no time left to learn more. Standing in front of the WHO head office in Geneva a distinguished visitor from abroad was being conducted by the director himself, out of curiosity asked, "How many people work in this building? The bemused director, who must have heard such benign questions before replied, "Hardly twenty percent!" Our brain has tremendous potential and capacity to work; we hardly use twenty percent of it! We forget that now, no one has to travel on foot to Baghdad or ride on a horse's back to China to learn a procedure. Our ancestors about whom we say they had all the time in the world learnt, not only medicine but also physics, chemistry and astrology and had to work harder unaided and had to travel a lot just to collect bits and pieces of knowledge, which with Internet now is available to us at the flick of a finger. What is stopping us to learn today? We do not have to struggle a fraction of what our forerunners had to, for acquiring knowledge not only of medicine, science, art, music but everything. Keep your mind open, start learning and never stop till the last breath: You will know enough if not everything depending upon how much effort you put in.

We accept that despite the exponential growth in knowledge, the knowledge has a shelf life. So, while the knowledge is being added, a lot of it is becoming obsolete and is being taken off from the shelf on its expiry date. In our days the expiry period on the average used to be three years; it is fast shrinking. A few decades on, I am sure people will be saying exactly same thing that we are saying today that there is an exponential growth of the knowledge and we have too much to learn, and generations before us had an easy time as; we say about our predecessors.

In medicine I can see further sensational involvement of technology in future. The day is not far when each one of us will be carrying a smart health card like credit cards that will contain one's entire life history. This inscription on the health card may even be stamped in the human anatomy like in the forehead. Your health vulnerabilities imprinted on your DNA will be read by retrieving it with a click, as they bill your groceries in supermarkets! Doctors will not only be able to know your vital statistics and generic background for spare part surgery if need be but also run your latest CT, MRI, Angiography or Endoscopy films of any internal examination, flash it on the screen and seek help from across the farthest corner of the world. With further progress in genetic engineering, one may not only have one's genes sorted out, but also clone the finest brains of top athletes and intellectuals and pick and choose the qualities of your progeny.

The Minimal Invasive Surgery has reduced collateral damage to the bare minimum. Heart surgery, fully awake and without cutting open your chest, removal of stones through Lithotripsy, without big whacking incisions. Unlike in the past, big surgeons no more give big incisions; it is an era of keyhole surgery. With the involvement of machines, computers and robotics, integration of visualization and therapeutic techniques, image guided surgery the developments in medical field are no more futuristic; these are right here now and one wonders; whatever will they think of next. Twenty first century miracles are making surgeons superfluous. How can one afford to remain aloof from such an exciting world?

Young daughter of a friend, studying in a medical school complained of headache. Her mother gave her couple of aspirins and did not take much notice of it as her examination was at hand and she was studying very hard for it. Next morning, she complained of a splitting headache and passed out. Alarmed parents took her to a hospital where a subtraction Angiogram revealed a leaking aneurysm in the brain. The girl gradually recovered consciousness, but the father knew that she was sitting on a volcano. Numerous neurosurgeons were consulted, all advised surgery. Different options were considered how to approach the leaking vessel, and everyone was scared listening to the possible complications. While working in London I remember a famous Neurosurgeon, Dr. Pennybaker who started a new treatment by destroying certain nuclei in the brain of patients suffering from Parkinson disease, with a probe driven through the skull of a conscious patient. Once he was explaining to the patient, lying on the operation table, "I am going to insert a pin in your head and then I will fire a flare to burn a part of your brain with its tip and hope your tremors will stop immediately if I burn the right area of the brain. If it is not the precise area, I may leave you paralyzed. So, at the two ends of this pin there are going to be two very frightened people."

The neurosurgeons planned to shave off the beautiful locks of the girl and different incisions to get to the trouble spot were visualized; scared stiff how not to cause any collateral damage that could leave her paralyzed while tackling with the berry aneurysm. One of the friends of the family suggested consulting a neurosurgeon in London. She was taken to a teaching hospital and the neurosurgeon managed to seal the bleeder by passing a probe through one of her arteries without a grisly operation. The girl returned home within a week, sat in her professional examination, and passed. Now a doctor herself she has never looked back.

The science of miniaturization, the Nanotechnology is going to revolutionize the world of medicine. Nano-medics, where the future treatment will be least invasive and directly targeted to the offending point; like to a cell whose behavior is aberrant, where a cancer may be brewing. Splicing of genes for, such as delaying aging process or changing the fate of your next generations, are exciting new frontiers. The removal of cancer by surgery as we practice today would look macabre butchery and medieval.

Scalpel wounds will be soon a thing of the past and in future the scalpel will be shown to the bewildered young students by the curators in the museums!

The quality health care also will not be a privilege of few but a right of everyone. And health care will be, quality, accessibility, and accountability.

The thing that scares me about suffering from tube-vision and medicine going robotic is that one will miss its humanistic outlook. With all the gadgets, sophistication and instrumentation of the modern world, the old concept of humane medicine and of a physician is changing. A doctor or an engineer will become a technician and so much dependent on technology that it may become difficult to tell a man and a machine apart! The only way to avoid that is to broaden one's horizon and learn as much as possible, not only of science and technology but also of humanity and philosophy.

Paradoxically the more information is available in the public arena, the more vulnerable and anxious people have become. On the Internet there are 800,000000 websites on 'health,' and still ticking, 250,000000 in UK alone. The public is more knowledgeable but more confused, more informed but more worried, more independent but more reliant on others. People are living longer but increasingly worried about dying. They are healthier but more concerned about ill health. The more they hear about science the less confidence they place in it. They are increasingly mistrustful of science – scientists, but more anxious to utilize the fruits of scientific endeavor. The more evidence-based medicine becomes, the more the public turn to complimentary and alternate medicine – much of which is not evidence based. They are more dependent on experts but less trusting of them. Doctors in providing medical care to the 'expert patient' (internet educated–cyberchondriacs) are suffering from work overload, change overload and information overload. The onslaught of technology is upon us and like it or not, no one can stop the invasion.

And now we are riding on a tiger. Artificial intelligence (AI) is going to devour the rider once it dismounts.

For a full life both the mind and the body should be in optimum shape. While the mind continues to develop if the sensors and input are right, the body needs to be looked after. The principles of healthy life are well known. Lead a simple life, stay in close harmony with mother earth, eat less and exercise more. Give more than you ask for from this world. At least try to pay back the rent for the space you occupy, the air you breathe, the water you drink and the food you eat of mother earth. The real pleasure is in giving. Whatever you give will come back to you in multiples. If you distribute love, you will receive it back many folds, if you give hate and rancor, it will come back to you in many guises. People are remembered for the love in their hearts. There is joy in giving. Confucius said centuries ago, "He who wishes to secure the good of others has already secured his own good."

In African continent there are multiple chain stores owned by Europeans, Arabs and even Indians. The airport personnel once stranded one such owner of a chain, in Lagos Nigeria, due to a strike. His private jet in which he was to return to his home in London could not take off and he was stuck for a few days in the plush five-star local Sheraton. Out of compulsion he had to consult me for an impending diabetic gangrene of one of his toes. While in London the very snooty Harley Street consultants used to be at his beck and call.

I was only a small fry, but he had little choice, and I was asked to see him. He was a middle-aged person and had multiple problems. His life story was remarkable. He started his career as a petty clerk in Kenya where he went from India in forties. After a few years he was made redundant, and he started a small business as a peddler and the business gradually grew due to his hard work. When he was well set, he was thrown out of Uganda. He started from a scratch in England where he had taken refuge and now ran a chain of super stores in most countries of African continent.

He suffered from Diabetes, Hypertension and already had triple bypass surgery. His big toe was bothering him for a while. He had a pill for every symptom. I gathered he must be a billionaire. His worries were awesome due to his vast empire, in addition to the anxiety, lack of sleep and impending circulatory problem of his foot. I felt sorry for the poor man. I asked him about his food. He described his 24-hour intake, a few crumbs of bread and cups of unsweetened tea. I was amazed at his spartan diet. This much food would fall of a branch of a fruit tree in a jungle, if he chose to live there, yet the breakneck speed he worked to increase his chain of stores left no time for him to think about himself.

Humans, I feel should be grateful to such maniacs. The opportunities that this man alone had provided for an enormous number of his employees and their families that made their living because of him ran in thousands; even dogs and cats and the pets who received their sustenance because of him. It is due to contributions made by such professionals, scientists, entrepreneurs, industrialists, and the crazy lot that this earth is so beautiful today. How little do they require for their personal needs?

History is replete with examples of noble people, who made a difference to this world, who gave much more than they asked for. People like Nelson Mandela, Mother Teresa, Edhi, Bill Gates, Warren Buffett and many more, who will always live in people's hearts and will never die. More than the material help; what counted was that they donated a part of themselves for a noble cause— -how to make this world less miserable and a better place to live. Behind the effort it is the thought that counts. Their acts of human kindness will always illuminate this world.

"We live in deeds, not years; in thoughts,
not breaths; In feelings, not in figures on a dial.
He most lives
Who thinks most – feels the noblest – acts the best."

PJ Bailey

This noble state of mind that you experience when you are one with Him and His creation. When seeing sufferings and injustice your heart bleeds, it is the ascension of man beyond the ethereal heights where even the angels dare not tread. And the Creator felt proud reproaching Satan about Adam, "I know what you know not." For want of an exact translation of the word in English dictionary, Sufis, Dervishes, and mystics seem to have monopolized this trait called 'Ishq'—Divine love, as an Eastern sentiment. Can it be translated as 'humanism', 'spiritualism' or 'mysticism'? As with a lot of concepts dealing with spirituality some substance is lost in translation but in short Ishq is when you treasure your fellow beings more than you treasure yourself.

But you do not have to be Bill Gates or Bill Clinton to make a difference. Anyone who lights a candle helps lessen the darkness; anyone who can work up a smile, smites sadness. Anyone who acts noble is making a difference. Do not let go any opportunity howsoever small you may think it is. No noble act is small. And do not wait. Reach out and touch some one's heart. Make a difference now. So said Dale Carnegie: -

I shall pass this way but once.
Any good that I can do
or any kindness that I can show to any human being,
(Animal or even a plant) let me do it now.
Let me not defer or neglect it.
Because I shall not pass this way again.

So, what is success? Is it prestige, position, or tons of money? All that is only a part, the real success is peace of mind that encompasses all spheres of life. Happiness is the epitome of success; one is at peace with his soul, the fellow men, and the Lord. The successful man is one who has been noble, steadfast in his faith, has patiently practiced and preached righteous deeds.

Isse kashmakash mein guzerain meri zindgi ke raatein
Kabhi sozo saz Roomi kabhi paich o tab Razi
May my life be a blend of best of my head and heart. (Aqil and Ishq)

Iqbal

Rabba na atena fid Dunnya hasnatanwan wa fil akherate hasnatanvan wa qina azab an Naar

Al- Quran

Lord, bless us wisdom and faith--with which to toil and turn our lives haven, here and in the hereafter, and save us from hellfire.

22

Faith

For Asian expats, working in Africa was an amusing experience. Though not aired openly but easily perceived, that in the apartheid regime we were not white enough and now, after Mandela not black enough to be affirmed alike. Children however are very genuine. They suffer no affectations and have no reservations in speaking the truth --"but the king is naked!"

After work, while walking from the hospital to my apartment, I used to come across strident young urchins playing odd games in the street with a plastic ball, worn-out beyond recognition. Every time I walked past them, they used to holler and loudly chant an African rhyme in chorus:

"Oyibo pehpeh if you eatee pehpeh you go yellow moh moh!"

Oh, pale one, if you eat pepper you are going to become more yellow.

Revealing proudly African heritage. I would ignore their rant, smile, and walk away. Despite their poverty, they seemed a happy lot, hollering merrily and laughing loudly, they seemed to be enjoying their lives.

Whenever I sauntered past them, I could not help noticing a forlorn kid who would be sitting aloof. He wore rather tattered shoes close to bursting, tied with raw jute string to keep the shoes intact. Once it occurred to me to give him a surprise. I had seen him so many times I guessed his shoe size and bought a new pair. Next morning as luck would have it, I found him alone sitting on a log. He was rather a sad-looking boy feeling sorry for himself. As I approached him, he stood up genuflecting as a mark of respect to the elders. I asked him to take off his old shoes and opened my pack and fitted him with the new ones. I felt pleased with myself for selecting the right size, as he stood comfortable in the new shoes. He seemed delighted and, also puzzled at the same time, genuflecting again, this time to show his gratitude.

I wanted to leave quickly so as not to discomfort him when he suddenly grabbed my arm in his little hands and asked, "are you God?" I was taken aback and put my hand on his shoulder and did not know what to make of it, but mumbled, 'no.' Feeling a bit embarrassed, I asked him, "Why do you say so?" He said, "Last night I prayed to God for new shoes, and since my prayer has been granted, you must be God." I laughed and hugged him. He shyly recoiled and squirmed out sayings. "If you are not God, you must be a friend of God." With my eyes misty, I said, "Yes, I wish to be a friend of God," yearning all the time in my heart that God also may deem such feelings. And as I snaked off, I wondered what went through the head of this little boy. And how easy it seemed to become a friend of God!

I reflected on what sort of concept of God this innocent boy harbored. Then I thought what sort of concept I have. My head swarmed with all the tender feelings in life—Love, compassion, beneficent, merciful; every good quality one can think of. Different people give different names according to their caliber. But it is the same God with different abstract adjectives. But it does not matter. Let Shepard's God be Shepard's and Moses' God be Moses'.

23

Kismet

Do events control our lives? Do our decisions determine the events? What is in our hands, and what is in God's? Has some supernatural force, God, already has ordained our lives and we are just pawns? These are the questions no one has the answers to.

While Bill Clinton was still in White House, he with his wife happened to be in Chicago on an official errand. They were staying in a hotel with very tight security. Hillary Rodham was brought up in a suburb, Parkridge, some fifteen miles away. She suddenly had a romantic idea, reminiscences of her younger days. She thought of showing her husband around her old dwellings. They stole a few moments from their busy schedule of official meetings and even managed to hoodwink and escape their security staff. They secretly drove to Parkridge. His wife Hillary took the president to her home for old times' sake to relive the tender dating days. She took out her old car from the garage and drove him around with no one knowing. that it was the president in the old car. She drove him around old lanes and down the memory lane, showing him her old school and coffee shops, she used to socialize in. Suddenly she realized the car was running out of gas. She pulled in a gas station and asked the attendant to fill her up. An unkempt middle-aged man obliged. When she was paying the bill, he suddenly hollered in excitement and hugged her passionately. Looked like they knew each other and then suddenly recognized each other. They broke into wild laughter and became very excited. They seemed old friends, perhaps had gone to the same school.

Sitting quietly in the car, the president was enjoying watching the get together. After she came back to the car and started the engine, she told the president that the man used to be her old boyfriend who had taken her out a couple of times while they were in school. The president mused pensively and then asked, “Hillary, had you decided to marry this man then, what would it have been like?” Undeterred, she answered, “Had I married this man, he would have been the president of United States today!”

The story, even made up—expresses what kismet is all about!

Abdul Fatah (John) Jandali was an immigrant from a well-off family from Homs in Syria. He got admission in Wisconsin university after graduation from American university at Beirut for a PhD in economics. There he met a class fellow and decided to live with her in a cabin against the wishes of her very staunch Catholic father. After she conceived, Jindal left her to nurture the child on her own. Finding no one to support her baby, abortion being out of question on strict religious grounds, she set her baby for an adoption on a condition that the future parents should be at least graduates from a college. When Steve was born, the young childless couple refused to accept the baby, as they wanted a baby girl. That was when the Jobs appeared on the scene. Although not graduates, they were very keen in wanting to adopt a child. The mother relented, and they raised the child with tender, loving care beyond the expectations of the biological mother. In fact, he was raised very well. Later, Steve Jobs found out about his biological father not very far from his place of work. Abdul Fatah ran a restaurant that Steve Jobs visited a couple of times without knowing the connection. Later, even when he did, the feelings were far from compassionate, and he never showed any desire to meet him in person. In fact, he felt very bitter about the whole scenario.

Facts are more fascinating than fiction. How this child became the icon in communication.

October 2003

It was Steve Jobs' kidney stone that became the reason for detection of a shadow over his pancreas, purely a chance finding. The urologist had advised a CAT scan for the kidney, and there it was—a definite shadow over the pancreas. A biopsy through an endoscope revealed it to be pancreatic neuro-endocrine tumor or Islet cell tumor, one of the lesser fatal tumors of the pancreas and almost curable with surgery, especially if found earlier like in his case, which was diagnosed for CAT scan for his kidneys.

He decided to go against the advice of his doctors and refused surgery. Went back to all the many paths that had been taught by his Indian guru Neem Karoli baba. Vegan, juices, purging, and acupuncture. How a drowning man clutches at straws—and that too, a scientist! How can he be so naive—leaving scientific judgments, opting for obsession diets and weird routines of purging, and fasting. Common Eastern fads, Gandhi's doctrine: "Keep your mind clear, bowels empty, and trust in God!"

"When I was diagnosed with tumor in October 2003, I made my arrangement with God or whatever, which was that I truly needed to see Reed [his son] graduate."

So, he saw him graduate! He said, "I am around fifty-fifty beyond any doubt about the vicinity of God!"

"The body exists to serve the spirit," Mrs. Jobs told Steve to convince him to have surgery.

July 2004

New CAT scan—the tumor had grown.

31 July 2004

Now nine months too late, he finally agrees. Surgery at Stanford Medical Center. A modified Whipple procedure was the best the surgeons could do. The writing was now clearly on the wall.

29

Epilogue

After Rambling the world, I can vouch for that bass voiced singer Louis Armstrong, "It is a wonderful world." And the earth plans to keep it that way. Pristine and beautiful— qualitatively and quantitatively; whatever it takes. Even as a boy I loved wandering and wondering in the woods and on occasions would wrap my little arms around a beautiful tree and try to intertwine my fingers in pure love. While studying in England over the weekends I would travel to Yorkshire and walk for miles the beautiful dales feeling so close to nature. On one occasion I trekked along the entire length of that scenic lake, Lock Ness from St. Augustus to Inverness. I can still savor the moments.

Despite the universal biodiversity everything in this world is interrelated. How well interconnected? I had no idea until I saw excellent documentaries by naturalists and environmentalists about the wonderful planet we live on. What is common between a camel and coral reef? Or between a wild wolf and the honeybee. Apparently, nothing. Dogs we all love, but their cousins—wolves are for hunting. We by hounding them have made the species nearly extinct. With extensive deforestation and concrete constructions, there is no habitat left for the humble bee.

Naturalists warn us that with just extinction of these two species, entire life of the populace on this planet is in jeopardy of being wiped out in a couple of centuries. Coral reefs that have turned white may look gorgeous, but these are dead skeletons and are threatening the sea life.

"We fell asleep in one world and woke up in another.
Suddenly Disney is out of magic,
Paris is no more romantic,
New York does not stand up anymore,
The Chinese wall is no more a fortress,
Mecca is empty of pilgrims."

The world was in a state of war without any geographic, social, or ethnic divide. A war without guns and bullets. A tiny invisible virus pitted against all the superpowers of the world, equipped with nuclear arsenal and other lethal weapons of mass destruction. And it was not winning the war against Covid 19. All the science and technology were humbled. People died like flies and were unceremoniously dumped in mass graves. It showed the utter helplessness of homo deus.

The only way left was isolation as in biblical times as Abu Sina's (980-1037) alarba sinnya, forty days of segregation. Later the term was deciphered by merchants of Venus as quarentena and then anglicized as quarantine. A vaccine for herd immunity was the only answer and the drug companies ran amok to find one.

The world however continued its journey oblivious of the carnage. The sun rose the same time with clockwork regularity, and the life went on. It put humans in cages. Hugs and kisses suddenly became weapons, and Not visiting parents, grandchildren, and the loved ones -- an act of mercy. The measure of love changed into social distance. The fear was social distance may not become emotional distance. Everyone treated others as suspect like a leper. The values were turned upside down.

Suddenly you realized that power, beauty, and money were worthless and could not get you oxygen that you were dying for. The oxygen that nature had been supplying us free without any discrimination of cast and creed—all our lives. From first birth cry to one's last hiss on death bed. And without sending a single bill!

There are about half a dozen ECMO centers in Britain where oxygen is perfused mechanically like in heart bypass surgery for very serious patients who cannot absorb oxygen through their consolidated lungs. The cost for one day running ran thousands of dollars. Oxygen we took for granted, nay as a birth right.

Mother earth was sending a message.

"You are no more necessary.
The air, earth, water, and sky are fine without you.
The air now is pristine.
The rivers are cleaner, and the woods are greener.
The sky is blue, and the glaciers are freezing again.

When (and if) you come back remember you are my transitory guests and not masters.
So do not overstep the hospitality."

But what has the humanity learnt from the pandemic? Coronavirus did not distinguish white from brown, black or the yellow. Or young for old, rich for poor. All lives irrespective of social status were equally inflicted. Walls were built to keep the have nots away, so that Europe remains white and US 'great'? Humans needed to grow up from such selfish callous attitude. Starting with "Love thy neighbor" and gradually enlarge the family circle to include all the humanity as practiced by our noble forefathers.

All people are children of one God on the only planet that we have.

Learn to share and care.

The earth is sending a stern warning for collective solutions to all its residents against pollution, wildfires, environments, climate change and water wastage: to rise above self, nationalism, provincialism, and parochialism and to think beyond borders and become World Sans Frontier in spirit.

Man despite tall claims is very reticent. Disease, loss and death scare him.

Did he learn any lessons and made amends? I think he did, albeit for only a fraction of time before revertng to his unwise nature.

In the later part of the last century, the world really opened up . People and nations were reaching out. Centrifugal forces like globalization, elimination of poverty, and climate changes were the slogans. Aliens were becoming associates. Europeans grew out of their old rivalries and hence the creation of EU. old interlocutors were embracing each other and shaking hands. EU became a model for rest of the world. Borders blurred in the continent of Europe, and people mingled freely without passports and visa restrictions. Liberalism was on the move.

America was outsourcing its products and technology to third world countries, resulting in a big boom in China and Far Eastern countries. Although economics was the basic consideration because of cheaper workforce in these countries, compassionate factors were also at play and were a major consideration. There were bilateral and multilateral agreements, collaborations with outsourcing and considerate pacts; people were getting closer. America was investing even in Vietnam! This free trade has helped both parties. It affected even acrid Indo-Pak relations. Prime Minister Atal Bihari Vajpayee of the nationalistic Indian BJ Party traveled by bus from Delhi to meet his counterpart in Lahore to bring about some sort of rapprochement between the erstwhile-warring neighbors.

In America, unthinkable changes were taking place. In pristine snow-white, White House, a black President and a dark First Lady became its residents, offsetting the centuries-old tradition of "For whites only." No one could think of a black man living in the White House, what to say become a president! History stood on its head. The world was heading toward globalization and "Love thy neighbor" was becoming the practice. United Nations was spending more and more of its energies toward alleviation of world problems like climate change and poverty. The leaders of the world were looking beyond solving their parochial glitches and became busy in solving global problems like climate change, food, and water scarcity. Problems that beset our planet were being addressed more vigorously with consensus and with one voice, like never before. the milk of humanity flowing freely, and one hoped more bridges than walls would be built.

I always appreciated the Scandinavian model—how decent and peaceful. Where the human rights were practiced according to tenets of humanity. People live their lives so peacefully, having full regards for the dignity and rights of others, particularly the weak and the have nots are respected like the privileged. Polite and nonviolent, good citizens; there is hardly any crime. Individually, each person is a specimen of humanity. A schoolgirl who should be in the class is leading the campaign for the world problems that beset the earth and putting world leaders and the elders to shame.

Darde Dil kae wastey paeeda kia insan ko
Warna atta'at kae liay kum na theein karo bian

God created man to feel and ease pains of others
Otherwise there was no dearth of angel to chant His prayers.

Iqbal

God conscious attitude becomes easy to follow if you follow a faith—any faith. Hindus and Buddhists clasp their palms of the hands to greet others like a deity.

Insan ke kissi roupe mein tazleel na karna
Phirta hai zamane mae khuda roop badal kar
Do not ever insult a man
He may be God himself in disguise

Muslim bless each other with Assalmo alaikum, Jews with Sholom and Christian greet each other according to the time of the day. My five days prayers as Muslim are not complete without veneration of Abraham's pedigree at least a dozen times every day.

Koi Khushbu jaise baat karo
Always say something nice
Perveen Shakir

Méd Sans Frontières is a beacon showing the way to the world. Doctors and nurses, putting their own lives at risk trying to save others'. Doctors and their teams volunteer to work in such hazardous locations where no sane person would venture to go, war zones and abject poverty.

Humanity wait for the utopian dream of World Sans Frontières to come true, where all men and women irrespective of color, cast and creed would have equal opportunities, rights and privileges.

Last silent prayer:

Kufar Kafirra wa deen deendar ra
Zara dared dil ata ra

Let the unbeliever not believe,
let the believers excel in faith

Lord bless me with a poignant heart that feels and heals.
Man's craze for more and more can destroy this planet as envisaged in Quran.

Al hakimo tukasar hatta zur tul maqabar

Man's greed for more and more is insatiable till he reaches his grave. Never underestimate man's stupidity!

****

Once the book was published, I was surprised at the outcome. How easily could I write over 260 pages without any glitch? I was no writer but now basked in the newfound flair; reflected radiance of the book. I could also discern some faint link and connection in my stray thoughts. There seems a method in the madness. As Dick Wilson said, all things in this world are interconnected. A silent prayer ensues. May God bless his soul.

Printed in the USA
CPSIA information can be obtained
at www.ICGtesting.com
LVHW041112270224
772917LV00001B/63

9 798891 741928